Our Sense of the Real

Our Sense of the Real

Aesthetic Experience and Arendtian Politics

Kimberley Curtis

Cornell University Press   Ithaca & London

First published 1999 by Cornell University Press

Printed in the United States of America

Library of Congress Cataloging-in-Publication Data

Curtis, Kimberley, 1956–
    Our sense of the real : aesthetic experience and Arendtian
politics / Kimberley Curtis.
        p.   cm.
    Includes bibliographical references and index.
    ISBN 0-8014-3577-3. — ISBN 0-8014-8640-8 (pbk.)
        1. Arendt, Hannah—Contributions in political science.   2. Arendt,
    Hannah—Aesthetics.   3. Aesthetics—Political aspects.   I. Title.
    JC251.A74C87   1999
    320.5'092—dc21   99-31256

Cloth printing   10 9 8 7 6 5 4 3 2 1
Paperback printing   10 9 8 7 6 5 4 3 2 1

For Phyllis Mae Curtis

and Hugh Paul Curtis

To write across the chalkboard, putting up there in public words you have dredged, sieved up from dreams, from behind screen memories, out of silence—words you have dreaded and needed in order to know you exist.

I mean all the times when people have summoned language into the activity of plotting connections between, and making distinctions among, the elements presented to our senses.

ADRIENNE RICH, *What Is Found There*

We could scarcely be silent without being tormented by the damning thought that speaking might have saved us.

THUCYDIDES, *The Peloponnesian War*

Contents

Preface

The outpouring of conferences, articles, and monographs devoted to the work of Hannah Arendt has been enormous. This body of criticism seems to suggest a shared sense that her work is of great import for *us*. Although I cannot speak for others, I suspect the deepest currents of her work kindle our contemporary souls in profoundly similar ways. At its most general level, this book is about that kindling.

To put the matter succinctly, Arendt is our poet of political life. She distills that life, condenses it, and offers us an idiom for its deepest impulse. An impulse itself essentially poetic, Adrienne Rich puts it best when she calls it "[The] impulse to enter, with other humans, through language, into the order and disorder of the world."[1] And Arendt promises, too. She promises, as we enter public life in speech and through deed, that our being in space and time will be confirmed with a potency only to be tendered there.

This appeals to us, allures us, for we feel ourselves, in this regard, to be fragile, brittle if not already broken. If we return to (the troubling work of) Hannah Arendt again and again it is, perhaps, for reassurance of an ontological kind. But it is also for the way her political idiom propels us toward a democratic way of life. In our post–cold war world, in which democracy has increasingly become synonymous with capitalism and markets, and citizen agency almost a chimera, we are in need of work that deepens and stimulates our ethical imaginations toward radical democratic practices. This book is a sustained examination of the way in which the aesthetic foundations of Arendt's theorization of politics do just that.

---

[1] *What Is Found There: Notebooks on Poetry and Politics* (New York, 1993, p. 6)

Acknowledgments

I have received many and deep forms of sustenance through the long germination of this project. Before all, my parents, each in a different way, taught me to be susceptible to and to yearn for beauty in the nonhuman world. They also taught me that such a susceptibility matters to the human project of living well. And so our family's weekend expeditions throughout northern California and our summer strainings in the mountains of the high Sierras are at the center of how I think about politics. My sister Robin Curtis has been a model to me of courage and fortitude in the face of adversity, and a sweet, unfailing voice of confidence in my work.

I was blessed with three brilliant undergraduate teachers at San Francisco State University. Together they seduced me to the life of the mind, and simultaneously introduced me to Hannah Arendt's work. Gerry Heather taught me that there is something deeply at stake in political-philosophical thinking; Matthew Stolz taught me by his example how to dwell in thinking; and Barbara Scott, in whose lectures I nearly always quietly cried, taught me that passionate concern and incisive intellection belong together. Each took me absolutely seriously at a crucial time in my personal and intellectual development. I hope they know what a gift that was.

I owe a great deal to Jean Bethke Elshtain, my chair, and Nick Xenos, William Johnston, and Peter Euben, the members of my dissertation committee, for their patience, encouragement, and insight throughout.

More recently, to colleagues at Duke and at the University of North Carolina at Chapel Hill I am very grateful. Michael Gillespie made crucial comments on my dissertation manuscript—comments that encouraged me to write an almost entirely different, though not unrelated (but better) work. I extend heartfelt thanks to Craig Calhoun and John McGowan for inviting me to participate in the UNC conference, Hannah Arendt and the Meaning of Politics. Both Craig and John, along with other conference participants, gave me needed criticism and encouragement. Special thanks in this context goes to Susan Bickford, whose friendship and generous and critical comments shaped this work and my thinking in very important ways. Members of the Duke Political Theory Colloquium helped me to sharpen parts of the final chapter, and Bonnie Honig gave it her usual astute scrutiny as well. George Kateb's comments on parts of Chapter 5 made me think more carefully, although he is still wrong.

I owe both John McGowan and Lisa Disch a tremendous debt: John for his faith in the project, and for his excruciating attention to my writing at the sentence and subsentence (!) level; Lisa for her perfect balance of encouragement, generosity, and exacting critique. Both gave themselves over to the process of turning the manuscript into a book. It is a far better work for their careful attention.

My editor at Cornell, Alison Shonkwiler, saw promise in the manuscript, believed in it, and throughout has given me steady guidance and the benefit of her always keen judgments. She has been an exemplary editor. Nancy Winemiller, manuscript editor at Cornell, has been tremendous—kind, astute, generous, and efficient.

Joy Pickett, Doris Cross, Elizabeth Powell, Carla St. Johns, and Lillian Fennell have, together, put many hours into working on this manuscript. For their secretarial assistance and their kindness I am very grateful. I have put Marissa Law through the ringer in the past year, relying on her patience, her humor, and her enthusiasm for the project, and not least for her secretarial expertise to get me through. John Zachman did precision bibliographic work and even offered some unbidden but astute editorial assistance. He also did superb proofreading. Meg Sweeny generously worked on the proofs when I really needed help, bringing her calm, supreme intelligence and delicious cinnamon rolls to make it all work. I am also very grateful for Tom Merrill's assistance with the index.

I am grateful for permission to cite portions of Pablo Neruda's *Canto General.* Edited and translated by Jack Schmitt. Copyright © 1991 Fundacion Pablo Neruda, Regents of the University of California.

My dear friends Suzanne Keller and Annette deFerrari, worked the talking (and sometimes the wafting) cure more than once. My mother and father-in-law, Maria Iannacome Coles and Gerry Coles, have given me love, advice, and confidence. They have also been models of how to live well, with humor, and to do disciplined political and intellectual work.

Finally, Romand Coles has given this work, as my life, his energy, passion, love, and abundant thoughtfulness. Our worldly roamings and mental musings together have breathed life into many, many of these pages. His exuberance, discipline, untiring will, and capacity to think at the edge have always inspired and sustained me.

List of Abbreviations

The following abbreviations to the works of Hannah Arendt are used throughout the book. *Thinking* and *Willing* are listed in the Selected Bibliography under *The Life of the Mind*.

BPF	*Between Past and Future*
CR	*Crisis of the Republic*
EJ	*Eichmann in Jerusalem*
HC	*The Human Condition*
JP	*The Jew as Pariah*
LK	*Lectures on Kant's Political Philosophy*
LMT	*The Life of the Mind: Thinking*
LMW	*The Life of the Mind: Willing*
MDT	*Men in Dark Times*
OR	*On Revolution*
OT	*The Origins of Totalitarianism*

Our Sense of the Real

1 On Gates and Oblivion: Ethical and Political Challenges in Late Modernity

> Man's dignity demands that he be seen (every single one of us) in his particularity and, as such, be seen—but without any comparison and independent of time—as reflecting mankind in general.
>
> —HANNAH ARENDT, *Lectures on Kant's Political Philosophy*

There is a gate on the Puente Negro, the railroad bridge that links the Mexican town of Juarez to the U.S. town of El Paso, some thirty feet away. In 1965 the Mexican and U.S. governments agreed to begin the *maquiladora* system, which allows foreign-owned (mostly American) companies to operate assembly plants in Mexico and to count the products as Mexican exports (although virtually none of the parts are made in that country), thereby avoiding high tariffs while benefiting from cheap local labor. Since that time, this gate has opened for goods and shut against people.

A symbol of the eerie configuration of capital-driven human intertwinement—the result of economic globalization—the gate is surrounded by commuter routes that freely bring some two to three thousand American managers into Juarez from El Paso and back each working day but are assiduously guarded against unpapered movement north.

The fourth largest city in Mexico, Juarez is an "economic miracle." In 1994 its economy grew 6 percent, a rate that doubled the next year. Home to some 350 foreign-owned, mostly U.S. factories, its achievements benefit the American consumer handsomely. As writer-investigator Charles Bowden puts it, "Juarez is in your home when you turn on the microwave, t.v., see a film on a VCR, slide into a new pair of jeans."[1]

It is mostly young women and children working for just above starvation pay who labor in the *maquilas*. Job turnover is between 50 and 150 percent per year because the work is so quick-paced and body breaking. There is no safety net in Mexico, hardly any independent unionization. Millions of Mexico's poor have moved to Juarez in the hopes of finding work in these factories. Industry there is thriving, and labor is virtually limitless. In 1995 at least 150 girls disappeared. Dead bodies began to turn up; often they were *maquiladora* girls who had left their beds for work before darkness broke. There are 200 gangs in Juarez. They, not the government, are the authorities in this city. They employ people to sell drugs; they kill and steal to eat and to protect turf. They are not a progressive force, but they are a growing one in this Mexican border town. As Bowden says, "We are not talking about darkness on the edge of town or a bad neighborhood. We are talking about an entire city woven out of violence."[2] After the North American Free Trade Agreement (NAFTA) was enacted, *narcotraficantes* began buying maquiladoras, joining American executives and stockholders in the largesse of free trade.

Strangely, despite all this interconnection, Bowden reports that when he goes to the United States, "no one ever mentions this place."[3] Days can pass without a single news story about Juarez in the El Paso newspapers (although there were 520 murders in Juarez in 1995, among other possible noteworthy events). No signs of intertwined cultures here; in fact, oblivion abounds, indicating the superfluous status that certain human beings are accorded. As Bowden has put it to a U.S. audience, "We all have a deep need to ignore Juarez." But, as he also warns, "places like Juarez…are growing quietly like mold on the skin of the planet."[4]

To their U.S. neighbors, people in Juarez are chimeras, optical illusions, mirages on the borderlands. Places like Juarez hauntingly challenge our capacity, politically, in late modernity, to take in the particularity of others with whom our lives are entwined—whether we wish them to be or not. The political problem with this market-driven global interdependence is that the forces of capital alternately mobilize, manipulate, and crush political will, configuring human relations in a way that is completely devoid of corresponding political spaces. Absent are the institutional spaces and relations in and through which newly interdependent constituencies might countenance one another and generate power in the interest of their freedom and capacity to solve mutual problems.

But we should put this more strongly. The phenomenon before us is not merely an absence or some radical lack. The problem is, rather, the active conditions that nourish oblivion on the part of those who benefit and the radical enclaving of those who do not. Such are the conditions in which human beings are made superfluous.

The effect of this market-driven globalization on the shape of politics is not negligible. Cut off from the complicated reality of those we must countenance if we are to make good political judgments, citizens are left vulnerable to tyrannous, antipolitical solutions. These are the directions in which U.S. policy moves, for example, in regard to the drug trade, illegal immigration, and an increasingly desperate border culture.

So a profound challenge to democratic politics in late modernity is this radical, antipolitical, and increasingly widespread enclave effect of globalization, an effect symbolized by the Puente Negro, on which one Juarez gang, the *pandillas*, have painted a mural in the style of the old-master muralists of the Mexican Revolution. Along the bottom of the mural peasants are marching; above them are the girders and machines of modern industrial life. Blood is spilling down from this future.[5] Each time U.S. border agents slide the massive steel gates open to let a train through, the optics tell a story to Juarez: It is a story of Mexican peasants being mowed down by the inexorable engine of progress.

This points to another overlapping feature of our world, one that should make us tremble as we interrogate the political and ethical challenges we face. That feature is the unabating if uneven growth of the gap between rich and poor, a gap whose defining feature, from our angle, is the gate that creates a remoteness unwanted by most but actively sought by growing numbers.

Close to home, we see this phenomenon reflected in U.S. citizens' desire to live gated, in private enclaves and in retreat from the public realm. The fastest growing residential communities in the United States are so-called gated communities.[6] Long popular among the rich and retired, these closed communities are increasingly sought by middle-class families. They are generally governed by a private community association and often have their own schools and police forces. In some cases private communities have incorporated as cities but remain closed to the public. Developers promote these communities with promises of security, predictability, and open space. Most have many meticulous regulations in order to keep these promises. Focus groups conducted with members of gated communities found widespread disgust for the idea of paying for common goods outside of their communities.[7] Gerald Frug describes the effect of this privatization of public space: "The village was open to the public. [It] did not have these restrictions. The village had poor people, retarded people. Somebody could hand you a leaflet. These private communities are totally devoid of random encounters. So you develop this instinct that everyone is just like me, and then you become less likely to support schools, parks, or roads for anyone else."[8]

Such behavior creates a hermetic world—hermetic not just because people know and encounter people like themselves in too many respects but also because the very nature of their encounters with these others is itself made as predictable as possible. The unexpected is rooted out. Under such conditions the reality of others who are different is difficult to comprehend in any politically and ethically significant (positive) manner. That difference comes to be perceived as threatening at the same time that the very regularity and relative predictability of experience stymies the imagination.[9] The motor that might otherwise move a self out into the world of others sputters to the rhythm of a tired old lawn mower. This is a world designed as a stronghold against heterogeneous experience.

The political effect of enclaving is not negligible. Such social behavior makes it exceedingly difficult to sufficiently illuminate the problems of a shared world, a world whose reality remains stubbornly in existence no matter how far we may draw behind the ramparts, how high into the citadel, how deeply into the fortress. Especially obvious problems are crime and environmental degradation, although the same is true in varying degrees of all political problems.

Finally, a third kind of gated condition has become a significant ethical and political challenge in late modernity—the enclaving of the criminal. Indeed, it might be argued that the only public projects enthusiastically supported by "citizens" of these new private cities and communities are those that are part of what Mike Davis calls "the prison-industrial complex." The prison industry in California, for example, with its twenty-nine "campuses," is currently more expensive than the University of California system. Inmates are double-celled, but in the wake of "three strikes and you're out" legislation and a 1994 state ballot initiative to require double sentences for second-time felons and a mandatory twenty-five years to life for third-time felons, triple-celling is being considered until more prisons can be built. Twenty-nine *new* prisons are needed to meet the projected 1999 inmate population.[10]

This "human storage" problem shows no signs of abating, especially since the California Correctional Peace Officer's Association, the union representing the state's correctional officers, has become the most powerful in the state. It operates California's second largest political action committee (PAC), which led the fight for the three-strikes legislation and, according to writer Mike Davis, has managed to create "a permanent law-and-order hysteria" in Sacramento.[11] The Rand Corporation's fiscal analysis of the three-strikes legislation concludes that, "to support implementation of the law, total spending for higher education and other government services would have to fall by more than 40 percent over the next eight years.... If the three strikes legislation remains in place by the year 2002, the state government will be spending more money keeping people in prison than putting people through college."[12]

The deleterious effects of such gating are hard to deny, for it is a politics premised on the profound dehumanization of a growing number of the nation's citizens.[13] As a prominent California state senator put it, "We dehumanize criminals and the poor in exactly the same way we did with so-called 'gooks' in Vietnam. We just put them in hell and turn up the heat."[14] And this, of course, is a fairly radical form of forgetfulness.

Globalization and gated communities, spawned by the growing gap between rich and poor, are increasingly common features of our political landscape. The world they represent is a privately rather than publicly articulated thing for which we, as citizens, can be responsible. Where there *are* public-political relations, both the conversation and the acts that follow from it have become moralized and self-righteous, the political universe populated by innocents or moral monsters—phantoms in either case.

The contours of this world similarly appear, though in a different register, among the social scientists who speak of a substantial loss of so-called social capital over the last twenty to thirty years. Decreased voting and other forms of political participation—such as declines in membership of church-related groups, unions, fraternal and veterans organizations and the PTA—has steadily, and in some cases precipitously, eroded "the networks, norms and social trust that facilitate coordination and cooperation for mutual benefit."[15] Of course it seems certain that not all social capital is of a piece, either in the *way* it facilitates coordination and cooperation or in whether and to what extent the mutual benefit it creates underwrites open, equal, and participatory politics. We should perhaps rue less the declining number of closed groups (for example, the Shriners) and rue more the parallel decline in participation in public groups like the PTA. Likewise, we should be wary of a burgeoning civic-renewal movement in which philanthropy often figures more prominently than forms of civic participation that bring diverse citizens together face to face. Although for these reasons we ought to view with suspicion the very term *social capital,* coming as it does from a political lexicon that commodifies all relations and thus drains them of their important distinctiveness, the social capital theorists certainly also capture something of the effects of our gated political landscape.[16]

I mean to indicate the difficulty of politics for us, if by *politics* we mean the capacity to collectively and freely respond to shared problems—if, that is, we understand politics as an essentially democratic, participatory undertaking. Why turn to Hannah Arendt for theories that might help us shape a political response to such conditions and the problems they generate?

Ethical Challenges

Defining and driving Arendt's political theory is the claim that the "horizon of experience" that frames our central ethical problems is and remains the totalitarian form of rule—rule in which "unbearable pain," as she once put it, has come to be, over killing and death, the most terrifying possibility, the worst evil (*MDT*, 127). The pain that cannot be borne is that which we feel when human particularity is rendered superfluous. In the Nazi death camps and to a lesser extent more generally under totalitarian conditions, individuals were reduced to "living corpses" (*OT*, 447), all human particularity extinguished. The primary principle of political organization at work was terror. A principle of radical enclaving around groups but perhaps even more ominously around individuals, terror was the means by which to achieve mass loneliness and human superfluousness. The point here is not that totalitarian politics was the first time genocide was practiced but that for the first time making human particularity superfluous became a political *ideal*.[17] Extinguishing the human condition of plurality—the fact that "we are all the same, that is, human, in such a way that nobody is ever the same as anyone else who ever lived, lives, or will live" (*HC*, 8)—became a goal of politics.

Implicit in Arendt's work is the contention that this historical moment remains the experiential horizon of our deepest ethical challenges, both practically and philosophically. This is not only or even primarily because totalitarianism stands as the highest manifestation of evil but because meditation on the essence of its evil now so "brightly" illuminates our world more generally. Our gates and our enclaves, the oblivion and sometimes radical forgetfulness they enable are defining features of our late-modern political condition. We live in a world—nontotalitarian for the most part— which, with instruments often more subtle than terror, seems nevertheless increasingly designed to achieve the same end. And though Arendt contends that this end is a pain worse than death, she is highly aware that we cannot rely on the assumption that people will feel this pain. As the totalitarian experiments demonstrated, the human being is a conditioned, shockingly malleable thing, capable of feeling pleasure in a disturbing multitude of ways.

The greatest casualty of the world Arendt describes is our sense of reality.[18] In this, our new world, inaugurated by the totalitarian experiments, our ethical challenges take on a novel, elemental quality—namely, how to take in and remain provoked by the real. How, as Arendt puts it in numerous and diverse places in her work, do we remain "fully alive"? This, I would like to suggest, is the primary ethical dilemma of our times. Our paramount ethical challenge is how to save human particularity, how to create a world in which it can appear and flourish, how to cultivate our passion for it.

Thus we turn to Arendt because her extended concentration on totalitarian politics—its essence and meaning—gives us an articulation of our greatest ethical and political challenges. Her ethico-political compass is exacting. But there is more. Totalitarianism marked, in Arendt's view, a radical break between an old world and a new one both politically and philosophically. Her conceptualization of politics, for which aesthetic experience is so central, is a monumental effort to reconceive the political world and to write for political possibility in the aftermath of totalitarian experiences. In their wake, Arendt rightly contends, neither our political hopes and possibilities nor the elemental foundations of political togetherness can receive true nourishment from the metaphysical certitudes that political philosophers since Plato have offered. Let me develop these themes and contentions.

In a difficult speech delivered in 1959 to the Free City of Hamburg on the occasion of accepting the Lessing Prize, Hannah Arendt recalled the Greek doctrine of the passions.[19] Before this all-German audience that had assembled just fourteen years after the war's end, she distinguished between passions that are truly pleasant and those that are evil on the basis of the *amount of reality* the passion transmits, as distinct from the *force* with which the passion affects the soul. Evil passions may be felt keenly, sharply; they may overwhelm us with their force. But those that are truly pleasurable have the capacity to intensify our awareness of reality, to make our sense of the real fuller, deeper (*MDT,* 6).

Arendt's political-moral lesson was aimed not only at those (former) enthusiasts of National Socialism for whom the thrill of being submerged in a movement of world-historical importance had, at least initially, drawn them in. It was also aimed at those who were, as Arendt called them, "inner emigrants" during the war, at those who exiled themselves from the irreality of a world grown too brutal for an interior life, a life certainly more sane but only apparently more real. The lesson in both cases was a sharp reminder that however intense or real our feelings and our inner life may seem, however poignant and piercing, a full sense of reality is possible only in a world capable of supporting, sustaining, and stimulating multiple and conflicting voices and strivings. That is, it is possible only in a world not governed by forms of retreat and the practices of oblivion they sustain.

Arendt's remarks and distinctions that day in 1959, then, looked back onto Germany's darkest hour. But her words were also aimed at the present, at the audience before her, for what Germany surely meant as a 'conciliatory gesture' Arendt saw as a failure of responsibility, an effort at oblivion.[20] Gotthold Ephraim Lessing (1729-1801) was one of the greatest figures of the German Enlightenment, a leading humanist who affirmed both faith in divine justice and belief in the capacity of reason, in time, to perfect the human species. The difficulty for Arendt was that during this politically important time of German reconstruction it was as if the German people thought, in offering her the prize in Lessing's name, they could, with a single gesture, welcome the German-Jewish refugee home, mend Germany's rent political fabric, and reinstate its proud intellectual tradition. With this gesture the lost world could be restored, and so too, Germany's innocence. By positioning Arendt as heir to the intellectual tradition of the German Enlightenment, the events between 1933 and 1945 could be mastered.

How can Arendt answer this public summons? How can she return to the metaphysical dream state of Enlightenment thinking, in whose tempting trance she would symbolically recant the political-philosophical centerpiece of her analysis of totalitarianism—namely, that this unprecedented political event definitively showed the futility of efforts to secure human rights in transcendentally derived principles?[21] At play in Germany's gesture are the same kinds of evil passions about which Arendt warned in her speech—those that overwhelm us with their force but do not make our sense of the real fuller or deeper.

Arendt resists these formidable passions to belong, to be home, to return, and to smooth over by foregrounding, even staging the event of her appearance before the public of Hamburg. She speaks patiently and persistently about herself, about the group to which she belongs, about her generation, and about friendship between Germans and Jews. Resisting her public's effort to assimilate her, she warns, "Nothing in our time is more dubious, it seems to me, than our attitude toward the world, nothing less to be taken for granted than that concord with what appears in public which an honor imposes on us and the existence of which it affirms" (*MDT*, 5). To resist the concord was to invite her German audience into a luminous if frightening public space in which the nature and terms of their novel moment in time could receive articulation, in which their sense of reality could be made fuller and deeper. The political-theoretical point made by Arendt at Hamburg was that the Enlightenment's metaphysical principles could only at this historical moment instantiate a place of oblivion and retreat, suturing the world shut against precisely those experiences that, by virtue of their being unprecedented, urgently required political reflection of a most elemental nature.

Arendt ingeniously and somewhat deceptively[22] calls on Lessing, of all people, as she attempts to affirm the disaccord between herself and her German public and to describe their new world and the passions they must cultivate to live together in it. Lessing was, Arendt argued, a partisan for such a discordant world. His partisan activity took the form of "scattering into the world" what he referred to as "*fermenta cognitionis*," thoughts designed both to strengthen opinions so embattled that their very existence as an angle on the world was at risk, and to stimulate the emergence of new ones (*MDT*, 8). Lessing was a polemicist for the multidimensionality of the world of discourse. The passion that drove and sustained his partisanship was an openness, a real gladness in the recalcitrant and plural quality of the world. The pleasure he felt, and that so attracted Hannah Arendt, was that induced by tragedy. Thus "tragic pleasure" born of a passion for agonism of the type Lessing practiced was a pleasure, Arendt pointedly told her audience, of which "we" are very much in need (*MDT*, 6–8).[23]

But of course Lessing could help us only so much, for the drama that engages us as a "we" is more dramatic, more difficult to face, and more difficult to perform. However much we succeed in feeling this pleasure by scattering our *fermenta cognitionis* in the manner of Lessing, our sense of reality will remain thin and attenuated without a world stable and ordered enough to render the multiplicity of Lessing's *fermenta* meaningful, to make it more than a playful (but perhaps not too fun) game of profusion that thrives on disruptions in the order of reason, on instabilities, on paralogy.[24]

Yet it is just such a world that our fate has denied us. Our drama is distinctively marked by a postmetaphysical condition in which the "pillars of truth" that have historically secured such a world are no longer effective. Neither God's commandments historically revealed, nor *ius naturale,* nor the self-evident truths of reason can serve as the transmundane sources of authority, sources whose eternity had, until the nineteenth century, bestowed relative permanence on positive law, enabling it to serve, its own changeability notwithstanding, as a stabilizing factor for the "ever-changing movements of men" (*OT*, 462). Without such eternal "pillars" we seem unable to give form and coherency to something stable enough to call a shared world. And without such a world all that multiplicity will vanish like a phantom, wasted into the stream of meaninglessness, taking our sense of human reality with it.

How does Arendt respond to this terrible paradox she so relentlessly articulated—of needing a shared world to render our *fermenta* meaningful yet simultaneously lacking the resources necessary for its constitution or securement? Are we doomed to have an attenuated and politically dangerous sense of the real? Convinced that the known forms of tradition, authority, and religion could no longer anchor a common world or orient us ethically, Arendt looked elsewhere.

Aesthetic Experience

Arendt's thought, like that of many in the twentieth century, takes an aesthetic turn. This book is a sustained interpretation of that turn and an argument for its ethical power and political relevance to vibrant, participatory democratic politics. Arendt's political theorizing, as her performance on that day in 1959 with the free citizens of Hamburg, can be understood as an effort to cultivate our pleasure in the feeling of reality intensified through a constant attentiveness to the wonder of human particularity and to the specificity of the world to which it gives birth. Her theory is a kind of pedagogy about the wonder of human plurality and our obligation to it. A many-sided pleasure, this wonder is perhaps best elucidated by the Greek term *deinon,* as used in the opening line of the second choral ode in *Antigone:* "There are many *deinon* things, but not one of them is more *deinon* than the human being."[25] That which is *deinon* inspires wonder and awe because it is somehow strange, unsuspected, and causes, perhaps, fear. As Martha Nussbaum says, "One is surprised by it, for better or worse [and thus] this opening of the Chorus' ode on the human being is a deeply ambiguous praise."[26] Still, praise it is—praise for the spectacular appearances of the being we call human—and as such it expresses the tragic sensibility that, following Arendt's discussion of Lessing, I will refer to as the aesthetic sensibility of tragic pleasure.

The aesthetic experience underlying this sensibility stands in sharp contrast to Western philosophy's prevailing experience of beauty, which has so influenced ethical and political reflection. In the following, for example, Plato dreams this experience: "What if the man could see Beauty itself, pure, unalloyed, stripped of mortality and all its pollution, stains and vanities, unchanging, divine…the man becoming, in that communion, the friend of God, himself immortal;…would that be a life to disregard?"[27]

Arendt turns decisively away from this dream experience of pure, because immortal, beauty to an experience of beauty that cannot be had in the unalloyed dream state. Here "Beauty" is experienced in the profusion and the inexhaustibility of the world's appearingness. Not a dream, it is the world's particulars *and their pregnancy,* their fullness that moves us, catches our breath. Let me take my example from our pleasure in nature's beauty.

In stillness, bending into the sweet face of the rose, one smells, feels, and sees Plato's unstained eternity. But there are other aesthetic pleasures in nature. As we move through a mountain forest, wet with the morning's rain, our eyes plunge into the moist, darkened tree trunks. Riveted, caught in their thrall, we stop momentarily. In their almost sovereign particularity they *become* the mountain forest, overwhelming—or better yet—defining all its other possibilities. Still, the very liveliness of life—the imperceptible flicker of our eye, the changed angle of sunlight on the leaf's water droplet, the tick making its way across our flesh, the throttling drill of the woodpecker—each draws us on to other forests, on to plunge into other possible manifestations of the same forest world. Things in all their sovereign particularity are, as Maurice Merleau-Ponty says, "rivals for my sight."[28] Our perception of the world is tumultuous, transgressive, a ribald succession of plunging and eclipsing, always manifesting astonishing variants on the same pregnant world.

We pleasure in this experience of the forest: its miracle, unmasterable fullness, its ever-changing aspect exceeding our grasp, holding us in wonder. It has a kind of breathtaking beauty. Still, neither these wonders nor our pleasure in their beauty are solely benign. There is here pain and horror: translucent wings torn from the living being, swarms of ants sucking the cicada's body dry, exquisite tiger swallowtails feeding on the decaying carcass of a beaver drowned by the earlier swollen and raging waters and at last come to rest wrapped around the tree at river's edge. These, too, are integral to the fearsome beauty of the forest and our pleasure in it; these, too, rival for our sight.

Like our experience of the forest, our experience of beauty in the human world is revealed to us by rivaling particulars. Here it is particular others who are the shimmering light on the water droplet, the woodpecker, our very movement on the forest floor, our responsiveness to them allowing us to plunge into another angle on our shared world, bending, widening, making more thick, intensifying, as Arendt put it, our sense of the real. And this, as Arendt's appearance before the public of Hamburg shows, is often a fearsome thing.[29] And so the experience of beauty I invoke rises up in response to something fearsome, surprising, something *deinon* in ourselves and others as well as to the plural and recalcitrant quality of a world always "stained" by human finitude and human plurality.[30] In both respects a tragic pleasure is induced which deepens our sense of reality.

In her political theory, Arendt seeks to re-sacralize our feeling for human particularity, to teach us to feel quickened, awed, and pleasured by it through the cultivation of a specific aesthetic sensibility. This sensibilty is ethically rooted in, and must be evaluated in relationship to, an analysis of those evils which, in our time, most menace our capacity to form human lives. That this aesthetic-ethical task is peculiarly appropriate to and dependent on political life will be made clear as this work progresses. But unless we deeply comprehend the centrality of this quality of aesthetic experience through which our sense of reality can be intensified *to* Arendt's political theorizing, we will minimize its ethical force and relevance. It arose explicitly and abruptly in response to a new phenomenon in the twentieth century: political evil, by which I mean the organization of political life around the ideal of the superfluousness of human particularity.

Still, it is by no means unmediated pleasure at the *deinon* quality of human particularity, nor is it just any quality of vitality at which Arendt's aestheticism aims. Were this so her aestheticism would be of interest only as danger. Rather, it aims for a world sufficiently common that human particularity and human plurality can be cherished and saved, for a world whose texture of realness has the particular quality of fullness as opposed to force. She judges harshly those political demands and political institutions that, though themselves instances of human particularity, either squelch or squander human uniqueness because they are not designed to save and cherish it. Thus in a world whose continuity, identity, and stability have been severely shaken by the collapse of traditional metaphysical foundations for political life, Arendt's aesthetic turn is also propelled, in a somewhat more traditional fashion, by the relationship between beauty and durability. She wrote, "Beauty is the very manifestation of imperishability" (*BPF*, 218), meaning that one of the most singular qualities of our aesthetic pleasure is that what we find beautiful we wish by definition to save, to help remain in being. In a world so devoid of its traditional "pillars," this quality of beauty becomes extremely interesting at both a theoretical and practical level. It also becomes important ethically, for it suggests that there may indeed exist, carefully cultivated, nonfoundational, nonmetaphysical "pillars" that might sufficiently constitute a horizon of the common. The basis of such commonality lies not in appeals to universal truths. It lies in the peculiar quality of durability. Beautiful things can perdure not because they are the same to all of us, timeless and true in that universalist way, but because they are powerful but specific time-bound responses to universal dilemmas embedded in the human condition. In this sense, beautiful things have a coercive and contingent quality; their durability, as their beauty, derives from their capacity to illuminate both the historically specific and universal shape of our human dilemmas. From this aesthetic reflection on the horizon of the common, our oppositional habits of mind are challenged to reconfigure the relationship between the universal and the particular, between otherness and commonness, the one and the many.

Still, Arendt's aestheticism is far from indiscriminate. She argued, with the Greeks, that it is a mark of barbarism to love all beauty indiscriminately, that it is the mark of a cultured person to develop a specific aesthetic sensibility and not to succumb to limitless aestheticism (*BPF,* 214). Judgments of beauty, specifically culturally formed, appear in her work as acts that can save, from the evanescence of human comings and goings, beautiful deeds, words, thoughts, and creations. Around such things and such judgments, Arendt believed, our world might become sufficiently common to give human experience the measure of stability it needs.

Arendt's political theorizing, as I read it, seeks to cultivate in her contemporaries a specific aesthetic sensibility whose political and ethical relevance lies both in its love for and attentiveness to human particularity and in the powerful relationship between judgments of beauty and the passion to save that beautiful things evoke in us.

If our deepest ethical challenge is how to save and cherish, to feel pleasure in human particularity, and if totalitarianism represents our deepest ethical challenges because it brightly illuminates the problems of our world, we might determine that our political problem is how to take in and remain attentive to the reality of those who are part of our political world, how to solicit the specific uniqueness of others into the light of our day as we make judgments and engage in action.

Phenomenological Account of Politics

It is in stimulating a politics in response to these challenges that Arendt's work is so rich. Hers is a theorizing that seeks the essence of politics. Her most elemental (and most important) questions are, How are political things, as distinctive phenomena, possible? How do they occur? In pursuing these questions, the most singular thing she does is to descriptively rediscover our "direct and primitive"[31] experience of our presence to one another *as* it gives birth to a public-political realm—a realm she describes as a space of appearance. Arendt redirects us, then, from an epistemic concern with the facticity of things political and teaches us to recognize their facticity in a phenomenal sense.[32]

The essence of public-political life, phenomenologically speaking, is that it is a shared space of appearance: "Being seen and heard by others derive their significance from the fact that everybody sees and hears from a different position. This is the meaning of public life" (*HC*, 57). Arendt's thought reaquaints us with the thick dimensionality of political life born of the mutual active witnessing between particular others who share the world. Her greatest debts are perhaps to the Greek tragedians who, in their sovereign refusal to reconcile conflict, to close off by epistemic means the radical perspectival appearance-quality of human togetherness, resurrect in artistic form the complicated density in and through which alone political phenomena are constituted. As readers of *Antigone,* we do not so much learn as experience the profound particularity of perspective that arises from the very different worldly positions that Creon and Antigone occupy and that must be countenanced if the public-political world is in fact to exist.[33] In tragic drama, of course, this countenancing is not achieved, hence the ensuing dissolution and destruction. But we are made to *feel* Creon's position: He is a new and thus uncertain ruler; a ravaging civil war has just occurred; threats to his power from within seem real; the decree forbidding burial of the traitor Polyneices is a comprehensible response. The ruler's fears and anxieties are hot upon him, and they take us up as well. Yet we are also made to feel with Antigone, who stings with a sense of outrage at being denied one of the most important public and private obligations her city grants to citizen women: to honor the dead. The politically relevant point is that there is no overarching truth to mediate here. The essence of politics is not about this; it is not, in its most elemental sense, an epistemic phenomenon. We will misconstrue our phenomenon if we persist in this vein, and the painful irreconcilability we experience as readers indicates how difficult it is to create and sustain a public space of appearances, how easy the gate and tyrannous fortress in our world in which the finitude of our perspective is densely entwined with differences of power and worldly location.[34]

It is this density brought so faithfully to life in tragic drama that we encounter when we concern ourselves with things political, this to which we must belong. As Arendt argues, it is in this density alone that our sense of reality is intensified. And what she means by this is something of the intense but strange exhilaration we feel upon completing a tragedy. Having, by means of this dire art form, experienced the dense and sheer irrefutable facticity of others in their particularity, our sense of our world is fuller. We can *see* what is needed for a public space to be constituted. Having felt the great finitude or circumscribed nature of human perspective, and having experienced something of the ineradicable temptation to be oblivious, we experience precisely our profound need to *be* in the presence of others, our profound need for public freedom, for the chance to answer back publicly through our witnessing responsiveness to a world always already succumbing to the temptation of the gate. Arendt writes *for* this upsurge of human responsiveness as it keeps in being the possibility not only of sharing but of comprehending the world, a comprehension that is a precondition for any adequate illumination of shared problems.

Arendt's political theorizing concerns the heroic ("heroic" because never fully possible) effort to move outside the gate, away from oblivion toward the presence of others. She writes of a possible experience of political life that is an ethically important response to the central features of late modernity. As I have indicated, aesthetic experience is a key part of her success in doing so. Only a reading that takes aesthetic experience not as an analogy for an account of political life, but as a central feature *of* it *as* a space of appearances, can adequately address both the ethical importance of Hannah Arendt's work and its relevance to our world.

My reading of Arendt is informed foremost by the ontological reflections she undertook at the end of her life. I reread her earlier work through the lenses of this later, more fully developed ontology, for, from this angle, the ethical directions toward which her work points are far more compelling than those suggested by her earlier political theorizing alone.[35] In this, I am thinking in some sense beyond Arendt by thinking through her. There are three interrelated rewards of this approach.

First, in the later work, Arendt offers an account of the appearing nature of the world in which mutual responsiveness, provocation, and eliciting self-display are the central terms through which she conceives our capacity to sustain and engender a sense of reality. This represents a shift from an earlier, more exclusive accent on self-display and virtuosity that lures readers away from the profound way Arendt theorizes our dependence upon the presence of others for our sense of the real. Her later work foregrounds this previously shadowy relationship. *The Life of the Mind,* Arendt's last book, was written after she seriously engaged for the first time the phenomenological work of Merleau-Ponty, together with the work of biologist and zoologist Adolf Portmann.[36] The ontological arguments of *The Life of the Mind* are inflected with their respective and overlapping accounts of the phenomenal world. The upshot of this is the ethical aspects of Arendt's theorizing rise to the fore.

The second reward of this focus on Arendt's ontological concerns is the way it helps us reconfigure the relationship between human particularity and a commonly shared public world. Dominant strains of liberalism have understood the latter to provide necessary fences so that individuals might, in liberty, develop the former. Proponents of civic republicanism tend to treat the need for a shared moral and political framework in static terms: They cannot adequately accommodate theoretically or ethically those outside their frame. Much of Marxist theory, while critically concerned about the collective foundations of individuality, is preoccupied with these foundations exclusively as causal preconditions; it is less attentive to the ways in which the collectively shared world itself squanders human particularity. For its part, postmodern theorizing, influenced by a Nietzschean account of nihilism, centralizes, like Arendt, the need to re-sacralize *this* world: its contingency, particularity, multiplicity, and ontological discord. What animates and gives postmodern reflection its ethical relevance is, as Steven White has summarized, its "responsiveness to otherness."[37] White refers to this, I think rightly, as its moral-aesthetic sense. Thus postmodern theorizing is centrally concerned with human particularity or "otherness" and highly suspicious of invocations of commonality. Rightly fearing the violence done to otherness in such appeals, postmodern theorists nonetheless have only recently begun to seriously engage the question of what kinds of shared institutions, practices, and sensibilities might positively instill a sense of our belonging to one another.

Central to Arendt's reconfiguration of the relationship between human particularity and a commonly shared world is the contention that our ability to experience and constitute a world shared in common is utterly dependent on that world appearing to us *through* the eyes of others. What guarantees our capacity to share the world, to instantiate it *as* something in common, is our responsiveness to the particular views of others and thus to the perspectival quality all things acquire in an appearing world. Responsiveness to human particularity is thus not ethically important for its own sake. It is important also so that we might continue to actively achieve a sense of belonging to a common world. And for this, for the world to be renewed as something vividly shared, we must solicit the presence of others. This, as I shall argue, is the essence of the public sphere as Arendt theorizes it, and it is the basis of our ethical responsibility in politics.

The third reward of my focus on Arendt's ontological concerns is that we can better articulate how the aesthetic-ethical impulse she theorizes relates to pragmatic political considerations. One of the greatest puzzles of Arendt's work has been that "the endless *palaver* in [Arendt's] *agora*" seems shockingly unrelated to achieving specific pragmatic ends.[38] That is, her conception of the public sphere as a space of appearances for beautiful words and deeds seems to be strangely devoid of content.[39] I am not unsympathetic to the existence of this problem in Arendt's thinking. Still, if we foreground her ontological concerns, the practical import of the aesthetic dimensions of her conceptualization of politics come into view as well, for if I am right that Arendt reacquaints us with the manner in which the phenomenal richness of things political are born, if she invites and challenges us to feel pleasure in the perspectival density of our shared world, then the pragmatic significance of her work lies in the way she theorizes our capacity to be attentive to those others—their outlook, concerns, sense of the world—with whom we share the world. Such attentiveness is significant not only for ethical reasons but also because practical purposes often founder on the reactive responses of the disenfranchised, the overlooked, the superfluous.[40] Perhaps even more elementally, our very capacity to formulate effective courses of action requires such vigilant and open attentiveness. For pragmatic reasons, too, then, our sense of a shared world must not rest unnecessarily on forms of domination and oblivion. And against these problems the aesthetic-ethical dimensions of Arendt's work are formidable conceptual weapons.

Arendt's Aestheticism: Debates

It is, of course, precisely the ethical content of Arendt's aesthetic account of political life that has caused such unease among her contemporary critics.[41] An early debate that occurred during Arendt's lifetime between Lionel Abel and Daniel Bell centered on her portrait of Adolf Eichmann and the actions by the Jewish Councils during Nazi rule. Abel charged that, in both cases, Arendt's analysis was guided by aesthetic considerations at the expense of moral and even political actualities.[42] Bell responded that Abel had mistaken Arendt's concern with justice in the form of her adherence to a single standard of universal order for aesthetic judgment. It was her concern with justice, Bell argued, that gives Arendt's writing a tone of coldness, not aesthetic considerations. Because, however, aesthetics and justice "derive from a singular preoccupation and are also separate from morality and also have a formal quality," Bell concedes that although Abel's is a cruel mistake, it is a comprehensible one. Argument centered, in this case, on whether Arendt had breached a boundary between concerns with justice and aesthetics that should never be breached.[43]

In another early article, Martin Jay sustains the clear-cut distinction between aesthetics and ethics, sounding a theme that continues to trouble

Arendt's readers. Jay argues that Arendt's "aestheticization of politics"—by which he means the disjuncture she makes between political and "any rational, utilitarian, historical and social foundation"—makes her greatest affinity to the political existentialists of the prewar years, especially to the decisionists. In this context he goes on to intimate that in succumbing to the "dangerous charms" of the political existentialists who "have been seen by most historians as having prepared the way for fascism," Arendt's aestheticization of political life shares elements of fascist ideology.[44] In a more sustained, less certain vein, George Kateb has explored the parallels between Arendt's work and fascist thought. Despite his lack of resolution concerning the parallels as he identifies them—a common anti-utilitarianism, a reliance on mutual pledging that he comes close to equating with oath-taking, and the aim of interrupting the automatism of all processes by asserting the unnatural or artificial against the natural or everyday—Kateb clearly does not believe that, in the main, Arendt places sufficient moral limits on political action. His objections are closely bound to her aestheticization of political life and to what he calls the existential supremacy Arendt grants to action—by which he means its capacity to justify and redeem human existence.[45]

The aesthetic antirationalism of Arendt's political theorizing is the subject of a somewhat different, more recent set of debates regarding her conception of political action and her public-realm theory. This is a debate between proponents of a consensual communicative politics, on the one hand, and those who argue for a more agonistic performative politics, on the other. For both, Arendt's work makes a crucial contribution to revitalizing the distinction between *praxis* and *techne,* and thus to restoring to political life its distinctive and emancipatory potential. The consensualists, however, tend to appropriate Arendt's public-realm theory for their consensual-universalist ends, ignoring or rejecting Arendt's agonistic aesthetic account of action in which, as they see it, "immoral and political greatness, heroism, preeminence are revealed, displayed, shared with others."[46] The agonists, by contrast, appropriate just this aspect of Arendt's work— namely, the ideal of "agonistic subjectivity,"[47] the embrace of political life as uniquely individuating through the "self's agonal passion for distinction."[48] This theorization of political life is held to be crucial, as it represents the greatest hope against the contemporary forces of normalization, subjectification, and the effects of a totalizing will to mastery. This postmodern-inflected reading finds precisely in Arendt's aestheticization of political life a strong emancipatory moment. Substantial differences regarding what politics can and ought to be govern this debate, ranging at the extremes from a form of communicative rationality to episodic eruptions of resistance in a darkened, fragmented world.

The problem with this sometimes clarifying debate is that unless we hold both agonistic and consensual moments of Arendt's account of political life in a common, if tension-filled frame, we will miss the essence of the ethical concerns that animate her political theorizing. Dana Villa, himself deeply influenced by a postmodern sense of the world, moves positively in this direction by arguing that Arendt both theorizes "the self-containedness of action," in which the value of action is not its instrumental quality but its greatness or beauty, *and* that she was impelled by a concern to tame and bound the agonistic performative dimension of action.[49] This she does, Villa perceptively argues, not by reasserting instrumental constraints or by making transcendental moral appeals but from within aesthetic experience itself. Arendt develops "the receptive side of virtuoso action"[50] through a Kantian account of judgment, "not by abandoning the aestheticization of action but by completing it."[51]

There is a problem, however, with this effort to read Arendt's aesthetic theory of judgment as taming the *agon*. Although such a reading reintroduces and holds the intersubjective element in Arendt's theorizing together with the agonistic subjective one (and thus goes a good way toward combating a reading of the aesthetic in Arendt's political theory as amoral or immoral), it treats aesthetic experience—whether in the account of judgment or of action—as a model or an analogy.[52] If we interrogate the importance of aesthetic experience in political life itself, the ethical power of Arendt's political theorizing will come to the fore.

My Arendtian provocation then is that, in the first and most elemental sense, we need a vigorous and diverse public and democratic life not for the sake of individual glory, or of winning immortality and defeating a nauseating futility,[53] nor for the sake of "making the world beautiful" so as to redeem appearances,[54] or of acting in concert,[55] or of sheer survival. Rather, we need such a public realm to sustain and intensify our awareness of reality. And this is a profoundly ethical need. Without such an awareness we can neither belong well to a world of others nor care for them well. Indeed, implicit in Arendt's work is the contention that whether we are, in fact, *humans* in any specific sense at this point in our history depends on our capacity to belong to and care for one another in such a way as to make our sense of the real fuller and deeper. This is what proves so moving to us brittle but not yet broken democrats, despite Arendt's own considerable reservations about the extent to which radical democracy is possible today,[56] despite her failure to adequately theorize politics as an everyday purposeful activity,[57] and despite her almost complete lack of theoretical tools with which to see issues of social and economic equality as political.[58] Despite all of this, there is, nonetheless, an important incitement toward radical democratic political life rooted in her ontological concerns and aestheticism.[59]

Thus, as I argue, it is by no means unmediated pleasure at the *deinon* quality of human particularity, nor is it just any quality of vitality or feeling of being alive at which Arendt's aestheticism aims. Her aestheticism is mindful—indeed, driven—by the need for a world sufficiently common that human particularity and plurality can be cherished and saved, a world in which the texture of reality is fullness as opposed to force.

If our greatest ethical challenge is how to intensify our awareness of reality, we must begin with Arendt's account of our capacity to experience reality in our postmetaphysical appearing world. This forms the subject matter of Chapter 2. No longer confirmed through a Christian *ens creatum* or a Greek *physis*, how does our sense of the real emerge in an appearing world? My primary concern is to argue that aesthetic experience is central to Arendt's pursuit of this question, and in so doing, I focus on the relationship between plurality and our sense of reality as it is illuminated by aesthetic experience. I develop what I refer to as Arendt's ontology of display. The centerpiece of the argument is that in an appearing world, our sense of reality depends on a mutual aesthetic provocation between actors and spectators—that is, it depends on the urge to see and be seen, to hear and be heard, to touch and be touched in a world of plural others. I then extend this basic relationship between plurality, reality, and aesthetic provocation to a consideration of Arendt's preoccupation with the *vita activa* and the *vita contemplativa*. In both cases Arendt's predominant concern is with how each domain of experience and the relations between them might best contribute to our capacity to intensify our awareness of reality. In both cases, then, Arendt's work is guided by essentially ethical concerns.

I am concerned in Chapter 3 with a discussion of these ontological concerns as they bear on Arendt's theory of the public sphere and her critique of the modern age. Arendt places an enormous ontological and existential burden on the public sphere as a space of appearances, arguing that it has an unmatched capacity to engender and confirm the reality of what appears in it. In particular, it is the one domain in which freedom can become a tangible experience, and consequently in which human particularity can be felt, witnessed, and saved. As such, the public sphere is the site for the miracle-like capacity of humans, in responsive provocation, to begin a new course of action and thus stand out against a world whose profound inertia always threatens their freedom. Further, it is in the public sphere that our sense of the world as a place, shared, and with a certain temporal continuity is perpetually won and renewed. In short, the public sphere is the fertile ground in which a sense of human reality and meaningfulness can grow.

Arendt's argument here has a certain historical urgency. That is, the modern age is characterized by both the slow demise of the ability of metaphysical truth to gather and sustain a sense of a shared world and the emergence of certain philosophical, scientific, and political events that have made the creation and maintenance of the public sphere, as Arendt theorizes it, extremely difficult. World alienation is the central condition of the modern age. Arendt's political idiom helps identify the forms of suffering and depravation peculiar to and so widely extended in this condition. Her political theory is fired by a feeling, not for the many forms of suffering social injustices inflict, but for the suffering that accompanies the injustice of living in obscurity precisely because of the way it attenuates the power of the mutual aesthetic provocation through which our sense of the real is born. Thus I argue that this form of injustice is prior to the forms of social injustice that preoccupy the modern political imagination, and I close by making the case for privileging a public sensibility attentive to the depravations of obscurity, but one that fruitfully mediates the tensions between the public passion for distinction and concerns for social injustice.

If the public world is to carry the burden Arendt places on it, it will need to provide some degree of permanence, some "willed continuity in time" (*BPF*, 5). In Chapter 4 I elaborate on the nature of our own historical predicament as it concerns both the loss of and the prospects for worldly permanence and stability. I begin with a discussion of the relationship Arendt draws between beauty and durability. I then turn briefly to her analysis of the practice of authority, through which human affairs were powerfully enclosed and stabilized. I argue that it was the beauty of acts in a far-distant past that became sacralized and that anchored this form of authority. No longer possible *for us,* we must sacralize a different kind of beauty if our world is to attain relative durability. And this concerns our human capacity to begin. Turning to Arendt's account of judging, I argue that in this practice we experience our mutual vulnerability and need for one another as beings capable, through initiative, of constituting a world. What may give our world a measure of durability is the way our capacity to augment the human condition of natality moves us, the way we find it pleasurable and beautiful. And for this we need the high degree of responsiveness to human particularity that judging requires; it draws us into the density of the world, and in so doing fosters the ethical stance that Arendt's ontology demands.

But how do we stay alive to this density? What kinds of worldly relations, public encounters, and mental traveling are required? What are the specific difficulties we face as we seek to sustain our awareness of reality in the dense plurality of our appearing world? Ours is a world structured by finitude—a finitude of time and place always already overlaid with forms of power that create, institutionalize, and enforce various kinds of human oblivion. In Chapter 5 I pursue the relationship between dimensions of human finitude and the temptations of oblivion as it bears on the mental practice of judging and on practical-political engagement. I pursue the former by carefully analyzing two different sets of political judgments that Arendt herself made, the latter through an examination of the remarkable political friendship that developed between a black civil rights activist and the Exalted Cyclops of the Ku Klux Klan in Durham, North Carolina, in the 1970s. Through these cases I develop an Arendtian-inspired argument concerning ethical responsibility in politics. I call this the obligation to renew, to cultivate those sensibilities and practices that enable us to hold open the space of the world in a renewing invitation to others to act, for without their deeds and judgments we cannot sufficiently interrupt and challenge those that prevail: Our sense of the world rigidifies, too readily reproduces itself, and our feeling for its reality and the reality of others is diminished. Each move in this direction is a move away from the understanding citizens need to further the pragmatic tasks of democratic political life.

2 Aesthetic Provocation, Plurality, and Our Sense of the Real

> The sad truth of the matter is that most evil is done by people
> who never made up their minds to be or do evil or good.
> —HANNAH ARENDT, *The Life of the Mind: Thinking*

As a reporter for the *New Yorker* at the 1963 trial of Adolf Eichmann
in Israel, Hannah Arendt closely observed a key functionary of the Nazi
regime whose political ideal, she argued, had been to render human particularity superfluous (*OT,* 457). What most struck her about Eichmann was
what she called his "remoteness from reality" (*EJ,* 288). He was, she argued,
protected by "clichés, stock phrases, adherence to conventional, standard-
ized codes of expression and conduct...against reality, that is, against the
claim on our thinking attention that all events and facts make by virtue of
their existence" (*LMT,* 4). Long before this encounter, Arendt had been preoccupied with the problem of reality: Her entire critique of the modern age,
as I argue in Chapter 3, had been oriented toward an analysis of those developments—philosophical, technological, and political—that contributed
to an attenuated sense of reality. The existential weight that she attributed
to the public-political realm as a realm of appearance also wells out of this
deep concern with the problem of reality. Even further back, Arendt's critique of romanticism in her first postdoctoral writing, later published as
Rahel Varnhagen, coheres around a critique of the worldless irreality of the

romantic outlook and sensibility. Finally, her analysis of the assault on our sense of reality that occurs under totalitarian conditions remained a constant thread throughout her work on the subject.

Neither Arendt's understanding of the problem nor her thoughts on how to face it are simple, nor do they receive systematic formulation.[1] Certainly the nature of the evil she believed she observed in Eichmann was tied, in her view, to a profoundly impoverished capacity to experience reality. And clearly Arendt believed that this kind of evil was increasingly prevalent in the modern world. The well-known thesis she pursued was that evil of this kind was the result neither of dark malevolence nor deeply willed malice. Rather, it was born of social conditions that increasingly made it possible for selves, without determinate decision to do so, to evade experiencing reality. That is, evil was the issue of a world designed to protect us from the plural heterogeneous quality of experience, from the intrusion of the surprising, the unusual, and the new. In such a world neither particular others nor events call us. We go about as if numbed to the profuse provocations of a hungry plural world. Knowing little of this hungering world, our sense of obligation and of responsibility cannot be born, as they must be if they are to be born at all, amidst our efforts to respond. There is only stillbirth.

Such evil, then, as Arendt found it before her in the person of Eichmann, and as we may find it in less obviously perverse forms before and in ourselves, is exhibited in lack—lack of responsiveness, of depth perception, of moral imagination about the lives of others and about diverse facets of human experience—in "remoteness from reality."

Arendt's meditation on this form of evil leads us toward an exploration of the relation between plurality—one of the central concepts of her political theory—and reality. Her philosophical and political-theoretical concerns, I suggest, center on the need to enhance our attentiveness to the condition of plurality. Arendt conceives this condition on multiple levels, but there are two primary conceptualizations: the human condition of plurality—meaning the condition "of living as a unique and distinct being among equals," the fact that "men not Man live on the earth"—and the plurality of the human condition—meaning the multiple and distinct practices, needs, and capabilities of human beings that correspond to the various conditions of our human existence. Arendt defines these conditions as "life itself, natality and mortality, worldliness, plurality, and the earth" (*HC*, 178, 7, 11). Perhaps Arendt's central thought is that it is responsiveness to plurality in this twofold sense that gives us our sense of reality: *that* things are at all, and that they therefore may matter in some way or another—indeed, that they cry out to be countenanced by us. This thought points to a vital need for and reliance on others: Our very ability to experience the specific realness of another, an event, not to speak of ourselves, depends on mutual responsiveness to the particularity of others—and by extension to ourselves and plural voices within ourselves. Attentiveness to plurality gives rise to a certain density within our experience. It intensifies our awareness of reality. To be in this density is, I believe, to be in the place of ethics.

Moving toward this density, however, requires a certain kind of aesthetic experience. This is the central argument of this chapter and an unstated proposition that I believe undergirds Arendt's ontological and political reflections. In the following discussion I examine the relationship between plurality and our sense of reality as it is illuminated by aesthetic experience. I first address Arendt's ontological reflections so as to develop general features of her account of our capacity to experience reality. I then turn to the *vita activa* to develop the argument that we need to experience the plurality of the human condition to sustain our sense of reality. I close by delving further into this relationship between attentiveness to plurality and our sense of reality as it occurs in contemplative life, focusing on the activity of thinking.

In organizing my discussion in this way I aim to draw attention to the profound way in which Arendt's ontological concerns guide her incursions into both the *vita activa* and the *vita contemplativa*. Reading her from this vantage point, it looks as if her entire intellectual effort was devoted to understanding how each domain of human experience and the relations between them might best contribute to our capacity to move toward and reveal the density of human experience, how they might contribute to intensifying our awareness of reality. In each case, as I argue, aesthetic experience is central.

Before turning directly to Arendt's ontology, we should recall her belief that, historically speaking, our postmetaphysical condition is at once new and also a return to a beginning. This she captures by culling the *experience* behind the central story of beginnings in the West: "We know only 'male and female created he them'—that is, from the beginning this plurality poses an enormous problem."[2] Today, as once before, we stand nakedly in the plural—naked because the doctrines and traditions of meaning that have clothed and "civilized" this awesome plurality have collapsed, leaving us with, as Arendt puts it, "the elementary problem of human living-together" (*BPF*, 167).

It is from this uncertain situation—one forced upon us, in Arendt's view, by modern events—that she takes her bearings. That is, this condition of naked plurality becomes for Arendt the beginning of all ethical possibility.

In a strikingly positive formulation, Arendt asserts, "Plurality is the law of the earth" (*LMT*, 19).[3]

Ontological Reflections

> It is in the very nature of every new beginning that it breaks into the world as an "infinite improbability," and yet it is precisely this infinitely improbable which actually constitutes the very texture of everything we call real.
> —HANNAH ARENDT, "What is Freedom?" (*BPF*)

Arendt's ontological reflections are captivating and stand, in my view, at the creative center of her work. The questions that drive her and that her work engenders are ethical: What kind of beings are we that our sense of reality, our sense for the real objectivity of the world—including that of ourselves and others—can be so degraded, so blunted that we do not feel its impact? How do we attain and maintain a sense of reality such that human existence is illuminated? How is our perceptive sensitivity stimulated? What are our challenges and disabilities with respect to this crucial capacity?

At the core of Arendt's ontological reflections are various forms of repetition and automatism that course through human existence and form the background against which the eruption of the new and distinct appears. This experience of eruption against repetitious background is a crucial part of what makes it possible for humans to experience a sense of reality and thus to illuminate human existence.

Prototypical of this background automatism, and really the primordial experience of it, is biological life itself and the forms of labor in which all human life must in one way or another engage to sustain itself.[4] Arendt refers to this as the realm of necessity, shorthand for those most elemental life processes in which humans qua *animal laborans* toil in eternally necessary and repetitious cycles of production, consumption, and procreation. From this angle, human life appears as a relentless cycle of compelling multiplicitous needs—a cycle bounded on one side by appearing (birth) and on the other by disappearing (death). Here humans experience a world of intense functional necessity where the beat of life wells out of the crush to survive. In the form of the life process, nature presses inexorably on all living things, its mode compulsion, often violence. It is independent of human will and neither progresses nor regresses. It has no temporality; it is the realm of "being forever" (*BPF*, 28), endlessly turning, ever recurring in its boundless fertility. Here, in some basic sense, everything is indistinguishable and the same insofar as all things are coerced by a profusion of incoherent and conflicting drives and needs in the service of the life process.

To dwell in the rhythms of necessity's relentless repetition can produce a sense of blissful belonging to the earth and to one another as nature's creatures. Born of the shared assurances with which need arises and must be satisfied, this form of togetherness is not entirely politically irrelevant. But in this context its importance is that it constitutes one of our prototypical experiences of the probable, the reliable, the eternal relentless whose unremarkability forms the repetitious but dependable background of automatism before which the remarkable might appear and distinguish itself as such.

Our other prototypical experience of the probable and reliable emerges in relation to the ability of *homo faber* to make novel objects for human use and pleasure. "The work of our hands" yields artifacts that have a stabilizing function, one that has an important bearing on our sense of reality. Arendt writes, "In contradiction to the Heraclitean saying that the same man can never enter the same stream—men, their ever-changing nature notwithstanding, can retrieve their sameness, that is, their identity, by being related to the same chair and the same table" (*HC*, 137). Thus the relative permanence of human artifacts provides a world of the familiar and dependable. In habitual intercourse with this world, its stability anchors us in relation to a merciless temporal stream. Without such moorings, Arendt suggests, we would not be sufficiently identical with ourselves to even experience the quality of objectivity (*HC*, 137), and this, of course, is a crucial precondition of our capacity to experience reality.

If these experiences form, variously, the coercive, probable, and deeply pervasive features of human existence, how does Arendt theorize the nature and possibility of "the infinitely improbable"? Here her concern is not with the mortal but with the natal, eruptive nature of human existence—with the fact that we possess, as she puts it, a capacity for miracles, for initiating new beginnings.[5] I explore this in elaborating what I call her ontology of display.

In developing this late ontology, I am drawing primarily from the first section of Arendt's final and uncompleted work, *The Life of the Mind*, entitled "Appearance." Her overriding concern in this section is to offer a phenomenological account of the primacy of appearances against the two-world theory of metaphysics and its elementary presumption of a higher order of reality lying behind or above the merely appearing world. She writes, "*[We] are of the world and not merely in it*" (*LMT*, 22), and it is here that together, as creatures uniquely fitted for such a world, we engender and confirm our sense of worldly reality.

The concept of appearance, of course, had been central to *The Human Condition*, in which Arendt developed her unique conceptualization of the public realm as a space of appearance. In that text, however, her concern with the appearingness of the world had been confined largely to her account of action, and her emphasis was on the courageous, agonistic insertion of oneself into a world of others in the effort to make one's appearance explicitly as a unique being among others. Arendt's reflections on judgment were also concerned with appearances but were preoccupied with the spectator of appearances as the one who receives and confirms them in being.

In her final work Arendt extends her account of the space of appearance to become a full-fledged ontology and, importantly, theorizes the *relation between* actors and spectators. Here all animate beings are simultaneously subjects of perception and objects perceived, and it is in and through their active reciprocal intertwining that beings in an appearing world come to exist.[6]

The richest sources for this development in Arendt's thinking are the writings of Adolf Portmann and Maurice Merleau-Ponty. Arendt read both for the first time in the same period late in her life in preparation for writing *The Life of the Mind*. The fascinating work of Portmann, the Swiss biologist and zoologist, gives Arendt further and more decisive evidence for articulating what Portmann called "the value of the surface" for the primacy of that which appears. She finds in his biological research confirmation of an urge to appear and to display—an urge that binds and relates all living beings. Indeed, for Portmann's new science, the research problem was "not *what something is*, but how it appears" (*LMT,* 28).[7]

Merleau-Ponty's influence on Arendt's thinking is somewhat harder to trace because she clearly had, also, fundamental disagreements with his work. Still, apart from secondary works, Arendt read exclusively from Merleau-Ponty's final period, in which his project was to develop a "new ontology."[8] The central and new concept of this later ontology was reversibility: the claim that all being is simultaneously sentient and sensible. As Merleau-Ponty says in one radical and enticing formulation, "As many painters have said, I feel myself looked at by things... so that the seer and the visible *reciprocate* one another and we no longer know which sees and which is seen."[9] Indeed, Merleau-Ponty sought to suspend the opposition between subject and object in the "chiasm" or reciprocal intwining of the sentient and the sensible.[10] His was a philosophy at the joints where sensed and sensing crossed over, encroached, reciprocated. He called this kinship *flesh*, a word with which he sought to designate, without untangling, the chiasm or crossing that he considered our primordial relationship to the world. We are, as he puts it, "Visible-seers," and it is this wild primordial reversibility through which our appearing world emerges into being for us.[11]

What is striking about the first section of *The Life of the Mind* is that although in the second paragraph Arendt introduces the essence of Merleau-Ponty's notion of reversibility—a notion that is entirely central to the meaning of the section—she neither cites nor works explicitly with Merleau-Ponty's term, never once refers to his "new ontology," even while throughout the section she quotes extensively from the only two works in which Merleau-Ponty developed it.[12] This is all the more interesting when we consider that it is precisely because of this primordial reversibility, because we are "at the same time...subjects and objects—perceiving and being perceived" (*LMT,* 20), that Arendt argues we are beings fitted for, geared to, an appearing world. Hence Arendt resists while being profoundly indebted to Merleau-Ponty's "Wild Being," with its central concepts of flesh and reversibility.[13]

Two primary theoretical differences help account for the silence of Arendt's indebtedness. Merleau-Ponty's notion of *flesh* was both too "wild" and too universal. First, Arendt must have found his assertion that "man exists only in movement,...that the world and Being hold together only in movement" too totalizing, and as such forebodingly at odds with the importance she placed on permanence and stability in human existence.[14] Even while writing of profound reciprocal intertwinement, she retained, perhaps clung to, the language of subject and object—language Merleau-Ponty completely abandoned in his late period. Second, Arendt theorized more autonomy for the thinking ego, resisting Merleau-Ponty's effort to extend the chiasm to the relationship between mind and body by defining "the mind as the *other side* of the body," since "there is a body of the mind, and a mind of the body and a chiasm between them," as he put it.[15]

Still, her indebtedness to Merleau-Ponty's phenomenology is palpable in their shared sense of the drama of perception, of the profuse dimensionality in and through which things in an appearing world come to be, of the relative, perspectival essence of such a world, and the active reversibility between the sensed and the sensing. The central terms of Arendt's ontology—eliciting self-display, mutual responsiveness, and provocation—bear much of Merleau-Ponty's wild sensibility, if not his explicit formulations. Such influences adumbrated, let me turn to a direct account of Arendt's ontology of display.

In *Thinking,* Arendt opens: "In this world which we enter, appearing from a nowhere, and from which we disappear into a nowhere, *Being and Appearing* coincide.... Nothing and nobody exists in this world whose very being does not presuppose a *spectator*.... Not Man but men inhabit this planet. Plurality is the law of the earth" (*LMT,* 19). In these few lines the ethical-aesthetic texture of what I call Arendt's ontology of display is laid forth. Here already it is evident that Arendt's answer to how our perceptive sensitivity is sustained and stimulated will be deeply dependent on certain relations with others, that the possibility, in an appearing world, of actualizing the specificity of an individual's existence, its infinite improbability, depends on plurality. Arendt's basic approach to the nature of reality is phenomenal, and the central metaphor that carries the weight of her phenomenological conception is that of the theater. Like the reality created on the stage, things and creatures of the world are appearing in nature such that what appears is "meant to be" perceived—seen, heard, touched, tasted, and smelled—by sentient creatures.[16] Furthermore, without this perceptivity, without sentient spectators "able to acknowledge, recognize and react to what is...meant for their perception," nothing *is* (*LMT,* 19). Hence plurality is the "law of the earth" in the sense that, for anything to be at all, the basic unit of plurality—actor-spectator or thing-sentient creature—is presupposed. Plurality brings into being "what is."[17]

But the intentionality of the world is not merely spectatorial. All creatures, Arendt goes on to say, simultaneously appear and perceive others, are both in this sense objects and subjects. And it is this reversibility that makes all sentient beings "fit for" this world in which Being and Appearing coincide. Critical to this sense in which things are fit for the world is Arendt's suggestion that we cannot make sense of the enormous richness of what is presented to the senses in functional terms alone, as, for example, the need of the organism for self-preservation or reproduction. When it comes to appearance, there is a "sheer functional *superfluity*" in what is displayed (*LMT,* 27).[18] Experience intuitively confirms such claims even at the most simple level of life, as when we cast our eye along the edge of the sea alighting on the almost fluorescent orange of the starfish clinging to dark rock and find, as we kneel for a closer look, that we quickly pass over its pale purple sister, drawn toward the delicate translucence of the sea anemone's emerald fingers, and still on to marvel at the blood-red urchin's prickly spines. What can such colors be *for*? we wonder. Arendt suggests we not seek an answer to this question alone, or even primarily, in a functional direction. To do so is to reduce the richness of "what is" in the manner of a philistine whose hallmark, as she puts it in another work, is "an inability to think and to judge a thing apart from its function or utility" (*BPF,* 215). Our experience of the surface profusion of the world invites us to understand it at a fundamental level in terms of display.

We find a more active sense to this display quality of the sentient world in higher animals, reaching a climax in humans. In these higher forms of life, Arendt argues, we can speak of what she calls the "urge to self-display" (*LMT*, 29). Here Arendt follows the work of Portmann in suggesting that there is a spontaneous impulse to show or exhibit the self, a response to "the overwhelming effect of being shown" (*LMT*, 21). She writes, "*Whatever can see wants to be seen, whatever can hear calls out to be heard, whatever can touch presents itself to be touched*" (*LMT*, 29). Here, too, Arendt's theatrical metaphors carry her meaning. Just as the actor, on stage before the eyes of all, feels the thrill of being seen and responds spontaneously to it by excelling, so higher forms of life are possessed by an urge to self-display—not the urge to express some inner authenticity but the urge to make its *presence* felt, to be recognized and acknowledged "as an individual" (*LMT*, 29).[19] Here Arendt tries to articulate what she calls "the expressiveness of an appearance," which is of a different order from the commonsense notion that, when we *express* something, it is something inner that is "pressed out" (*LMT*, 30). This urge to display and self-display, which is the very essence of things in an appearing world, by contrast, expresses *itself*, makes an effort to shine forth, to excel in its particularity before others. To be sure, concealment is always a passive and, in some creatures, active event in the appearingness of the world as well. Arendt quotes Merleau-Ponty affirmatively in this context: "No thing, no side of a thing, shows itself except by actively hiding the others" (*LMT*, 25).[20] My point here, however, is that inasmuch as things appear, they demand recognition, long for reaction, desire to be countenanced.

It is in this sense, too, that we should understand Arendt's thought that plurality is the law of the earth. That is, sentient creatures, according to their complexity, possess an *active* response to being perceived—in the form of an impulse to distinguish themselves. Thus "what is" is constantly contributing to and bringing forth the wild spectacular quality of the world.

Here, then, to summarize, we find an ontology of display suggesting that reality in an appearing world is something born out of a highly charged mutual sensuous provocation between actors and spectators that is essentially aesthetic in nature. All living creatures are in this respect linked together in a continuous though developmentally differentiated whole. Arendt uses the language of "impulse," "urge," and "spontaneity" to underline the mysterious "given" quality to this conception of the nature of the world. Here we have a universe alive with yearning to sense and be sensed, a universe that perpetually gives birth to its own plurality and profusion.

Yet there is discontinuity between the nonhuman natural and the human world as well, for "purely" natural things "emanate" this profusion, they have "no choice but to show whatever properties a living being possesses" (*LMT,* 36). Against this backdrop of emanation, humans prepare and make this profusion "fit for" the world of appearance. In humans, the urge to make our presence felt through self-display is manifest in the effort to "present [ourselves] in word and deed and thus indicate how [we] *wish* to appear, what in [our] opinion is fit to be seen and what is not" (*LMT,* 34).[21] We present our response, our take on the world, and this response always demands both active display and active concealment. It is because of this active capacity to display and conceal that we bring forth the plurality of the earth in a unique way; it is this capacity that marks the radical discontinuity of the human species with the rest of the natural world. We conceive of this relation best as a continuity out of which discontinuity arises, as a "difference in identity," to use a phrase Arendt coins in another context (*LMT,* 187).

This ability to *present* ourselves is of course Arendt's way of saying that humans alone have the ability to be free. And the way Arendt theorizes this freedom appears indeed to rely on this ontology of display.[22] That is to say, our capacity to take undetermined action, to begin something new is rooted in the unprecedented fact of our own naked appearance in an already existing world. It is rooted in the human condition of natality. Having the quality of the miraculous, appearing from a "nowhere," statistically speaking improbable and without model, our capacity for action is a "response" to this unprecedented fact of our birth (*HC,* 177). It is a response to the unprecedented we feel ourselves to be and that others perceive in us and solicit of us—as if the shock of birth itself elicits response. So this sensuous provocation, this active urge to self-display is also the engendering root of our own capacity for freedom. As Arendt somewhat mystically but compellingly puts it, "Because he is a beginning, man can begin; to be human and to be free are one and the same" (*BPF,* 167).

Hence the capacity to begin in which we undergo a kind of "second birth" by "confirm[ing] and tak[ing] on the naked fact of our original appearance" (*BPF,* 176–77) is distinctive to humans as natal beings. Yet this does not mean that we humans create ourselves. Arendt does not share in this Hegelian-Marxian premise. Her dissent is rooted in her identification of a structure of finitude that refers, in the first instance, to "the sheer thereness of being" (*LMT,* 37). By this she means the elemental fact that the world long preceded our appearance and will long outlast our disappearance. In the second instance, it refers to the inevitable concealment that passively accompanies all events of appearance, a phenomenon rooted in plurality itself. That is, because we exist only in the plural in an appearing world, the *only* mode through which things can be acknowledged is in the way they seem. Here again the metaphor of the theatrical stage carries her meaning. That which appears, in its sheer thereness, is common to all, yet it is observed by spectators, each of whom occupies a slightly different "seat." It-seems-to-me, *dokei-moi*, as the fundamental mode of appearance, means that everything that appears, whether it chooses or not, having been received by a plurality of others whose "particular perspectives [are] determined by location in the world as well as by particular organs of perception," will acquire a kind of "disguise" (*LMT*, 38). This inevitably thwarts our ability to control how our self-presentation affects others, as well as our ability to know others in any definitive sense. Here the point is that disguise is an inadvertent, inevitable accompaniment of every appearance in a world of plural others.

Thus, as a consequence of this structure of finitude, there is a dense and recalcitrant quality to our experience of the world in which plurality reigns. But this density also teems, is expectant and pregnant. The appearingness of the plural world lures us beyond any given presentation it offers. Thus to return to the issue of human freedom conceived as *self*-presentation, in our eliciting self-presentation we suffer a beautiful vulnerability. That is to say, our perception of the world, which is always the substance of our self-presentation, is profoundly disputable, profoundly and endlessly provoking, however uniquely our own it may be. And this is true as much for what it presents as for what it conceals. Arendt's conception, then, of this effort at self-presentation (which she calls "glory" in her "Greek" works) is not a unidirectional, megalomaniacal urge to be admired by others. Rather, while clearly an urge to be acknowledged and a hope of being praised, this urge at the center of our being is, in its very essence, "world open and communicative" (*HC*, 168). As the reference for the actor on a stage is always a specific audience, so, too, do our efforts at self-presentation always "play" to a specific community.[23] Intrinsic to our effort at self-presentation is a deliberate response to and moving out toward the plural world of others. We offer ourselves—that is, our take on the world in eliciting presentation—and depend on our world's perceptivity, on others' own urge, in turn, to make their presence in the world felt through self-display. Thus the very quality and character of our particularity emerges, if it emerges at all, in the interstices of the human world and is perpetually evading transparent knowledge and control—that of others as well as our own.[24] We are essentially in this regard nonsovereign beings, beings embedded in a profound finitude that is the very condition of the appearing world's fecundity.

Our urge for self-presentation may result—indeed, more often than not does result—in many forms of distortion on our part and on the part of those we seek to provoke. Such distortions exceed the inherent semblance, disguise-quality that accompanies all appearances. I have in mind lies, manipulation, ambition, self-deception, willed ignorance,[25] and other forms of oblivion. These are the enduring dangers and temptations of an appearing world, and they point to the fragility and vulnerability of all our efforts to offer ourselves to the world. I reflect in a sustained manner on these dangers and temptations in Chapter 5, in the context of an argument concerning ethical responsibility in politics. They are, however, not of central concern just now.

Thus far I have argued that for Arendt the engendering ground of the real is the mutual provocation that occurs between appearing beings whose sensual apparatuses and desires and urges "fit them" as spectating subjects and observed objects for the phenomenal world: "[We] exist only in the plural" (*LMT*, 99). The specific reality of appearance *is* only in the plural, and that wild, spectacular plurality, as our individual reality itself, is engendered through a kind of mutual sensuous provocation that is aesthetic in nature.[26] I do not here argue against the contention that intersubjectively formed cognitive interests are also important in giving birth to the world's plurality. Arendt, to be sure, speaks of the fact that humans alone make our presence felt by exercising "deliberate choice" about how we *wish* to appear, and, as I have indicated, speech is our primary means of doing so. My point is that we do not cognitively decide to "make our presence felt." The way Arendt theorizes this phenomenon is nearer to an aesthetic-existential drive that manifests itself in the world in multiple forms, among which are, importantly, cognitive-purposive aims.[27] Conceptually speaking, the urge to make our presence felt and to feel that of others—what I have referred to as mutual aesthetic provocation in which we, responsive to an appearing world, offer ourselves in an eliciting display—is the *conditio sine non* of the world's plurality.[28] Here we begin to see the first elemental link between the aesthetic ground of Arendt's account of reality in our appearing world and the ethical concerns with particularity and human plurality that govern her political theorizing.

Yet as Arendt also argues, "Reality in a world of appearances is first of all characterized by 'standing still and remaining' the same long enough to become an *object* for acknowledgment and recognition by a *subject*" (*LMT*, 45), and, "Every living thing depends on a world that solidly appears as the location for its appearance" (*LMT*, 21–22). In what sense does Arendt think this "solidly" and this still-standing and remaining the same? Here the question is not how appearances are actualized but how the reality of their thereness is confirmed, guaranteed. The problem we are concerned with is our "sensation of reality," our feeling for the realness of ourselves and the world *writ large.*

The reality of what we perceive in an appearing world is, Arendt argues, guaranteed by its "worldly context" (*LMT,* 50), by which she means at the most general level what we share in common. Thinking of this in the most basic of ways, all sensuous creatures despite or amidst the "surprising" diversity of the world's appearances and the "astounding diverseness of sense organs among animal species," have both "appearances as such in common," as well as the elemental fact of their specific coming and going (*LMT,* 20). We share, as Arendt puts it, a common stage (*LMT,* 21). Yet this fact of sharing the same stage does not of itself impart a sensation of reality, does not make the world feel solid and sufficiently identical with itself to confirm our sense of it and of our own reality. This depends, on the one hand, on a sixth sense that guarantees that my utterly different five senses sense the same object and that makes my sensing of the object communicable to others. And it depends, on the other hand, on what Merleau-Ponty has called "our perceptual faith." In describing this faith, Arendt writes, "Our certainty that what we perceive has an existence *independent of* the act of perceiving, depends entirely on the object's also appearing *as such* to others and being acknowledged by them" (*LMT,* 46; my italics).[29] But this formulation may be misleading. What does Arendt mean by saying that our sensation of an object's reality depends on its also appearing "*as such*" to others? By "as such" she certainly does not mean "as identical." Precisely to the contrary: Our perceptual ability to transcend the subjectivism of our own seeing and thus gain a sensation of the object's reality depends on the perceptual acts of distinct others. In an important passage in "The Concept of History" where Arendt's considerations are less ontological, the point I think becomes clear. She writes, "The Greek learned to exchange his own viewpoint, his own 'opinion'—the way the world appeared and opened up to him...with those of his fellow citizens. Greeks learned to *understand*—not to understand one another as individual persons, but to look upon the same world from one another's standpoint, *to see the same in very different and frequently opposing aspects*" (*BPF,* 51; my italics).[30] The point here is that our ontological assurance in the act of perception depends on the perceived thing taking on a certain kind of objectivity, an objectivity that can be won only if our perception is embedded in (and piqued by) the multiplicitous perspectival quality that all things acquire in an appearing world.[31]

When Arendt argues that our sensation of reality depends on a world shared in common, a world that "solidly appears" and can become the "location" in which appearances can "stand still and remain the same," this is a solidity and a sameness born through the responses and provocations of witnessing spectators and sensuous actors for whom the spectacular display quality of the appearing world is paramount.[32] The crucial point here is that our capacity to experience a world in common, to constitute a certain worldly solidity is utterly dependent on the engendering ground of plurality itself, on aesthetic provocation among multiple, distinct appearing beings. The eruptions that this provocation elicit "save" perspective, if you will, from degenerating into repetitious sameness; they renew the world as something both vivid and shared. If, therefore, we can locate the common world at all, it is paradoxically to be found only where this eruptive eliciting provocation flourishes.[33] And while aesthetic provocation is not a sufficient ground for our ability to experience a world in common and thus to have a sensation of reality, it is a crucial dimension of that ability.[34] As such, because the existence of a world in common is a precondition for any appearing thing to be confirmed in being as such—and here human particularity is our first concern—this relationship between aesthetic provocation and the possibility of a common world forms the second elemental link between Arendt's account of reality in our appearing world and the ethical concerns with particularity and human plurality that govern her political theorizing.

If, in sum, we look carefully at Arendt's ontology of display, we encounter the argument that our capacity to sense the real depends on a mutual provocation between appearing beings, which is aesthetic in nature. Both our ability to actualize the plurality of the human condition as well as our ability to give experience some permanence by establishing a minimal sense of a common world rely on the vitality of this mutual aesthetic provocation. We are, then, in great need of one another's sensual yearning for one another in this sense.

Arendt's ontological reflections suggest that our sense of reality is something born of our experience of the driving coercive cycles of the life process, and of an overflowing sensuous profusion and diversity that perpetually brings itself before itself and into being. There is something of a ground/figure structure to the relationship Arendt draws between these mortal and natal aspects of human existence, with the artifacts of *homo faber* creating a sufficiently stable, humanly created environment from which ground and figure, probable and infinitely improbable might be distinguished.[35] And yet Arendt suggests that the substantiality of our ability to sense the reality of necessity has in significant degrees receded. To an unprecedented extent in the twentieth century, those of us who are in a position of privilege are now faced with having to choose to be present to the reality of necessity. That is, our experience of the compelling quality of existence itself has become in some sense optional; its very appearance in the world has come to depend greatly on aesthetic provocation between actor and spectator, on witness and testimony.[36] Electricity, the combustion engine, atomic science, and the promises of genetic science, for example, push back our direct experience of necessity, and the danger lies, as Arendt points out, in our forgetting that while these capabilities hide necessity from our senses, they in no way do away with it (*HC*, 125). So, if we, for example, think of a slew of problems associated with modern technology that have become political problems of the first order (for instance, nuclear waste, genetic engineering, ozone depletion, and water degradation), it becomes clear that our dominant social forms, ideas, and practices are intimately bound, to a novel extent, to denying the factuality of necessity.[37] All of these problems underline how great our need is for a world in which the plural unit of actor-spectator can give testimony and perform receptivity. The sheer factuality of the world—both socially and naturally understood—is in danger. And the power of Arendt's ontological reflections in this context lies in her insistence that there *is* a *there* to which we must not submit but which we must *encounter*. To deny this "there" is to risk paying a price blindly. At the very least, Arendt's formulations remind us that deliberate judgment is called for.[38]

In many respects, then, Arendt's ontological reflections point to a newfound fragility in our capacity to sense reality, to be present to "what is" under postmetaphysical conditions. And this is, of course, of profound concern, as the first requirement of all ethical discernment is "declar[ing] the presence of that which is present"[39] in its compulsion and profusion. We have neither the ancient Greek *physis* nor the Christian *ens creatum*. What we have is aesthetic provocation under conditions of plurality, a challenging and vulnerable ground, for what I have been suggesting we find in Arendt's work is an account of how our sense of the real is engendered in an appearing world, not that it is a natural constant as such. Arendt theorizes what I am calling "aesthetic provocation" and the initiative to which it is tied in the following way: "It may be stimulated by the presence of others...but never conditioned by them" (*HC*, 177). If this is so, and I believe it is, the aesthetic-existential urge to provoke and be provoked by appearances is a feature of ourselves as appearing beings that can never be conditioned away absolutely; still, the effective force in our lives of aesthetic provocation and the initiative to which it is tied is extremely mutable, subject to varying conditions, institutions, sensibilities, practices, and forms of power. This means, of course, that our sense of the real is likewise mutable. And, as I discuss in Chapter 3, it is Arendt's contention that our own historical conditions dangerously attenuate the power of what I am calling "aesthetic provocation" and have done so explicitly and increasingly since the onset of the modern age. "Modern sensibility," she says, "is not touched by obscurity" (*OR*, 70).

Our need is to cultivate our tragic pleasure—our pleasure in the feeling of reality intensified through the provoking presence of particular others and the recalcitrant and plural quality of the world thus engendered. We need strong particular others, by which I mean people in love with, stirred by Lessing's tragic pleasure. As I argue in Chapter 3, it is this need that makes us uniquely and historically vulnerable to the presence or absence, strength or weakness of public-political life. Indeed, our need should propel us toward the publicity of the public realm, for while Arendt clearly recognizes that all forms of human togetherness give us some sensation of reality insofar as self-disclosure or the unique particularity of appearing beings is implicit in everything one says and does (*HC*, 179),[40] the potential for intensifying our awareness of reality, making it fuller and deeper, is greatest, Arendt contended, in the merciless brightness of the public realm. And this is because such human togetherness constitutes the widest possible way to be seen and heard and to see and hear, and thus to let most fully appear the "living essence" of each unique person as each encounters the world and elicits, in turn, the world's countenance (*HC*, 50).[41]

Despite this existential weight with which Arendt burdens our public-political lives, however, other primary dimensions of human experience are also essential to our capacity to sustain and intensify our awareness of reality. I next turn to Arendt's account of the *vita activa*, offering a reading of her understanding of our need to experience the plurality of conditions essential to human life, focusing in particular on her controversial account of necessity. Thereafter I turn to the *vita contempletiva* to explore Arendt's account of the performance of thinking in which the self who, in a world of appearances is one, becomes pluralized into the duality of the thinking experience. In both domains of experience I show how aesthetic provocation under conditions of plurality draws us toward a density of human experience that is essential to our capacity to engender, sustain, and intensify our awareness of reality. In the former case, I am concerned with the plurality of the conditions of human existence; in the latter, with the plurality or duality of the thinking ego.

Underlying my analysis of Arendt's work here is the contention that her undeniable focus on the unique reality-intensifying capacities of public-political togetherness has diverted attention from the aesthetic sensibility of tragic pleasure in the plurality of sensibilities, perspectives, aims, wants, interests, capacities, and desires that animates her approach to human experience. This plurality, with its conflicts, encroachments, and mutual provocations, we must feel, indeed be vividly haunted by, if we are to be, again and again, drawn into the difficult density of human experience. Here alone can we articulate a sense of responsibility and obligation adequate to the condition of human plurality. If plurality is the law of the earth, it is from this law alone that we might begin to adequately conceive ethical responsibility.

The *Vita Activa,* Necessity, and the Plurality of the Conditions of Human Existence

> We walk with alien feet; we see with alien eyes; we recognize and greet people with an alien memory; we live from alien labor.
>
> —PLINIUS, *Naturalis Historia*

Arendt's reflections on necessity are among the most troubling and least appreciated aspects of *The Human Condition.* Her invocation of Plinius— who is describing the kind of loss experienced by Roman slaveholders who used other human beings to shield themselves from the crushing toll on their bodies and spirits exacted by life's necessity—should caution us away from a common reading of Arendt's views of necessity. On this reading, Arendt is thought to hold that because the essence of the life process is ceaseless compulsion, necessity must be dominated so that we can lead a fully human life in which we are freed for a life of speech and action. Like Aristotle, to whom Arendt is much indebted, the ontological status of necessity, it is argued, is far lower than the life of speech and action. The apparent insensitivity Arendt exhibits toward the life of *animal laborans,* her failure to find much specifically human and thus exalted about it, and her concomitant celebration of politics as something having little to do with life's necessary and compelling dimensions are at the heart of the moral objections to Arendt's work and to the charges of aestheticism and formalism many levy at her conception of the political.

Such concerns have been sharply articulated by feminist theorists attempting to identify the many facets of patriarchal power. Some have argued that Arendt's apparent devaluation of bodily existence and the concerns, practices, experiences, and outlooks peculiar to it actively obscure this important theoretical task.[42] Related concerns about Arendt's largely ahistorical and essentialist reading of necessity emerge from theorists deeply influenced by the Hegelian-Marxist account of labor as the key historical activity through which, in dialectical interchange with nature, our specific humanness is socially produced.[43]

While both concerns do point to enormous deficiencies in Arendt's conception of necessity, I am not concerned here to offer those arguments. Rather, my purpose is to develop the insights and warnings that Arendt issues from her phenomenological position.[44]

Arendt's primary concern is not with human subjection but rather with human domination. What Plinius calls attention to, what cries out in his words to be addressed, is loss—loss accrued to the dominant and the privileged who dedicate themselves to escaping the compelling life force that besets humans as creatures of nature. Committing "violent injustice" against their fellows, the "enormous" price they pay is "the substitution of vicarious life for real life" (HC, 119–20). The salient feature of this vicarious, alien life is loss of vitality and liveliness. Arendt considers this loss with utmost seriousness, and would have Plinius provokingly haunt her readers. This is the intention of her text here, an intention that has gone largely unnoticed amid the critical responses that these aspects of her work have (rightly) provoked. I intend to argue why and how we ought to let Arendt, through Plinius, haunt us.

My approach to Arendt's phenomenological understanding of necessity as articulated in *The Human Condition* is that this understanding forms an important part of her effort to see and value the human condition in its naked plurality.[45] What this naked plurality means in terms of the need humans have to orient and make ourselves fit for appearance in a postmetaphysical world, a world without a fixed center, is that, with Einstein, we must deny that "at a definite present instant all matter is simultaneously real" (HC, 263). This general relativity of all things means that it is the specific quality of the real to be evasively multidimensional. In such a world we need a theatrical agility, an ability to experience the world from multiple standpoints if we are to sustain our greatest possible attentiveness to it. I think of this as theatrical agility because, for the full impact of any play to occur, all involved—playwright, actors, spectators—must accomplish this kind of difficult but exhilarating inhabitation of multiple standpoints. Such agility involves taking pleasure not only in the harmony but also in the discordance that exists between dimensions of human existence as they reveal and conceal themselves to us from varying standpoints. As we practice this agile movement, our sense of reality will be heightened. The promise is that we can thus be more fully present—more responsive, more attentive to the world, and in this, somehow more fully human.

Thus if Arendt can be said to have a method in *The Human Condition,* it is to inhabit what Shiraz Dossa has aptly called the "sensibilities" that govern the three activities most fundamental to human life: labor, work, and action.[46] Arendt herself sometimes referred to these sensibilities as "mentalities," and she personified them in the actor, *homo faber,* and *animal laborans.* These figures allow her reader to more deeply experience the respective orientations to the world brought about in and through these activities. It is critical to note, however, since it is the source of much misunderstanding of this text, that these figures do not represent whole persons or classes of persons but are competing, conflicting, and interdependent sensibilities or standpoints within the self toward the world.[47] This of course is not to say that one sensibility may not dominate a particular historical period or a particular class of persons. In fact, the balance of these sensibilities in our time was the impetus that led Arendt to write the book.[48] Her aim in inhabiting variously and somewhat erratically these personified sensibilities is to rectify the imbalance she diagnoses as peculiar to our time in which the aims and outlook of *animal laborans* have come in her view to dominate.

Thus in *The Human Condition* Arendt is clearly concerned as a deep "occasional" thinker with reinvigorating our capacity to act in speech and deed in public life because, as the most free activities, they more fully embody, in her view, the specifically human ability to make our unique presence felt through our eliciting-offering gestures toward others. This high evaluation does not, however, come at the expense of every other activity, for even in a book in which she explicitly says she is not attempting "an exhaustive analysis of the activities of the *vita activa*" but is engaging in a more limited effort "to determine...their *political* significance" (*HC,* 78; my italics), (a fact rarely noted by her readers) we find significant positive evaluations of both the activities on their own terms and the meaning and necessity of the tensions existing between them. Even, therefore, in this "political" book there is a vision of what it means to be fully human—a vision that is achieved, in Arendt's view, not by being wholly freed from necessity for the life of speech and action but by sustaining the reality of the various conditions under which life was given.

If we look, then, at the realm of necessity, the home of *animal laborans,* we see that while it clearly stands in conflict with the specifically human life of speech and action, the relationship is not a simple one of domination and subordination. To be more fully human, we must heed the warning implicitly issued by Plinius.[49] We must not only be drawn to escape the violent, compelling nature of necessity but also be responsive to the losses entailed by the very effort to secure ourselves against life's necessity. These losses certainly stem from the violent injustice we do to others when we use them as a means of our own escape. But these losses also stem, as we shall see, from an accompanying attenuation of our sense of reality.[50] To be responsive to such losses, compulsion must not be wholly alien to us; we are in need of feeling its impact. This is one of Arendt's dominant thoughts about necessity, and, as I elaborate it, it will be clear that there is a multidimensionality to her conception of it, just as there is to each of the conditions of human existence on which she reflects.

In *The Human Condition* Arendt alternatively considers labor, work, and action, those activities most fundamental to human life because each corresponds to one of its basic conditions: labor to life itself, work to worldliness, and action to plurality. "Labor" and "life" constitute the realm of necessity that is shorthand for the most elemental life processes in which humans qua *animal laborans* engage in endlessly necessary, repetitious cycles of production, consumption, and procreation. In the realm of necessity, the human condition of life is reproduced. Here life's fertility is endlessly born with a force unmatched by other activities in the human condition.

Necessity stands, then, for the force of the life process that—unyielding—bears down on all living creatures insofar as they are creatures of the earth. In delineating this category of experience, Arendt is not trying to establish that the laboring activities driven by the life process cannot acquire different sociohistorical meanings. She is careful to say that all human activities have the quality of freedom and initiative to some extent.[51] Hence, for example, reproductive life is not a wholly coercive thing; it bears the marks of our cultural-historical and individual distinctiveness. And this of course could be traced and analyzed, although Arendt does not do so.[52] Her primary point is that what distinguishes between the three activities of the *vita activa*—labor, work, and action—is the measure of freedom in which each partakes. The category of necessity indicates those activities in which the force of life makes its impact most acutely felt through its primary modes of pain and suffering. It is of all activities *least* free. With her strict delineation of the term, then, Arendt insists that despite the tremendous variations in cultural meanings given to the activities driven by necessity, and despite the tremendous achievements of *homo faber* in reducing the pain and suffering that these activities cause us, there remains an irreducible compelling dimension to our experience which we ignore at our peril.

This compelling quality of the force of life is viewed differently by the three figures in the *vita activa*. To the political actor who represents the human need to communicate not merely what we want or need but *who* we are through deeds and especially speech, the toilsomeness of life is enslavement. The political actor needs liberation from the processes that beset us as creatures of nature—from the body's endless involvement in the cycle of consumption-production, from life's need to reproduce itself, to stave off death, decay, and unbearable bodily pain, and so on. The political actor needs liberation from nature's compulsion *for* a life in the world of human affairs in which speech and action are at stake. It is in this context (and this alone) that Arendt says we must be "freed from" necessity and the immediacy of its demands. The political actor needs a certain (uneasy) sense of alienation from and even hostility toward life.

From the point of view of *homo faber* as well, the impact of life must be kept at bay. Indeed, this is largely the aim of work: to build a more permanent artifice within which the world of human affairs can exist and attain relative durability vis-à-vis the relentless appearing and disappearing that characterizes the life process. Made by the purposive and limited intervention and destruction of nature through human technologies, the most important task of the human artifice, as Arendt puts it, is "to offer mortals a dwelling place more permanent and more stable than themselves" (*HC*, 152). The standards of such a human-made world are not the urgencies of the life process but those of utility, beauty, and permanence, and the things of that world form the objective in-between of a human world stabilized by their quality of objectivity. As Arendt puts it, "Without a world between man and nature, there is eternal movement but no objectivity" (*HC*, 137). In pursuing "his" ends, *homo faber* develops an instrumental sensibility toward nature and the realm of necessity. What *homo faber* sees, however, is not some confining force to be freed from but "the almost worthless things" out of which to build a world to house human affairs (*HC*, 135).

By contrast, from the point of view of *animal laborans*, thoroughly ensconced in the cyclical rhythms of life's demands, nature appears as the "great provider of all 'good things' which belong equally to all her children" (*HC*, 135). *Animal laborans* alone experiences what Arendt calls "the sheer bliss of being alive" (*HC*, 134), a kind of elemental happiness that can only come from the "prescribed cycle of painful exhaustion and pleasurable regeneration" (*HC*, 106). She writes, "The reward of toil and trouble lies in nature's fertility, in the quiet confidence that he who in 'toil and trouble' has done his part, remains a part of nature in the future of his children and his children's children" (*HC*, 107).

On this reading, humans possess competing and conflicting sensibilities toward necessity and the life process, each important in its own way. Necessity is thus, a multiplicitous experience for humans; plurality governs or should govern us, too, with respect to it. Alert to its multiplicitousness, alive to our conflicting experiences and needs with respect to it, necessity itself appears rife with meanings, irreducible and full of voices. Thus necessity elicits, in its refusal to be fixed and dominated, our attentive responsiveness. It has a *deinon* quality, and Arendt, I suggest, both exhibits tragic pleasure in it and attempts to cultivate such a pleasure in her readers, for it is this, once again, that helps intensify our awareness of reality.

What are the fruits of this analysis? To flesh out and examine these, I want to more fully explore Arendt's effort to appreciate the sensibility that arises from the "toil and trouble" that *animal laborans* experiences. What might be lost by collapsing the tension between the life of the actor and that of *animal laborans* by taking a thoroughly dominating attitude toward the human condition of life in favor of the political life of glorious speech and deed? (Such an attitude is, of course, precisely the one for which Arendt's detractors criticize her.) Why, more specifically, might it be ethically important to keep this voice, among others, sounding?

To begin with, it is from this dimension of the life of *animal laborans* that a very fundamental sense of belonging to the earth is born. This feeling, which Arendt sometimes refers to as "bliss," is a critical part of our sense of reality, for it provides us with an elemental identification with the earth and its creatures (*HC*, 120). This sense is not simply attained, however. It is a consequence of our intimate experience not only of the profusion of life's fertility but also of its coercions and limiting powers that we experience directly as embodied beings.[53] There is, furthermore, an element of mystery in this sense of belonging, insofar as it is a belonging to a continuum of life that reaches back into a "nowhere" and affirms the strange solidity of what has been "given as a free gift" (*HC*, 39). Arendt locates the activities of the life process in a private, nonpolitical realm because she seeks not only to keep public-political life free from compulsions of this life process but also to protect this sense of belonging and the strange sense of reality it gives us. In the profuse thereness of the fertile process of life, the bodily-driven dimension of human existence represented by *animal laborans* offers respite from the confines and directives of the human-centered public world. The metaphors Arendt uses in this context—depth, darkness, dark background, and darker ground—capture the sense of mysterious belonging to a darkness outside the illuminations of space and time.[54] We might think of this sensibility to which the experiences of necessity give rise as something like a reservoir in the human soul where the very beginnings of a feeling of renewed possibility stir. Against the socially and politically organized world, the experiences of *animal laborans* may be vital sources of our ability to imagine and wonder a world different from our own, one that includes access to other cultures as well as access to the very specific and perceptually different worlds of others more generally. Thus, although Arendt's effort to protect "necessity" by relegating it nearly wholesale to a private realm conceived as antithetical to the public-political realm is insufficiently attentive to the political significance and historical variation of the activities of *animal laborans,* this should not blind us to her argument that the experiences of *animal laborans* need some measure of protection from human intervention on the grounds that both our sense of reality in terms of belonging and our sense of possibility may be at stake.[55] And lest it be forgotten, this is not some back-to-nature argument. The creation by *homo faber* of a more permanent world and the concern with durability are central preoccupations of Arendt as she critiques the modern age. Encroachment, taming the life force, is necessary, but it must remain in tension with the strength and relative autonomy of the life process.

To summarize, we have the idea that to be subject to the force of life is to experience a kind of bliss, a kind of belonging to something larger, something dark and mysterious that itself offers respite from a human-centered world and is also a source of rejuvenation for action in it. In a world entirely or even substantially humanly administered, this kind of belonging would be eclipsed. Such a reservoir is politically important because it is one of the principle resources on which humans can depend for imagining a different, better world. Nature's autonomy and otherness in this sense is crucial to our specific humanness insofar as this consists, as Arendt argues, in our capacity for initiating thought and action. That we are natal beings in the twofold sense of being part of the endless appearing and disappearing that characterizes the life process and that we are capable of new beginnings, of initiating action are deeply bound to one another in Arendt's thought. Hence the sensibility to which our experience of necessity's compelling and profuse qualities gives rise might help draw us back from the instrumental projects of *homo faber* or from the specifics of concerted action initiated by citizens. These experiences might indeed intensify our awareness of reality—of what we are doing and how we are living—in the manner of fullness.

The second set of reflections that emerges from Arendt's appreciation of necessity involves a different, perhaps more basic sense of reality it gives us—namely, the sense of being alive. Arendt argues that without experience of the relentless compulsion of the life process, the human sense of vitality would be eliminated (*HC,* 120). Indeed, our very capacity for initiative is tied to this sense of compulsion and "unfreedom." Without the impact of nature's compulsion bearing down on us, we have no way of distinguishing between a state of freedom and one of enslavement. This is of utmost importance because the technological innovations of the modern age, as I have already argued, seem to change the very nature of necessity itself.[56] Each new development seems to represent yet another door to freedom. As long as we live on the earth, however, the ability of *homo faber* to drastically reduce life's modes of pain and suffering does not do away with the compelling quality of the life process but serves only to hide it from our senses. What we lose, then, is not necessity but the bearings by which we are able to distinguish between freedom and necessity and the vitality and sense of reality that this distinction imparts. And this in turn may threaten, in a fundamental way, our sense for otherness, "[that] curious quality of *alteritas* possessed by everything that is," a sense without which human plurality and thought itself could not occur (*HC*, 176). What may be at stake is the ability to encounter that which we are not—understood in terms of nonhuman nature and also in sociopolitical terms. Such, in any case, are the questions and possibilities raised when we concentrate the experiences of *animal laborans* into a full sensibility or outlook upon the world.

My aim has been to foreground Arendt's treatment of necessity as an instance of the aesthetic sensibility of tragic pleasure that she attempts to cultivate in *The Human Condition*—namely, a fundamental pleasure and awed wonder at plurality, at the *deinon* quality of our experience of the world. In this text it is expressed as an appreciation of the outlook and contribution of each of the three activities of the *vita activa* and a kind of pleasure in their mutual hostilities, tensions, and provocations. The specific concerns and possibilities each presents provoke and incite us to constitute and experience, in their shifting, alternating unique claims on us, the dense texture of the real. And, once again, insofar as to be ethically responsible is to be responsible for "declar[ing] the presence of that which is present," this is of great importance.

I want to turn now to Arendt's reflections on the *vita contemplativa*, focusing in particular on thinking. Here we find the same preoccupation with plurality as the sin qua non of our capacity to be attentive to reality, but now considered in the context of the relationship between the invisible and visible worlds.

The *Vita Contemplativa*: Thinking

The experiences that led Arendt to reflect on the *vita contemplativa* occurred during the trial of Adolf Eichmann. As Arendt watched and listened to Eichmann, she became convinced, as I have suggested, that the one characteristic that distinguished him was "a curious, quite authentic inability to think" (*LMT,* 417), and she described this condition as one of being "protected against reality, that is, against the claim on our thinking attention that all events and facts make by virtue of their existence" (*LMT,* 4). Eichmann, it seemed, was incapable of countenancing the particularity of the world, neither his specific particularity (as when, Arendt relates, he responded to his own death with a funeral oratory cliché whose "lofty words…completely becloud[ed] the reality of his own death" [*EJ,* 288]) nor the particularity of others (as when he sat "for months on end facing a German Jew who was conducting the police interrogation, pouring out his heart to the man and explaining again and again how it was that he reached only the rank of lieutenant colonel in the SS and that it had not been his fault that he was not promoted" [*EJ,* 287]).

In Eichmann, then, Arendt found a person radically unresponsive to the way in which the world displays itself in a self-presentation that elicits, yearns for, and demands our particular response. Eichmann remained shockingly unprovoked, and in Arendt's effort to understand this, the following question, as she described it, "imposed itself" upon her: "Could the activity of thinking as such, the habit of examining whatever happens to come to pass or to attract attention, regardless of results and specific content, could this activity be among the conditions that make men abstain from evil-doing or even actually 'condition' them against it?" (*LMT,* 5).[57]

This question is really about the way in which the activity of thinking might itself help us remain attentive to the event-quality of the world, to its plural particularity, to, as Arendt put it, the impact of the new.[58] She is thus keenly interested in the relationship between thinking, by which she means "the quest for meaning as opposed to the thirst for knowledge," and our sense of reality (*LMT,* 78). Is there something in the thinking experience itself that, when habitually performed, conditions and forms us, something that enables us to be more attentive to the real? Does thinking's quest for meaning, which is always about generalities (for example, What is virtue, justice, evil?), paradoxically enliven our attentiveness to particularity? Does it intensify our responsiveness to the world's eliciting provocations? Is there an "inner connection between the ability or inability to think and the problem of evil?"[59] Such are Arendt's questions, and although they appear here in my text, as in her writing, without connection to other possible important and mediating conditions, they make no sense without these conditions. We need to remind ourselves in what follows that her question is whether thinking is "among the conditions" that keep us from evil-doing. The lack of a systematic account of these conditions is no doubt partly due to the fact that Arendt took up this investigation toward the end of her life, and her work remained uncompleted.[60] The final, unfinished volume of *The Life of the Mind, Judging,* was to provide the bridge between the contemplative and the active life. Furthermore, if we consider Arendt's work as a whole, it is quite implausible to believe that she thought her questions about thinking's ethical significance could by themselves suffice. At the very least, the relative vitality of the public sphere and the existence of friendship are, in her view, extremely important mediating conditions. My own interpretation presumes this much, and I therefore bear very seriously in mind Arendt's qualification that thinking may be "*among*" the conditions that keep us from evil-doing.

It was, of course, not only Arendt's encounter with Eichmann that led her to burden thinking with such ethical weight. Half in the spirit of Kant's exhilarating writings about the end of the mind's tutelage, which for him was the essence of enlightenment, and half with a darker Heideggerian sensibility, Arendt greeted the end of the metaphysical tradition. Terminating definitively with the horrors of totalitarianism, Arendt nevertheless saw possibilities for human emancipation in a situation whose defining characteristic was that not only professional thinkers but now everyone was faced with what she described as "the gap between past and future." By this she referred to the existential condition of thinking that she elucidates with Karl Jaspers's conception of life as a boundary affair: "Life itself, limited by birth and death, is a boundary affair in that *my worldly existence* always forces me to take account of a past when I was not yet and a future when I shall be no more" (*LMT,* 192; my italics). As such, existentially speaking, we always find ourselves in a gap in which questions of meaning impatiently crowd our being.

It was the experience of this gap that the power of the metaphysical tradition in the West had elided, in part by making certain questions central while entirely eclipsing others, and in part by giving each individual's life story meaning by drawing it into a powerful preexisting metaphysically derived narrative frame. It was faith in just such a world that relied on the plausibility of a reality more true and perfect than that presented through our bodily senses, that Arendt believed political experiences had definitively defeated. She heralded this end uneasily, fully aware that there are other, far more debilitating ways to quiet the impatient crowd of questions that, existentially speaking, press each of us. The most haunting testimony to this fact is totalitarianism, for silencing was achieved through the spread of an ideology that emancipated thought from the impact of experience by ordering facts into an absolutely logical procedure (*OT,* 468–74). Here the effort was not to offer answers to questions gravely countenanced, but rather to extinguish the birth of questioning itself.

Thus Arendt suggests that our situation in which the "gap" yawns is, as the new method of totalitarian ideology attests, at once a danger and a situation in which, for the first time in a very long time in the West, thinking might flourish. Precisely the recession of tradition makes room, in this foreboding century, for hope. For these reasons, too, Arendt burdens thinking with enormous ethical weight.

In pursuing Arendt's questions about the possible ethical relevance of thinking, we are, however, confronted from the start with paradox. What Arendt is claiming for an activity that requires withdrawal from the world of appearances, is aporetic, and that disrupts our common-sense understanding of the world and therefore seems altogether useless and unreal (*LMT*, 89), is precisely that the experiences it offers are crucial to our capacity to feel the impact of the real. If the world and our sense of reality is engendered through our eliciting self-presentation, whereby we seek to countenance and be countenanced by others, why should the silent worldless quest for meaning that goes on endlessly in the unreal nowhere place of thinking heighten our attentiveness to the particularity of the world, to its dense and plural quality?

To begin to answer this question it must be established that the kind of thinking with which Arendt is concerned is plebeian. Recall, first, that she describes thinking in almost nonchalant, certainly very ordinary terms as "the habit of examining *whatever* happens to come to pass or attract attention" (*LMT*, 5; my italics). Furthermore, not the province of the few, she argues that thinking is "an ever present faculty of everybody,... a natural need of human life" (*LMT*, 191). She speaks, as we have seen in the context of Eichmann, of a "claim" that, by virtue of their existence, all facts and events make upon us. Our thinking ego or, as Kant put it, "reason's need" is provoked by and responds to this existential and aesthetic claim. And this need is a need for meaning. It yearns not for "the *that* something is, but for the what it means for it to be" (*LMT*, 57). As such, Arendt argues that what moved philosophers to pose their metaphysical questions "is in no way different from men's need to tell the story of some happening they witnessed, or to write poems about it" (*LMT*, 78). From the get go it is as if the world yearns to be countenanced, to be questioned as to its meaningfulness. It makes a claim upon us, and we, all of us, without distinction, are creatures fitted to respond, to be claimed. This contention that thinking is a plebeian, which is to say universal, need is not a claim that we automatically do it. Rather, it is a claim that each human being possesses the mental faculty of thinking that need not, but only can potentially be, aroused by the world. Arendt puts it this way: "A life without thinking is quite possible; it then fails to develop its own essence—it is not merely meaningless; it is not fully alive. Unthinking men are like sleepwalkers" (*LMT,* 191). Hence the "fit" between a provoking world and "reason's need" is a complex, uncertain one, though all human beings possess the necessary requisites for it.[61]

Withdrawal from the appearing world is the first requirement of thinking. It is our initial answer to the world's provoking claim, on us, for thinking demands a surcease from the urgency and provocation we feel in the world of appearances. Because the aim of thinking is not particulars, but generalities, we must become, paradoxically, sensually protected from reality. For this reason the objects of thought given us by the world must be transcended if we are to think not *that* they are but *about* them, if we are to think what it might mean for them to be. To go beyond them in this sense requires a twofold operation inherent in the thinking activity itself. First, the thinking ego must "de-sense" the object of thought so that an image can be produced and stored in the mind. For this, imagination, in which we make present to the mind what is absent from the senses, is crucial. Here we repeat in the mind what the senses experienced. We "de-materialize." Then, when the mind is roused to think, it must actively remember and thus select from memory these "de-sensed" images. As the mind takes hold of them in concentration, these images undergo a second change to become thought objects. From a "mere image," they become a "vision in thought," as Arendt, quoting Augustine, puts it (*LMT,* 77).[62]

These are the "operations" or, elsewhere, "laws" inherent in the thinking faculty we all possess. They are part of the reason that thinking appears so out of order to our everyday common sense. Each contributes to the autonomous character of thinking.[63] But this is an autonomy nonetheless consonant with the preceding argument about the provocation of the thinking ego by the world, with the idea that reality exerts a claim upon our thinking selves, and that thinking itself, governed by its own "inner impulse" and "inherent laws," is fitted to respond to the world's provocation. Thinking, by this account, belongs to the world (and all of us to it), not in the sense of being determined by it but in the sense of being provoked by it.

This plebeianization of thinking is pitted almost wholesale against the professional philosopher's account. Arendt's target, specifically, is the Socratic-Platonic tradition in which thinking is held to be inspired either by an admiring wonder (Plato) or by Eros (Socrates), and whose objects are beauty, goodness, and wisdom. This tradition distinguishes the noble nature of the very few thinkers from the baser nature of the many; it is gripped by a two-world theory in which the baser natures are confined to a petty, discordant world of illusion while the noble natures alone have access, via contemplation, to a true world: perfect, harmonious, and real. Here we are called not to explore the complex fit between the plain or plebeian need of reason and the multiplicitous provocations of things in an appearing world. Rather, we are called to imagine that thinking is stimulated by a higher sensibility, that it is a capacity in the few for movement beyond the world's stormy plurality whereby particulars become transparent through the intuition of an underlying harmonious order.

Arendt based her rejections of these metaphysical conceptions on two areas of concern. First, they can give no account of the ontological status of evil. If the beginning of thought is admiring wonder or Eros, evil and ugliness have being only as deficiencies—that is, they are barely thinkable. There is, as Arendt puts it, "no place for the factual existence of disharmony, of ugliness, and finally of evil" (*LMT*, 150). Second, in these metaphysical accounts thinking seems to bear so little relation to worldly reality. It seems, that is, insufficiently related to the pondering reflection that the darkness of our splintered and ruggedly beautiful world invites in us and that most of us, at least sometimes, undertake.[64]

Thus, in rejecting this philosophical account, Arendt asserts both that thinking erupts out of the fit between reason's need for meaning and an animated event-world that stakes a claim upon us, and that responsiveness is a universal potential of all human beings. In making this assertion, however, Arendt must show how this plebeian thinking might condition us from evil-doing as well as account for the troubling fact that this potential fit between reason's need and the world of appearances often fails to be actualized. Once again her question must be, Why do some people appear not to feel the claim of the world?

To explore these issues, Arendt initially asks, What enables those who *do* feel the claim to do so? What, as she puts it, makes us think? (*LMT*, 129–93).[65] After that, is there something in the thinking activity itself that, paradoxically, keeps us attentive to the real? The answer Arendt gives in both cases points to something in the performance of thinking itself, a "property inherent in the activity...regardless of its objects" (*LMT*, 180). That property is the mind's capacity to become "plural" and carry on within *itself* the provocation possible only between the plural unit of two. Within this somewhat narrowed structural and formal focus, Arendt's reflections move. But, as I shall argue, they press out beyond these confines to intimations about the worldly preconditions for the thinking activity, as well as to considerations of the interrelationship between thinking and being in the world of appearances. The hope, again, that underlies Arendt's trains of thought is that if we examine the performance of thinking, we may indeed gain insight into why some do not think and why it may be that thinking is "among the conditions" that keep us from evil-doing. In all respects it is Socrates who provides her with the most important testimony to this silent, invisible, and yet lively activity.[66]

The Performance of Thinking: Socrates and the Mind's Duality

In taking Socrates as her exemplar, Arendt underscores the importance of her qualified thesis that thinking may be "among the conditions" that keep us from evil-doing, for her hope is pinned not on thinking in the abstract but on thinking *in the world*. Her hope arises in understanding thinking's proximity to and interchange with the other conditions and activities of human existence. In Socrates, Arendt finds,

> an example of a thinker who was not a professional, who in his person unified two apparently contradictory passions, for thinking and action—not in the sense of being eager to apply his thoughts or to establish theoretical standards for action but in the much more relevant sense of being equally at home in both spheres and able to move from one sphere to the other with the greatest apparent ease, very much as we ourselves constantly move back and forth between experiences in the world of appearances and the need for reflecting on them.... [He was] a man who counted himself neither among the many nor among the few (a distinction at least as old as Pythagoras), who had no aspiration to be a ruler of men, no claim even to be particularly well fitted by his superior wisdom to act in an advisory capacity to those in power, but not a man who submitted meekly to being ruled either; in brief, a thinker who always remained a man among men, who did not shun the marketplace, who was a citizen among citizens, doing nothing, claiming nothing except what in his opinion every citizen should be and have a right to. (*LMT,* 167)

Devoted to aporetic dialogue, driven by the fundamental question "*What do you mean when you say?,*" moving back and forth "with ease" between internal dialogue and dialogue with others so as to have his own thinking engaged and to engage that of his fellow citizens, Socrates, in Arendt's view, represents the "natural need" of all (*LMT,* 185). Socrates is our "everybody" as we attempt to grasp thinking in its nonprofessional plebeianized sense. It is of utmost importance, therefore, to note that Arendt's model always remained "a man among men" and that he did so with ease.

Only the thinking of one who is "at home" in both spheres is, Arendt believes, ethically relevant.[67] With this in mind, let us turn to her elaboration of the internal experience of thinking qua performance.

The crucial evidence Arendt considers comes from two positive propositions Socrates left behind. Both are to be found in Plato's *Georgias*. They are first, "It is better to be wronged than to do wrong," and second, "It would be better for me that my lyre or a chorus I directed should be out of tune and loud with discord, and that multitudes of men should disagree with me rather than that I, *being one,* should be out of harmony with myself and contradict me" (*LMT,* 181).

Although both of these Socratic propositions have been interpreted as "purely" moral propositions, Arendt suggests we consider them more correctly as subjective statements of the thinking ego. That is to say, they are insights, from the point of view of the thinking ego itself, into the structure but also the wants and needs that govern the thinking life.[68] Thus the disagreement between Socrates and his interlocutor Callicles as to whether it is better to do or suffer wrong is one that arises because Socrates loves the thinking life, whereas Callicles's passion is for what all of Greece would have agreed is the life of a man as opposed to that of a slave. As Arendt says, "What becomes apparent is that Callicles and Socrates are talking about a different 'I': What is good for one is bad for the other" (*LMT,* 181). Here, then, Socrates testifies to the existence of a thinking ego with its own pleasures and interests, its own bearing on the world, a bearing that, moreover, conflicts with and is distinct from other elements of the self.

The second proposition also testifies to the existence of the thinking ego, giving us insight into its basic structure. It is evidence for what Arendt calls the duality inherent in the thinking performance (*LMT,* 185). To think not *something,* which we do merely as conscious beings, but to think *about it,* we must begin a questioning dialogue with ourselves. Here "I" is both the one who asks and the one who answers; here we have a two-in-one, difference in identity. Hence the thinking ego's concern is not for harmony with the world but for harmony with itself. And the crucial point here is that harmony can never arise from a single tone. The phenomenon of thinking requires a duality. As soon as we attempt to gather the meaning of things as spectators of the whole, an otherness rises up within the self. It is this otherness and difference, "such outstanding characteristics of the world of appearances as it is given to man for his habitat among a plurality of things" (*LMT,* 187), that are the conditions for the very existence of our thinking ego as well. Without this splitting in two, in which a difference rises up within myself, my thinking cannot be. In this sense, in the thinking activity itself life has deposited its fundamental plural beat. Arendt writes, "Nothing perhaps indicates more strongly that man exists *essentially* in the plural than that his solitude actualizes his merely being conscious of himself... into a duality during the thinking activity" (*LMT,* 185).

So Arendt's answer to the question of what enables those who *do* think to do so is this plurality within the thinking self, this actualization of difference that everyone possesses *in potentia*. This is not a surprising answer, and its scope is still limited. But Arendt pursues its implications further: In withdrawing from a world of plural others into the solitude of thinking, we are far from being radically severed from that world and its governing features of plurality, relativity, contingency, far from being released into a world of perfection, truth, identity. To the contrary, we are drawn into the density of the thinking ego that shares, on an invisible plain, the visible world's general features. Drawn toward this similarity, in a suggestive, somewhat cryptic, but I think key passage, Arendt writes, "As the metaphor bridges the gap between the world of appearances and the mental activities going on within it, so the Socratic two-in-one heals the solitariness of thought; its inherent duality *points to* the infinite plurality which is the law of the earth" (*LMT,* 187; my italics).

With this passage we arrive at a slightly new way of posing Arendt's leading question—namely, Does the *way* in which the plural self of thinking "*points to*" the plurality of the earth help condition us from evil-doing? In other words, if we take seriously the experience of being a self that-is-not-one, feel its pleasures, know its interests and needs, if these experiences become habits crucial to our sense of well-being, do we become more attentive to the claim of reality? And if so, does this attentiveness, in turn, deepen our ability, in thought, to represent other viewpoints and subject positions, to actualize a denser, more multiplicitous internal dialogue? Is there at play an important recursive relationship that, if identified, can illuminate how the performance of thinking might be "among the conditions" that keep us from evil-doing? For exploring this relationship the two most relevant phenomena are conscience and what Arendt calls the destructive effect of thinking. I will treat each in turn.

Conscience

Framing Arendt's reflections on conscience is the contention that the totality of the moral collapse in Nazi Germany makes our traditional understandings of how conscience functions no longer plausible. The astonishing "ease" with which, under totalitarian conditions, "Thou shalt not kill" became "Thou shalt kill," and the traditional contents of conscience were silenced, erodes time-worn conceptions in which conscience has been thought to function in an automatic way—either because we possess a faculty whose voice speaks to us independently of law and public opinion or because we have a learned or inbred feeling of lawfulness.[69] Indeed, Arendt argued against the judgment in Jerusalem, which held that Eichmann had "close[d] his ears to the voice of conscience" (*EJ*, 126). On the contrary, she thought, his ears remained opened, and the only voices he could hear were those of "respectable society" that presented no objections to what he was doing or being asked to do.[70]

Arendt believed that the traditional understanding of conscience described not an activity but a passivity. If, when consulted, the so-called voice of conscience gives us the rules—learned or innate—we need only apply to particulars, if it is this habit we master, then we prepare ourselves not for independent moral judgment but for the practice of applying rules whose specific content we have learned to passively receive but not to question.[71] The difference between almost everybody and those very few who maintained basic moral bearings under totalitarian conditions was, in Arendt's view, that the conscience of those few did not function in this customary way. These were people with a different mental practice, a different mental life. Their obligation of conscience was not toward a voice giving rules. It arose, rather, from a certain "interest in the self" that is not self-evident in all people, although Arendt believed it to be an ever-present possibility in each person (*CR*, 64).[72]

This interest—the existence of which the first Socratic proposition I discussed attests—arises from the thinking ego's desire to keep the thinking dialogue in being. Although this is a dialogue "not thematically concerned with the Self but, on the contrary, with the experiences and questions that this Self, an appearance among appearances, feels are in need of examination" (*LMW*, 64), and although, therefore, the thinking dialogue or reason's need is provoked by a world yearning for meaning, it is not our concern for the world *alone* that generates our desire to keep the thinking dialogue going. That desire is also propelled by pleasure intrinsic to the internal dialogical experience. The point here is that thinking is born of and oriented toward a provoking world, but in terms of what keeps it alive as a practice, thinking has, at the same time, a certain autonomy. And that autonomy lies in the pleasure to which Democrates testified when he said, "[The mind] is used to getting joys out of itself."[73] What joys are these?

When we become two, when, as thinking beings, we become plural and "actualiz[e] the difference given in consciousness" (*LMT*, 191), what we are doing is engendering the plurality of the thinking ego and thus creating the only conditions under which the thinking life can be *and* have its being or its vitality *felt*. The pleasure we feel, then, lies precisely in the enormous vitality that this pluralized thinking ego imparts to the self as it unleashes the "sheer activity" of thinking. Thinking, Arendt writes, is "the de-materialized quintessence of being alive" (*LMT,* 191). The pleasure we take in thinking is the pleasure in the enhanced sense of being alive that the pluralized self makes possible.

Thus from the standpoint of the thinking ego, this relationship with myself as a plural being takes priority, and it gives rise to conscience, because, in order to sustain itself, the one who asks and the one who answers must remain, as Arendt puts it, on speaking terms, must remain friends (*LMT,* 188). A kind of communicative harmony must reign between them. And it is conscience that ensures this.

Hence the mental practice that gives birth to a conscience that might prove extremely important morally is the "sheer activity" engendered through the mutual provocation between two voices within the self. Far from practicing a passive receptivity in which the mind listens for the sound of a rule-giving, ever-present voice within the self, conscience is a by-product of this thinking experience. It is present only if and when we are in dialogue with ourselves, only if and when we "come home" (*LMT,* 191). In this sense, conscience arises, in the midst of thinking, as a witness, and what it bears witness to, what it brings before us and thus intensifies, is the pleasure and interest that fuels the thinking ego itself.

The voice in which conscience does so is an admonishing one. It tells us what to avoid so as not to jeopardize our vitalizing friendship with ourselves. Its guiding principle, Arendt suggests, is noncontradiction. Sometimes rendered in her work as the principle of self-consistency or, following Kant, "Don't talk non-sense," it is the latter injunction that is consonant with what is most interesting in Arendt's theorization of conscience (*LK,* 36). Unlike noncontradiction, which pertains to the domain of logic and thus would be quite a straitjacket on the thinking activity as Arendt conceives it, the injunction not to talk non-sense concerns meaning in a far broader sense. Thus what endangers the sustainability of a dialogue among friends is a kind of insanity (non-sensicalness) arising from an inability to keep friendship alive (*LMT,* 74). The danger arises not from contradictory and inconsistent thought trains, but from a lack of communication *among* them, communication that *might* result in resolution but that might also oblige us to hold the inconsistent thoughts in tension. It arises, thus, from a refusal to embrace and feel pleasure in communicative plurality as it occurs in mental life. In this respect, the rigorous thought experiments of thinkers such as Emerson or Nietzsche, full of contradictions and inconsistencies, look far less like the ravings of immoral madmen and more like the products of the interest, concern, and pleasure the thinking ego has in itself. These philosophers' experiments are the products of lasting friendship within and dedication to the self.

Such thinkers, we might argue, are admonished by a vigorous conscience, in Arendt's sense, for conscience is a witness without which thinking cannot endure. It is the part of the self that is *for* the sound of voices where otherwise there would be either silence and nothingness or sheer cacophonous babble. To suggest this vis-à-vis Nietzsche without qualification is not without its ironies. Yet there is in his perspectivism precisely such a conscience-driven commitment to the vitality that the plural self of thinking imparts. Indeed, this is the vitality that rushes unforgettably out of the opened pages of his work. If we are, I think, to try to explain Nietzsche's often intolerable inhumanity, we do far better to turn to the (increasing) paucity of meaningful friendships and worldly intercourse in his own life. Indeed, this is one striking difference between Nietzsche and Emerson.[74]

So conscience as Arendt reconceives it is a presence within the self that is attentive to and tries to keep plurality in being in mental life. It is a by-product of the thinking ego's interest in itself and the joy it feels at the inner provocation between the two-in-one of the thinking dialogue. If plurality is the law of the earth, conscience is its guardian in the domain of the mental activity of thinking. In this sense the duality inherent in the thinking ego "points to" the plurality that is the law of the earth.

Still, if conscience is a by-product of thinking, sounding its admonishing voice only if we begin thinking's pressing quest for meaning, and if thinking itself is indeed profitless and without result, what is the moral relevance of the voice of a conscience aimed at keeping such an activity going? How might this mental practice of thinking and its admonishing witness condition us against evil-doing?

In dark times, when the world speaks with virtually one voice, when the worldly experience of human plurality is foreclosed, those few who know the joys of thinking, who have this "interest" in friendship with themselves, feel obligated to its vitality. And this obligation may give them an ethically crucial autonomy from the world's tyranny, for this two-in-one has become accustomed to a certain responsibility toward its other: the responsibility of giving accounts to its friend—of why it does and thinks what it does and thinks. The thinker has developed the habit of going "home," and as Arendt succinctly puts the ethical point, no one wants to live with, be friends with a murderer (*LMT,* 190). Thus this moral autonomy is won by actualizing plurality as it occurs in thinking, preserving our *experience* of it—experience that the world has otherwise foreclosed.[75]

The mental practice of thinking in its plebeian form, together with its by-product conscience, opens us out upon ourselves as plural beings and, we might say, conditions us to feel the pleasures of intensification that are brought by the plurality of voices arising from the duality inherent in the thinking ego. From this conditioning we become entwined in an obligation toward *whatever* will keep that plurality in being. In this obligation the thinker's autonomy from the world's evil, from its monological tyranny, is anchored.

Having made this perhaps reckless point, let me fend off the possible objection that the obligation we may come to feel toward the pleasure in the duality of the thinking ego might indeed lead us, as it may have led Plato, to attempt to befriend tyrants in the effort to institute a form of rule that would protect the ever-endangered practice of thinking.[76] Such a form of rule, of course, would have none of the "plebeian" ethical consequences with which Arendt was concerned. Nor, however, is it likely, given the amount of domination its rule over the many would require, that this world would offer the quality of relationship to others necessary to sustain the vitality of thinking. The central question to which I am alluding is this: What worldly conditions do we need to keep a rich plurality of inner voices in being? What kinds of pragmatic, public engagements with different others do I need in order to keep the thinking dialogue between me and myself from becoming too solipsistic so that what I have in fact is the mere form of dialogue that shelters an activity more proximately monological? Arendt's argument for thinking's autonomy notwithstanding, all of her work points to a profound sense of the worldly preconditions for our capacity to sustain a rich plurality of inner voices. This is a difficult question to answer definitively. Still, we seem to have an astonishing propensity toward both benign and pernicious forms of oblivion and habitual perception, a fact that makes the question ever urgent.

Arendt's account of conscience is one of the aspects of the mental practice of thinking that she believes might help condition us from evil-doing. But conscience must be considered with another aspect of thinking, and this has to do with the effect that this pluralization of the self in dialogue with itself has on our sense of the world's reality, on our attentiveness to the world's plural particularity. To elaborate this I turn to the second sense in which this property of duality inherent in the thinking ego "points to" the plurality of the earth. Conscience grounds a certain autonomy from the world, while thinking's destructive effect turns us toward it. Both are crucial experiences that bear on the ethical relevance of the performance of thinking.

Thinking's Destructive Effect

Thinking is an experience that points to many possible meanings. It has, Arendt suggests, inevitably a destructive effect insofar as it "unfreezes" what was settled and solid. Things begin to "get slippery when we talk about their meaning, nothing stays put anymore, everything begins to move" (*LMT,* 170). Thinking arouses us to examine our unexamined opinions, purges us of those we cannot adequately defend (which, as the aporetic quality of the Socratic dialogues implies, is all of them), and leaves us with a perplexity that, from the standpoint of the world, looks like (and is) paralysis.

The sheer activity of thinking, in which the otherness within the self is actualized, thus undermines and assaults all the criteria and rules we have come to habitually rely on to guide us morally. It is in this potentially dangerous state that thinking's duality points to the plurality of the earth, for while we are momentarily paralyzed in our relations in the world, the invigorating movement of the quest for meaning simultaneously leads us toward a plurality of possible worlds.

But why should we embrace this understanding of thinking as being of great ethical relevance? From the world's standpoint there is a curious emptiness in such a mental activity. In itself it achieves nothing. In a less benign sense, there are dangers in an activity that destroys the often fragile stability of our worldly meanings and paralyzes the worldly actor as it does so. Indeed, it could be argued that Socrates' own failure with Alcibiades and Critias instructs us about the nihilism that inherently haunts the thinking experience insofar as it leads us onto unstable terrain. Precisely in the profitless, unproductive nature of thinking, in its failure to produce either doctrine or blueprint, we might argue, lies its danger. Arendt herself persuasively argues that this is fallacious, that nihilism is not produced as a consequence of thinking itself but is a refusal of thinking's exhilaration, a refusal to feel pleasure in the earth's plurality and the provocation that plurality exhibits in the domain of mental life. Nihilism, thus, is a product of existential weakness that shows itself in both individuals and cultures.

Still, as pleasurable as thinking is, and as crucial as it is in achieving the elementary movement away from the blunt presence of things, its irreality (despite the vitality it imparts) is, Arendt rightly argues, intolerable as a continuous state. The undermining, destructive, and dizzying effect of thinking propels the self back into the world. And the state we are in when we return is precisely that of reflective judgment. That is, it is a state in which we have no general rule to guide us in a world of particulars. *In the world,* however, we must judge. Thus when Arendt, in a somewhat immodest formulation, argues that thinking "activates judgment," all I think her thesis can bear is the (interesting) claim that thinkers return to the world *in the state of* reflective judgment. The mental activity of thinking, with its destructive effect on worldly meanings, teaches us to feel pleasure in precisely that state alone which, after not too long a time, lands us in the situation of reflective judgment, although this says nothing about what sort of *response* we will have to that state.[77] Whether we will successfully move out to visit others and resurrect the complex "objectivity" and reality of the world about which we must make judgments will depend more on our practical worldly engagements and on the vigor of the public-political world to which we belong.[78]

I have said this is all Arendt's thesis can bear, but there is something more. There is the promise of a possibility—namely, that having thought, we return to the world changed, that the thinking experience imparts a kind of intensification that may be brought to bear on our sense of reality in the world of appearances. Conditioned to feel pleasure in the multiplicity of the thinking experience but unable to dwell terribly long on its futile quest for meaning, we return to the world of particulars with a heightened sensitivity and attentiveness to what complex meanings an appearance, in eliciting presentation, might provoke. So our eyes, our senses are revivified; they reveal greater density and dimension. Arendt gives a simple but interesting example as she discusses the way that thinking unfreezes meanings and the effect that this experience can have on us when we return from the silent dialogue with ourselves. She comments, "At all events, this kind of pondering reflection does not produce definitions and in that sense is entirely without results, though somebody who had pondered the meaning of 'house' might make his own look better" (*LMT,* 171). But how do we decide? My suggestion is that this revivified eye, this opening out onto the plural density of worldly existence, may be accompanied by an urgent vulnerability, for, faced with decision in a world of many others, this is a self conditioned to feel pleasure in the plurality of dialogue. It is thus a self governed by nonsovereignty, a self moved to solicit others' points of view. Our return state, then, is one of communicative readiness, communicative need, for thinking conditions us to feel pleasure not for what pleases in an immediate self-gratifying sense, nor for pleasure in harmony as monological oneness. If there is harmony it is a full-part harmony, one that reaches its depth through tensions in which transgression and accord follow one upon the other. Arendt's pages are filled with praise for and pleasure in the sublime splendor of a world whose multiplicitousness frightens as it incites and provokes, for the *deinon* quality of human experience. This kind of "tragic pleasure" Arendt refers to as the "home" to which those who think are compelled to return again and again. And turning back to the world of particulars, the promise is that our human responsiveness to its provocations is more fervid and keen, toward things and events as well as toward others.

If we stand back now to pull together the threads of Arendt's explorations of the "inner connection between the ability or inability to think and the problem of evil,"[79] if we bring succinctly to view what in the performance of thinking might condition us against evil-doing, the "inner connection" is plurality, and the key experiences are the pluralization of the self and of the world's meaning, both of which occur in the thinking activity. This twofold pluralization conditions us to feel pleasure in plurality as it governs the thinking life. This is what the practice of thinking cultivates in those who think, and this may prove to be a bulwark against evil-doing because it conditions us to want to be in precisely that *state* in which the need for reflective judgment is called forth, *and* to "enter" it with both a certain autonomy and a communicative need. Thinking in *this sense* alone might be said to "activate" judgment. And when, propelled by thinking itself, we return to the world of appearances conditioned to feel pleasure in the plurality of meanings that dialogue engenders, our attentiveness to the world of particulars is enhanced, and with this our sense of reality may be intensified.

As I have said, however, this final effect on our being in the world is only the promise of a possibility. There is nothing automatic about thinking's effect on our sense of reality in the world. Its promise depends for its fulfillment, in a profound manner, on a receptive and provoking world of others. It depends on the world's organization, particularly on the existence of a vigorous public sphere or spheres and, at the very least, on pockets of friendship among thinking others. If there is no receptivity on our returning, if there is little communicative need on the part of others, if ours is largely a world of lonely isolates, then there will be no one and no place to invite into the world of appearances the effects of the thinker's enhanced attentiveness, no way to give those effects any reality.

And thus it is that, its relative autonomy notwithstanding, thinking's ethical significance is deeply dependent on the world—on the nature of our specific relationships with intimate others as well as on our collective, institutionalized community life because we are in need of others who can arouse us to the practice. We have great need to share a life in which the performance is stimulated. Indeed, it may well be that friendship with ourselves *begins* with our friendships with others, and that from that beginning we discern an interrelationship. Arendt writes, "What Socrates discovered was that we can have intercourse with ourselves, as well as with others, and that the two kinds of intercourse are somehow interrelated.... I first talk with others before I talk with myself, examining whatever the joint talk may have been about, and then discover that I can conduct a dialogue not only with others but with myself as well" (*LMT,* 188–89). The emphasis here is on the primacy of our experience of worldliness and the condition of plurality that constitutes it. And the sense of the temporal relationship seems to be not only developmental—that is, that in our talking friendships with others we first, as children, learn to mimic such dialogue in the withdrawn solitude of mental life.[80] It also seems that we revitalize this friendship with ourselves over and over again, provoked by our friendship with others, provoked by our mutually eliciting display in our wider world.

If we are to answer the question, then, of why some do not think, and of why some grow thoughtless, we must look primarily to the world—are they without friendship? Is their public life without genuine discourse? What is the quality, intensity, and duration of their world's discursive solicitations, challenges, provocations? These become the vital questions in our effort to understand the complex fit between the plebeian natural need of reason and our capacity to respond to the multiplicitous provocations and claims that the things in our appearing world make upon us.

Let me, in closing, turn to a consideration of what appears to be the most damning refutation of Arendt's theoretical claim for thinking's ethical relevance, a claim based, as I have noted, on the argument that plurality as we experience it in the invisible world of thinking will have a conditioning effect that will enhance our sense of reality in the world of appearances and prevent us from evil-doing. This is a consideration of the case of philosophers—those whose profession is thinking and, in particular, to the contrasting cases of Martin Heidegger and Karl Jaspers.[81]

If we look to these two most significant thinkers in Arendt's own life, this kind of conditioning effect appears implausible, for clearly Jaspers remained morally independent throughout the totalitarian period, whereas Heidegger, for a crucial ten months at minimum, lost his moral bearings, his capacity to refrain from evil-doing. Can we explain the difference and retain anything of the claim Arendt seeks to make for thinking?

Here again we must attend to Arendt's choice of Socrates as her exemplar. Socrates was a man among men: He felt the need to call *himself* to account by calling *others* to account; that is, this provocation among citizens, among very different others, this movement back and forth is crucial. Although Arendt remained extremely circumspect regarding Heidegger's Nazi activities,[82] we can piece together an implicit, compelling difference between his performance of thinking and that of Jaspers that has to do precisely with the relationship between thinking and worldly intercourse. The difference should be instructive. Let us look first at Heidegger.

The metaphors Arendt uses to refer to this philosopher in whom, as she says, rumor had it, thinking "ha[d] come to life again," are those of "digging" in an "underground," of "beating paths" on a "deep plane." Save for the ten months in 1933 when, during the reign of the Nazis, he became rector of the University of Freiburg, Heidegger's thought, as his life, remained uninvolved in the visible world. His abode, if we are to reflect on "who Martin Heidegger is," is that of the worldless thinker, caught by the winds of thought, passionately engaged in the endless task of "wondering at the simple."[83]

If Heidegger had indeed brought thinking back to life again, his thinking nonetheless suffered from what Arendt called a "*déformation professionelle.*"[84] That is, Heidegger was one of the few who could remain in the storms of thought, unpropelled by its irreality back into the world of others. Unlike Socrates, it was not Heidegger's practice to bring *himself* to account by calling others to account. He did not, strictly speaking, move back and forth between the world of the visible and the world of the invisible. Better, this was not essential to his thinking performance. The consequences were that the two-in-one of Heidegger's thinking self remained uninformed, unnourished by this practice. His was a self cut off from this kind of accountability with others. It was, shall we say, an underground self. The *déformation* involved was a deformation that comes from being conditioned to love and feel pleasure in a far more narrowly dimensioned, more abstract plurality than that which pleasured the plebeian Socrates, whose to and fro movement was so great. (Indeed, Arendt once referred to Heidegger's philosophy as egotistical and too romantically individualist.)[85]

If we return to our thinker who, having thought, is now poised to judge and to act in the world, and we replace that plebeian thinker who habitually moves back and forth with the underground Heideggerian, thinking's effect will be different. This thinker does not suffer the same sort of "urgent vulnerability," doesn't need others, is in this respect too autonomous, pleasures in a too self-enclosed plurality. Indeed, for lack of experience, this thinker hardly knows a difference between the plurality of the thinking ego and the "we" of the world's plurality; this person easily conflates the world's plurality with his own inner plurality.[86] This is a thinker, then, whose practice of thinking has rendered him vulnerable in a far different sense—vulnerable to evil-doing that comes from being unresponsive to human plurality. In *this* sense, indeed, thinking has no positive bearing on our capacity to be attentive to reality.

Not only, then, is Heidegger not the exemplar of Arendt's plebeian reason with its passions, interests, and vulnerabilities, he is even, in a circumspect way, her negative example. This is not the same as saying Arendt did not admire Heidegger's thinking. To the contrary, she remained profoundly influenced by and appreciative of his work, although not uncritically so.[87] Heidegger's life suggests that Socratic "ease" in both worlds alone makes it possible for thinking to be ethically relevant.

It is precisely this capacity to change residences "with ease" that distinguishes Jaspers's thinking. Arendt writes, "Jaspers's thought is spatial because it forever remains in reference to the world and the people in it, not because it is bound to any existing space. In fact, the opposite is the case, because his deepest aim is to 'create a space' in which the *humanitas* of man can appear pure and luminous" (*MDT,* 79). By this she referred to a quality that comes from the passion for the kind of light that shines forth from our efforts to freely explore, together with others, the world we co-inhabit. So Jaspers's thought exemplifies, perhaps even in a greatly heightened form, the interrelationship between thinking and worldly dialogue with others. Arendt's account of what enabled Jaspers, in extraordinary isolation from the wider world during the war years, to maintain his moral bearings also points to the vulnerability of thinking's ethical relevance to that worldly interchange. More specifically, it points to our need as thinkers to not merely split in two and carry on *some* kind of dialogue in the quest for meaning. We must, in that withdrawn nowhere place of thinking, be informed by the voices of those specific others who share the contemporary world out of which our thinking erupted and into which we will throw our voices if and when we return to it. And this we can do only if our lives have significant worldly involvement. That involvement for Jaspers, during the years of isolation in which the world was barren and spaceless, was, Arendt suggests, his marriage. Its significance, she thought, was that

a woman who is his peer has stood at his side ever since his youth. If two people do not succumb to the illusion that the ties binding them have made them one, they can create a world anew between them. Certainly for Jaspers this marriage has never been merely a private thing. It has proved that two people of different origins—Jaspers' wife is Jewish— could create between them a world of their own. And from this world in miniature he has learned, as from a model, what is essential for the whole realm of human affairs. Within this small world he unfolded and practiced his incomparable faculty for dialogue, the splendid precision of his way of listening, the constant readiness to give a candid account of himself, the patience to linger over a matter under discussion, and above all the ability to lure what is otherwise passed over in silence into the area of discourse, to make it worth talking about. (*MDT,* 78)

It is thinking in this sense, alive to the provocation of others' thought yet retaining an important autonomy from the world born of the pleasure in one's inner plurality, that might condition us against evil-doing by enhancing our attentiveness to reality. Its autonomy notwithstanding, thinking remains vulnerably dependent on our ability or our "great good fortune" to have friends or to live in a world in which public discourse flourishes. Thinking's moral relevance depends on the complex interrelationship between thought and the world, and, as far as ethical relevance is concerned, it is the human condition of plurality, the "law of the earth," that interweaves the loose but durable threads of that interrelationship.

3 World Alienation and the Modern Age:
The Deprivations of Obscurity

The poor man's conscience is clear; yet he is ashamed. His character is irreproachable; yet he is neglected and despised. He feels himself out of the sight of others, groping in the dark. Mankind takes no notice of him. He rambles and wanders unheeded. In the midst of a crowd, at church, in the market, at a play...he is in as much obscurity as he would be in a garret or a cellar. He is not disapproved, censured, or reproached; *he is only not seen.* This total inattention is to him mortifying, painful and cruel. He suffers a misery from this consideration, which is sharpened by the consciousness that others have no fellow-feeling with him in this distress.

—JOHN ADAMS, *The Works of John Adams*

Writing in the first year of his term as vice president of the United States, John Adams gives voice to a kind of suffering he thought peculiar to the poor. Such suffering creates, he wrote, "as severe a pain as the gout or stone [and] produces despair and detestation of existence."[1] Arendt was drawn to Adams's insights, moved by "the feeling of injustice" he expressed. Once self-preservation has been assured, she wrote, "the real predicament" of the poor is that they must suffer "the insult of oblivion," as she called it. "Darkness rather than want is the curse of poverty" (*OR,* 69). No one articulated more poignantly than John Adams what Arendt referred to as "the crippling consequences" of such darkness. And no political theorist has cared more about and wrote more passionately against these consequences than Hannah Arendt.

It is not, of course, that Arendt wrote against poverty or championed the cause of social injustice. Indeed, she seems somewhat tone-deaf to such concerns.[2] Arendt's political theorizing was fired by a feeling for a different kind of injustice—the insult of oblivion. This form of injustice is, I suggest, prior to social injustice in the sense that the degradation of obscurity is a primary precondition of our capacity to inflict and sustain the suffering involved in the many forms social and economic inequality take.[3] As I shall argue, the point is not only the uncertain moral claim that if we could but fully "see" others we could neither commit nor sustain social injustices against them. It is also that the condition of oblivion itself weakens those who suffer it in ethically troublesome ways. Thus, in what has been perceived as Arendt's insensitivity, even cold inhumanity, I find the essence of a particularly compelling humanism that owes much to her phenomenology and wells out of her concern with how to intensify our awareness of reality.

What, then, are the crippling consequences of this form of injustice? In the context of the American Revolution, Arendt wrote about the political predicament of the vast majority of the population who suffered not from want but from "continual toil and want of leisure." Here we can begin to trace Arendt's thought. The essential injustice suffered by this majority was that while, in varying degrees, they were represented and could choose their representatives, "these essentially negative safeguards by no means open the public realm to the many, nor can they arouse in them that 'passion for distinction'... which according to John Adams, 'next to self-preservation will forever be the spring of human actions'" (*OR*, 69).

Here Arendt hones in on the crucial triad: public space, arousal, and action. Excluded from the place where we appear to others and they to us, the play of arousal, the provocation between those who see and those who are seen, remains largely dormant. That aesthetic-existential urge to make our presence felt—the urge Arendt theorized as an active response to being perceived—is thwarted, the passion to excel unawakened. And with this comes suffering that is crippling.

It is tempting to interpret this crippling largely within the frame adopted by modern theorists of individual liberty who were influenced by the Romantic expressive tradition. John Stuart Mill, Alexis de Tocqueville, and Wilhelm von Humboldt, for example, argue that individuals denied the proper cultivation of their inward forces suffer distortions.[4] Here, however, the focus is on self-development, and although Arendt is not uninterested in this type of individual flourishing, her primary concern is with existential crippling. Those relegated to oblivion suffer a loss of feeling for their own existence, their own reality, as well as for the larger world and their relationship to it. They feel, as Adams put it, "despair and detestation of existence." It is this crippling of the urge to appear that makes the insult of oblivion prior to social injustice. In rendering the victim invisible, it disarms the impulse that is the spring of human action, creating a condition in which resistance to social injustice is unlikely.[5]

Although Arendt developed her understanding of the insult of oblivion, following Adams, in relation to the "curse" of poverty, it forms in her writing the central injustice suffered in the modern age more generally. Indeed, it is the normative standpoint from which she develops her critique of modern political thinking and modern social and political institutions and practices. Yet it is perhaps strange to call this an injustice endemic to the modern age, for if it is crippling, most of us remain dramatically unaware of its impact. "Modern sensibility," Arendt argues, "is not touched by obscurity" (OR, 70). Indeed, the odd thing is perhaps the lack of outrage, the *absence* of pain, despite Adams's passionate depiction. Thus we have the paradoxical argument for an elemental, widely suffered form of injustice that almost no one recognizes. I suggest that we understand the paradox in this way: that Adams is right, that the passion for distinction is a real existential need, but because it is intangible and requires institutional support, it is easily overwhelmed by substitutes. In the modern age, the allure of riches as the road to engaging the "passion for distinction" easily displaced the deeper path this passion can tread.

Arendt's political theory offers us an idiom with which to identify, even experience, perhaps, become more susceptible to this kind of suffering *as a phenomenon*. In this chapter I seek to elaborate this idiom through an examination of Arendt's conception of freedom, the public sphere, and humanism. I then turn to selected features of her critique of the modern age, highlighting her ontological concerns and approaching them with the seriousness I believe they merit. I discuss those modern conditions that widely extend the form of suffering with which she is concerned—conditions that dramatically attenuate the power of that mutual aesthetic provocation through which our sense of the real is born. I conclude by arguing for privileging a public sensibility that is attentive to the insult of oblivion but fruitfully mediates the tensions between the public passion for distinction and the suffering inflicted by diverse forms of social injustice.

The Arendtian Idiom

What is freedom? It is, Arendt elegantly says, "the freedom to call something into being which did not exist before" (*BPF*, 151). This capacity, she argues, springs from our own beginning in the world, is, as it were, a response to it. Hence to be free is to begin, and our impulse to freedom "animates and inspires" all human activities (*BPF*, 169).

Yet our question is more specific: What is freedom as it relates to politics? Although born of the same responsive provocation to being in the world, freedom as it relates to politics is distinct. It is not the same as the inner freedom we may experience in solitude as our mental life's two-in-one plays with itself. Neither is it the freedom of the artist whose responsive creativity precedes the product and thus does not show itself to others, except as reified testimony to and promise of the human impulse to freedom. Politically relevant freedom, by contrast, is manifest only amid the sensuous aesthetic provocation of speaking and acting beings. It emerges only where people are together in this manner. It carries some of the exhilaration of free corporeal movement, untied and uncoerced by direct need. Indeed, to be free requires first that we be liberated from the toil upon us as nature's creatures. Won either by coercing others or through the invention of implements to replace our own labor, we become freed for a togetherness governed not by interest or need but by the impulse to freedom.[6]

Arendt argues that this worldly quality of freedom pertinent to politics is testified to in both Greek and Latin. In both languages there are two words for action. In Greek, *archein* means "to begin," "to lead," "to rule," and *prattein* means "to carry something through," "to achieve," "to finish." In Latin, a similar structure prevails: *agere* means "to set something in motion," and *gerere* means, originally, "to bear." Arendt finds here evidence for the "original interdependence" of action: that the one who begins "depends" on others to complete what was begun, and that those who carry forth the act to completion in turn "depend" on the beginner for their opportunity to act (*HC*, 189). By contrast, our single term, *action*, has lost the second cluster of meanings, so that for us to act is synonymous with leading and ruling. We think of action on the model—indeed, the ideal—of sovereignty, and with this change we lose the politically relevant relationship of action to freedom.

As fascinating as is this etymological path toward reviving an older understanding of action, the discrete nature of the terms and the different selves to which, in any given action, they refer should not obfuscate the phenomenon of freedom as Arendt theorizes it. Freedom emerges through the active and reciprocal intertwining of appearing beings. "The actor," she writes, "always moves *among* and *in relation to* other acting beings" (*HC*, 190; my italics). That is, we simultaneously act and are acted upon, and this "reversibility," in which our urge to make our presence felt conjoins simultaneously with our sense of the presence of others, is the birth of freedom. It is the birth of the fearsome miracle upsurge out of human plurality of the new beginning. Freedom as it is relevant to politics cannot be specified apart from an account of this very profound reciprocal provocation on the part of appearing beings, this "original interdependence."[7] Indeed, it is this reversibility that gives rise to the *deinon* attributes of human freedom: action's essential unpredictability, its boundlessness, and its irreversibility, all of which are attributes alone of this nonmodern sense of freedom. Perhaps, too, one of action's most quixotic but essential qualities is also born in this reversibility—the capacity to generate power and mobilize people freely on behalf of a common cause.

Politically relevant freedom is thus, as Arendt theorizes it, never something we *possess*. It is, rather, a mode of being whose specific virtuosity shows itself in how well we, as nonsovereign beings, act to answer the world's demanding, often urgent call. Those too burdened by private need or interest are poorly capable of such responsiveness.

Like all performing arts, then, the appearance of freedom in the sense of the capacity to begin something new in word and deed is ephemeral. Freedom *is* only in performance, only in acts. It has a fugitive, apparitional quality, and hardly seems real. In Chapter 2 I argued that what reality things in our appearing world might have depends on the witnessing presence of others. Each appearance is simultaneously a solicitation that others might give testimony to and receive the impact of its coming into the world. Our sense of reality in general and the reality of specific phenomena is called forth in the theater of display and witness. In a profound way, this is true of all phenomena. Yet some phenomena require a more specialized theater for their appearance; some require a "publicly organized space" if they are to have much reality for us (*BPF*, 154). Such a phenomenon is the freedom with which we are concerned.

Indeed, one of the most important purposes of the public sphere is to give this capacity some tangible reality. Only in the beckoning publicity of worldly spaces designed for its appearance can freedom come out of hiding and give us confirmation of its reality. This publicity of a distinctively public sphere—the fact that things there can "be seen and heard by everybody" (*HC*, 50)—is both one of the uniquely defining qualities of that sphere in contrast to other spheres of life and one of the most elemental reasons for Arendt's preoccupation with it. The publicity of the public realm intensifies our sense of the reality of that which appears in it. Arendt's argument here is not that our sense of the reality of our capacity for freedom, more generally understood, will be entirely extinguished without a public sphere to solicit and confirm its being into the world. The capacity will survive in underground forms in most times of severe political tyranny and closure, and in this form we may not be unaware of it as a phenomenon. But in such forms it will be irrelevant to the task of making the world we inhabit a human one, for, as I shall argue, this is, in Arendt's view, an essentially political capacity. And thus, the weight upon the existence of publicly organized spaces of appearance so that freedom might be tangible is enormous.

We may well need to add further to this burden, for Arendt argues that it is from this political or worldly experience of freedom that our other experiences of freedom are derived. All forms of inner freedom—of thought, of creative design, of will, she argues—are "derivative" (*BPF*, 146). They develop out of this prior performative experience of freedom. The argument that freedom is primordially a worldly phenomenon runs along two different but parallel tracks—the one phenomenal, the other historical.

First, Arendt argues, we "become aware of freedom or its opposite in our intercourse with others, not with the intercourse with ourselves" (*BPF*, 148). The elemental movement out into the world, together with the freedom to speak and act in that larger world of others, are the experiences through which we first grasp the phenomenon of freedom. The "original field" of freedom, Arendt argues, is "the realm of politics and human affairs in general" (*BPF*, 145). Phenomenologically, freedom is first and foremost a worldly engagement, and from such original engagements "derive" our experiences of freedom in other domains of human experience.

The second sense in which our experiences of inner freedom are derivative is historical. In the West, Arendt points out, the idea of freedom was not applied to inner life until late antiquity. Reacting to the severe loss of political freedom, the Stoics transferred it to the inner domain, where it was transfigured into an experience of total control over the self. There, without worldly impediment or interference, freedom had found a new home. The ideal of this new inner freedom was no longer performative virtuosity but sovereignty, and it required retreat, reverie, and solitude. This paved the way for early Christianity's "discovery" of the phenomenon of the will, and, with the powerful writings of Augustine, freedom as free will entered the history of philosophy and became (and has remained) both the prevailing understanding and practice of freedom in the West.[8]

These arguments concerning the twofold derivative character of inner freedom raise the interesting question of how much the vitality of freedom in this inner sense itself depends on being replenished by our experience of freedom in its "original field." If, phenomenologically speaking, we first know freedom in the world with others, does our freedom of will, of thought, and of creative design become desiccated if the world offers us fewer and less and less potent invitations "to enter, with other humans, through language, into the order and disorder of the world," as Adrienne Rich puts it?[9] When the worldly opportunities to experience freedom have receded, are these derivative experiences threatened as well?[10] If so, Arendt's understanding of freedom illuminates the depth of lethargy and despair, the "detestation of existence" suffered by groups entrenched in the darkness of generational poverty.[11]

Thus to summarize "the crippling consequences" of obscurity we find the following. Denied that movement in relation to others in a public sphere, denied the dense and pressing presence of speaking and acting beings, our own urge to appear remains unprovoked. Our potential to call forth something that had never been before, to "change every constellation" is crippled (*HC*, 190). And if this were not sufficient cause for despair, the denial of this political freedom over time may well undermine our capacity for inner freedom as well.

Still, to leave matters here would not do justice to the full ethical import of Arendt's concern with this kind of suffering, for the incessant "palaver" in the *polis,* that press of self-display and receptivity as it gives birth to the new, also humanizes. Thus to suffer the insult of oblivion is to be denied the full capacity for participating in humanizing the world. To unfold this argument requires further direct engagement with the enormous ontological importance with which Arendt charges this ephemeral phenomenon of freedom and the publicly constituted space for its appearance. For, as we shall see, implicit in Arendt's humanism—nonessentialist, qualified and tentative though it is[12]—is the contention that whether we are, in fact, to be *human* in any specific sense in our postmetaphysical appearing world will depend on our capacity to belong to and care for one another *in such a way as* to make our sense of the real fuller, deeper.

If our capacity to sense reality emerges in the contrast between a repetitious background and an eruptive novel ground, if it depends on the appearance of "the infinitely improbable," then the existence of an organized sphere where the capacity to begin can appear and be confirmed is of greatest ethical significance. In the bright light created by the testifying presence of all, the shock of the improbable can be collectively felt. Here I speak, much as I did in

Chapter 2, of the capacity to register the elemental impact of existence that arises only in the face of the provoking, even incursion-like presence of others.

Such an elemental capacity to sense reality is of course possible without a public sphere, and this was one of the points of my account of Arendt's ontology of display. But the very essence of the public sphere is to arouse the impulse to freedom and to let it shine, and this it does, in contrast to other forms of social existence and private experience, as an *open* and *extended* domain of human plurality. As such, it offers a space in which the unrelated, the new, and uncertain events and developments can become relatable, a space in which those who share the public world can take stock, and meaning can be born.[13] Through the fragile, uncertain, often foreboding encounters between multiple, particular perspectives, our sense of a common world is won. When these encounters diminish, so, too, does our sense of the world as a specific, shared, and ongoing human project. Without public spaces to engender a world held in common, human existence is bewildering, and qualities of nonrelatedness and non-sensicalness prevail. And with this our world becomes dimly lit. In darkness we are inhabited by forces whose nature we hardly grasp.

So in these senses—that we better register and receive the shock of the improbable and actively constitute a sense of a commonly held world—the public sphere and freedom as Arendt theorizes them possess a particularly potent capacity to sustain and replenish our sense of reality. If a specifically human manner of living is to emerge, the existence of a public sphere in which freedom can appear is crucial. Now let me push further toward Arendt's humanism.

Arendt often referred to "the deeper significance" of the public-political realm. It was, she argued, also a "spiritual realm" in which can be seen not *what* you are (an inspired teacher, fat, from the middle class, a gifted mechanic, and so on) but *who* you are (*MDT*, 73). Implicit in all our relations but barely known to ourselves, who we are can appear fully only to others when we enter the public sphere (*MDT*, 73–74). It is a spirit-apparition and concerns a person's "living essence."[14]

We should not obscure the worldly nature of this spirit. Arendt seeks to name the essence of this *being-in-the-world*, and in so doing she is profoundly influenced by the phenomenological notion, so poetically formulated by Merleau-Ponty, that "the subject is a process of transcendence *towards the world*."[15] Who we are is born of our unique, ongoing, and difficult embrace of the world.[16] And it is in the public sphere in particular, Arendt argues, that this living essence can be humanized.

Those who enter the public sphere must be "speaking persons" (*MDT*, 79), and this places certain demands on them. Foremost among these are the courage and passion for the activities of dialogue: for the listening, the lingering over things, and the luring of them into existence that makes them worth talking about and responding to through action.[17] Through this commitment with which they abandon themselves to the public world—to its many strangers, its flux, its alien quality and often unwanted happenings, they can acquire the height of humanness, what Arendt calls "the valid personality" (*MDT,* 73). Not subjective, yet valid without being objective, this humanness wells out of an openness, gladness, even gratitude toward the world in all its density and recalcitrant plurality. When we say what we "deem truth," we humanize the world because *what we see* arises out of this profound conjoining with and "tragic pleasure" in the world. The world is the bearer, if you will, of our *human* particularity, and through our embrace there simultaneously occurs the upsurge of the world as a humanly meaningful place.

Thus without this venture out into a publicly organized space, the reality of what we do and who we are grows dim. Free action in the public sphere gives rise to a certain luminosity. And it is alone out of this deeper, spiritual sense of politics that our "sympathy," as Arendt put it, for human particularity can arise (*MDT,* 30). We must cultivate such sympathy to care for our world and one another in such a way as to make our sense of the real fuller, deeper. The insult of oblivion deprives us of the worldly relations through which this sympathy might dawn. And this is the same as being denied the opportunity to participate and live in a humanized, meaningful world. This, too, is one of the "crippling consequences" of this form of injustice. I turn now to Arendt's account of the conditions of the modern age that have made this kind of suffering so widespread.

Critique of the Modern Age

Arendt is well-known for her relentless attacks on the unworldly, antipolitical tendencies of modernity. Her erudite use of ancient texts, practices, and understandings as the instruments of attack has contributed to a view, shared by many of her readers, that she is a nostalgic thinker who glorifies a far-distant past, who underappreciates many important features of modernity, and whose political theorizing, although provocative, is of little practical or critical use to our present.[18]

There is some truth in this position. The rigidity of Arendt's conceptual distinctions between the public-political realm on the one hand and the social and private realms on the other, while indeed provoking, is far too taut either to explain satisfactorily contemporary political phenomena or even to fully celebrate political life as she aims to.[19] These rigidities serve to badly limit our conceptual license to grasp the way very diverse kinds of political action constitute significant public spaces in which political freedom might appear. This seems especially true of those insurgent counterpublics in which political relations are established outside the formal public sphere by otherwise (variously) disenfranchised groups. Excluded from "normal" politics, these groups find ways of constituting spaces of appearance in which their own worldly concerns and practices of freedom can make themselves felt.[20] This has been an especially common experience for precisely those groups about which Arendt is remarkably silent. Prominent examples are the many forms of women's political action, for these have often been concerned with calling public attention to what Arendt believed were properly private domestic affairs because they concerned human need in one form or another.

Interestingly enough, however, despite these rigidities, Arendt's ontology and her celebration of council politics suggest a far more elastic notion of the public sphere. This is also true of both her reliance on promising as the act that sustains public space and her understanding of the portability of this phantom space, as in her affirmation of the famous Greek words "Wherever you go, you will be a *polis*" (*HC*, 198). These aspects of Arendt's theorizing make her work particularly compelling as they sharpen our sensitivity toward the incitements of appearance and responsive display, enticing us to explore the many diverse ways in which people of different status and social location seize opportunities for freedom and for generating power in the world. Thus her ontology and her celebration of council politics suggest a far more protean understanding of political action, and they underwrite a more radically democratic politics than do the central distinctions of her explicitly political theorizing.

The paradox remains, however, that these limiting distinctions *at the same time* function to clear conceptual space for the crucial phenomenon that Arendt sought, against her time and the tradition of political thinking, to theorize—the peculiar capacity of political life as she understands it to intensify our awareness of reality. And this has been an enormous contribution, giving us a certain novel critical purchase on modern political understandings and practices, riveting our attention to the peculiar importance of various kinds of civic participation not because they achieve particular social ends but because there, in the common space created by speaking persons, our experience of our specifically human existence is intensified. What Arendt's overly rigid distinctions do achieve, I'm suggesting, is an opening for reflection on and appreciation of the ontological dimension of political experiences, and for an interrogation of historical forms of public-political life in terms of their capacity to contribute to or intensify our awareness of reality. Indeed, if we centralize Arendt's ontological concerns, as I do in this reading, it becomes clear that it was the ancients' passion for reality that made their political understandings of such vital interest to her—and this is especially true of their delimitation on the public-political world.[21] Thus Arendt tried to listen to them anew in the service of revitalizing a form of public-political life in which attentiveness to the reality and meaning of human doings is deepened. It is from this overwhelming ontological concern that I read Arendt's critique of the political prospects of our modernity.

World Alienation: Spiritual Consequences

If any one thing characterizes modernity in Arendt's view, it is its process character. The prototypically modern experience is one of being in the midst of natural and other inexorable processes. What meaning things bear is derived from their function in the overall process. Individual acts are dwarfed, stripped of their dignity, power, and meaningful place in a wider world. Hence the process character of the modern age destroys the conditions for the appearance of human particularity and for collective, meaning-giving acts. It makes the insult of oblivion a widely suffered experience.

The deepest sign of the modern age is loss of the condition of the world understood as both the subjective-in-between that intangibly forms between people who share a common life and the thing-quality or objective-in-between. The hallmark of Arendt's concept of the world is that, in both of these senses, people are at once related and separated. "The world" stands for the existential dimension of spatiality. By pressing people indistinguishably together, the modern age is an assault on the existential dimension of spatiality in its objective and subjective senses.

Modernity commences, Arendt argues, with three profound and different sources of "world alienation": the Reformation, the (so-called) discovery of America, and the invention of the telescope. Each event represents different forms of retreat from the worldly dimension of our lived experience, and each is significant to Arendt because in the ways of knowing and the form of life it instantiates, reality is neither verified nor engendered through the presence of others. Arendt singles out these events because they threaten the aesthetic provocation through which a human sense of the world is born in our postmetaphysical condition.

Thus, for example, when, with the Reformation, faith became contingent on unmediated relationship with God, the center of the self's activity became innerworldly life. And when large numbers of peasants were expropriated as Church property was seized during the Reformation, it created a group of worldless laborers relatively unbound to place. For its part, the "discovery" of America initiated a dramatic process of abolishing distance and space. To grasp the world in its aftermath required disentanglement "from all involvement in and concern with the close at hand and withdraw[al] to a distance from everything near" (*HC*, 251). Each event brought world alienation because each either entailed a loosening of attentiveness to place or to the presence of particular others close at hand. The self was required to habitually rip itself from its embeddedness in the world of things and others in its local and immediate world.

Finally, and in Arendt's view second to no other event, Galileo's discovery of the telescope initiated an assault on the adequacy of our "body-bound" senses to reveal truth. The "shock of this event" (*HC*, 273) was that "our senses, our very organs for the reception of reality" betray us, for they reveal not true appearances but illusions (*HC*, 262). At the outset of the modern age, then, being and appearing part company. And this was accompanied by a wholesale loss of self-evidence. The nightmare of the human mind on the edge of the modern age is that reality is only a dream, and God is not only unreachable but an active and evil deceiver, a *Dieu trompeur*, as Descartes put it.

The response to this nightmare is extraordinary. In a restless search for certainty, the modern mind withdraws from the deluding world into introspection. In this state, all objective, sensuous reality "dissolves" into subjective states of mind. The sensed object is made over entirely anew as an "object of consciousness." Because nothing other than what the solitary mind itself makes is involved in this process, the reliability of perception is guaranteed.

This represents a kind of hyper world alienation in which truth depends on the absolute abolition of relations to the appearing world; it demands that the knower be under "the condition of remoteness" (*HC*, 267). The question is no longer "What do you *see*" but "What did you *do* to arrive at these results?"[22] And the tools for this kind of project are the symbols and logical relationships of modern algebra, which, as Arendt put it, has "succeeded in freeing itself from the shackles of spatiality" (*HC*, 264–65).

But this freedom is accompanied by loss of meaningfulness. To illuminate the nonsensory experiences of mental life, philosophical language had always been metaphorical. Borrowing from the world of appearances, metaphorical words discover analogies—similarities of relations intuited between the world of appearances and the imageless world of invisibles.

This "carrying over" capacity illuminates, even establishes the reality of mental events and occurrences whose hallmark is their invisible quality. Arendt draws her example from the *Iliad:*

> The poet likens the tearing onslaught of fear and grief on the hearts of men to the combined onslaught of winds from several directions on the waters of the sea. Think of these storms that you know so well, the poet seems to tell us, and you will know about grief and fear. Significantly, the reverse will not work. No matter how long somebody thinks about grief and fear, he will never find out anything about the winds and the sea; the comparison is clearly meant to tell what grief and fear can do to the human heart, that is, meant to illuminate an experience that does not appear. (*LMT,* 106)

The point in our context is that inner experiences—be they the experience of an emotion or Cartesian introspection with its preparatory de-sensing process—have no capacity for self-illumination, so to speak. If these experiences are to be made accessible to human understanding, we must use a language that is born in the sensuous appearing world. Indeed, the irreversibility of the relation, the fact that we comprehend nothing of the wind and sea through our feelings of grief and fear, points to the primacy of the appearing world.

This loss of meaningfulness is accompanied by an additional loss, and this concerns the consequences of the radical withdrawal from others required by this path to knowing. Fortified against "objects *also* appearing as such to others and being acknowledged by them," the introspective mind cannot maintain a sense of its own reality (*LMT,* 46). Just as the "that-ness" of the world of appearances, through metaphor, illuminates the life of the mind, so the space of appearances created when we are in the presence of others brings into being and confirms the "*that* there is" of all human perception. In each case, when it comes to our capacity to sense reality and illuminate the meaning of existence, the primacy of the world of appearances is confirmed.

Thus, although the abyss that Galileo's discovery created between humans and the sensuous appearing world was the source of unparalleled innovations in science, it resulted in philosophical impotence. And this impotence prepares the way for what Arendt refers to as the "spiritual consequence" of world alienation. With faith in our "bodily vision" shattered, the spiritual hunger for knowledge and truth no longer satiable through the stillness of philosophical contemplation, trust was placed in doing. Only in actively intervening could deceptive appearances be identified and truth be secured. This was the work of *homo faber*. If we can reliably know only what we make, surely in the controlled conditions of the laboratory we can imitate the processes of that which we did not make so as to wrest nature's truth from it.

The fantastic flourish of activity that marks the modern age, then, had a spiritual, not practical genesis. *Homo faber* was driven by the need to satiate the hunger for true knowledge. But this dogged effort to fulfill the human spirit was premised on a radical disavowal of the world of appearances, and this meant also a radical disavowal of the revelatory power of language and of our presence to one another. Arendt writes, "In the place of the concept of Being we now find the concept of Process. And whereas it is in the nature of Being to appear and thus disclose itself, it is in the nature of Process to remain invisible" (*HC*, 296–97).

This substitution represents an elemental change of human self-understanding. Moderns began "to consider [themselves] part and parcel of the two superhuman, all-encompassing processes of nature and history" (*HC*, 307). Means-ends thinking, the very framework within which a thing's utility might make sense, was overwhelmed by the principle of process. The life process itself, Arendt argues, became the highest good.[23] And happiness derived from pleasure in life's sheer abundance became the raison d'être of human existence. To alleviate the pain and suffering associated with life provides spiritual satisfactions that override all other motivations for collective life.

Pain and suffering of this kind stand in sharp contrast to the suffering that so concerned Hannah Arendt. Indeed, not being *seen* cannot be recognized *as* suffering in a world in which truth and knowledge are secured through radical severance from the appearing world. For deep, spiritual reasons, the modern spirit does not register the insult in the condition of obscurity.

World Alienation: Practical Consequences

There are also practical reasons that the modern age is unmoved by the suffering of oblivion. The unprecedented processes of expropriation and wealth accumulation set off by the Reformation created profound experiences of world alienation. As Arendt so floridly puts it, this event "propelled Western mankind into a development in which all property was destroyed in the process of its appropriation, all things devoured in the process of their production, and the stability of the world undermined in a constant process of change" (*HC*, 252).

This story of capitalism concerns the "liberation" that accompanied the original depravation of a privately owned (or at least worked) place in the world, the liberation of the "force inherent in labor power" (*HC*, 255).[24] Historically bound to the circumscribed domain of the family-kin network, labor was liberated "to" the public domain of the factory, where dozens, hundreds, and even thousands of worldless laborers were brought together. This development changed the very nature of labor. From a cyclical, repetitive activity, labor became a rectilinear, swiftly progressing development, ever subject to revolutionizing advances in its productivity. A process without end, modern production nonetheless retains the fundamental aspects of the life process: its force, its urgency, its relentless consumption and its worldlessness.

The spiritually-driven focus on doing has its practical counterpart in the elevation of laboring to the highest rank among the *vita activa*, as collective life becomes organized around these devouring processes of production and accumulation. To account for the immense increase in human productive capacity, this ranking is reflected in modern political theory. John Locke finds in labor the source of all property, Adam Smith the source of all wealth, and Karl Marx the very process through which we recognize our humanity.[25] Labor becomes the legitimizing figure of their political theories because, rooted in the natural processes of the body, it alone among the three activities of the *vita activa* approximates the endless, apparently automatic progressing nature of the productive growth that marks the modern age. Both labor and this growth seemed natural; they seemed beyond, as Arendt puts it, "willful decision or humanly meaningful purposes" (*HC*, 106).

It is this wish to portray the process of accumulation as in the nature of things that unites theorists of capitalism and socialism, this which forms the deepest continuities of the modern age, politically speaking. Neither are concerned with what Arendt calls "the worldly character" of a produced thing—its function, location, and length of stay in the world (*HC*, 94). Nor are they concerned with the world in the sense of a commonly constituted space of appearances. To different degrees, dreaming the dream of liberating humanity from necessity, and overwhelmed by the explosion of productive social forces, the dynamic devouring social life process becomes, for all three, the highest purpose of collective life.

This devouring quality is the essence of the social realm that grows up around the new productive forces, and it is this realm with which modern political theorists have been so preoccupied. The rise of the social realm represents a terrible kind of deformation. Arendt uses the potent language of nature to make her point. She writes, "The social realm, where the life process has established its own public domain, has let loose an unnatural growth, so to speak, of the natural" (*HC,* 47). "Unnaturally," concerns of reproduction, production, and consumption crowd out and prevail over all other possible practical concerns.

In particular, the experiences and distinctiveness of private life succumb to the devouring processes of life. Progressively unable to satisfy the needs of mere life within its domain, the extended family has waned in its capacity to protect distinction and individual difference by offering respite from social life. The processes of conformity and normalization that have accompanied our modern "civilization of productivity" engulf and deform the private sphere as well.[26]

The public realm is also disfigured once it focuses its light on the life process of birth, decay, and death itself. It ceases to be an arena for the appearance of freedom, not because that triadic relation between the public, arousal and action is broken, but because action is reduced to finding further ways to alleviate life's pain and suffering. And for this we do not need to appear to one another as distinct and free beings. To the contrary, we must be seen, as Arendt argues we see one another under the guise of life, as species creatures subject in the same ways to life's necessity. Within this frame, to experience suffering is to be denied one's equal share of the goods. Collectively speaking, it is to impede the growth of society's productive forces. Although in different ways, the frameworks of both modern liberal theory and Marxist-socialist theory are defined by these two forms of suffering. In both cases, it is difficult to conceive that we might suffer when deprived of a public space of appearances. The experience itself is nearly inaccessible because the public sphere as that place for the arousal through mutual provocation of our passion for distinction has lost its raison d'être. Arendt finds both tragedy and irony in this condition in which the life process has become the very essence of a life shared in common—tragedy because it entails a radical loss of human relatedness, irony because it makes labor, the most private and least common experience of all the activities of the *vita activa,* the basis of collective life. We get at Arendt's un–self-evident yet important point if we reformulate the claim to read: Labor is the least authentically sharable experience. Here the question is "What does it take to have a common experience, to really share things together?" Arendt's answer, as I have been arguing, is "Identity in difference." That is, our sense of the reality of the world depends on plurality—a profusion of views—on intersubjective experience. The experiences of the production/consumption processes of life and labor can but dimly provide this because they are in essential ways the same for all of us, ensconced in the body's relentless repetitious needs. These are not experiences in which human plurality flourishes. They are less amenable to disclosive speech than are other activities. To make the production/consumption processes of *animal laborans* the common end is both tragic and ironic in that authentically common experience is either precluded or at least severely curtailed. The public realm is deformed.

There is further tragedy and irony, for the devouring, limitless nature of these processes undermine, as we have seen, the permanence of the common world in its objective sense. And this permanence, Arendt argues, is a precondition of freedom itself. So when the dream of abundance is elevated to the highest aim, public life receives a limitless foundation. In the unworldly "realm" of the social, *animal laborans* has little world-building capacity in either the objective or intersubjective sense. The contention underlying Arendt's thought here is that without a world of stable things that transcends individual mortality, human relatedness cannot gain sufficient stability. The specific capacity of humans to distinguish themselves through word and deed and thus to build and experience a distinctive common world is eroded and undermined. Such capacities have, again, lost their raison d'être. No less isolated and private for having made the life process the common end, the preconditions for the appearance of freedom are destroyed. Thus while it is certainly true that we can produce and consume in particular ways, *animal laborans* has little ability to challenge the primacy of the life process itself as the dominant aim of our common lives. And with this, the public realm is deformed.

Loss of the world that gathers and separates us, although not necessarily permanent, represents at least a temporary loss of the capacity to be specifically human. While Arendt thinks it is characteristic of humans that we wish to make our appearance explicitly, to deliberately choose *how* to appear, it is not a necessary condition of life for our species. Instead it is something that must be tended and cultivated, and for which worldly space, in the literal and metaphorical, objective and subjective senses, must be provided. It is precisely this to which modern political theorists, in Arendt's view, were almost wholly inattentive.

Thus it is on the ruins of both the public and private spheres and the experiences that they help preserve that the denatured social realm emerges. And despite the spatial metaphors, Arendt's argument implies that the "realm" of the social, strictly speaking, has no real spatial dimensionality. Its dimension is temporal and that itself reduced essentially to the future.

The practical consequence of world alienation is that the dream of abundance becomes the guiding force of collective life, the "unnatural growth... of the natural," our highest practical purpose (*HC*, 47). Underlying Arendt's arguments here is a loud lament that this unnaturalism has been "unleashed." The authority she musters through the language of "the unnatural" appears to serve a nostalgic return. That is, insofar as this phenomenon is unnatural and deforming, our project looks to be one of return or restoration. If this is true, Arendt's way of theorizing the liberation of labor and the predominance of concern with the life process is uninteresting, even irrelevant to our world, for this "unnaturalness" is a fact with which we must work, not wish away.

If, however, we pay attention to the structure of Arendt's argument, it looks less romantic in tone and orientation. That structure appears in the (Aristotelian) argument that certain activities and human experiences must find a home in particular domains of human life if they are to retain their distinctiveness (*HC*, 73), and furthermore, that this distinctiveness is important, as I argued in Chapter 2, to the challenge of retaining and intensifying our sense of reality. Despite her language of naturalism, it is not a metaphysically grounded argument that orients her or makes her critique of the modern age interesting and hard-hitting.[27] Her concerns are ontological, and her mode of argument presses our late-modern imagination to an interrogation of how best to preserve and make possible diverse forms of human experience.

Arendt's deepest quarrel with the social is the extent to which it *reduces* the plurality of human experiences and activities, is the sheen of irrelevance all other capacities acquire. Thus she writes, "Society is the form in which the fact of mutual dependence for the sake of life *and nothing else* assumes public significance" (*HC*, 46; my italics). This loss of human experience troubles Arendt as she looks back over the centuries of the modern age:

> It is not only and not even primarily contemplation which has become an entirely meaningless experience. Thought itself, when it became "reckoning with consequences," became a function of the brain, with the result that electronic instruments are found to fulfill these functions much better than we could. Action was soon and still is almost exclusively understood in terms of making and fabricating, only that making, because of its worldliness and inherent indifference to life, was now regarded as but another form of laboring, a more complicated but not a more mysterious function of the life process. (*HC*, 321–22)

And, perhaps honing in on the issue, Arendt writes, "None of the higher capacities of man [are] any longer necessary to connect individual life with the life of the species" (*HC*, 321). Human connection, the relatedness and distinctness between a particular person and the larger whole, between self and others, requires only social labor, and although this necessitates a high degree of coordination and organization, it does not require the kind of presence to one another through which human distinctness and relatedness is engendered. Nor does it require the solitude and mastery of *homo faber* or the withdrawal into the lively duality of the thinking ego. The point here is that human connection is a largely crippled possibility in such a world, for the diverse perspectives arising from key dimensions of human experience that might provoke our attention are largely absent, having become superfluous. With this, we suffer a loss of a sense of reality.

Just such a world, we might argue, needs public spheres in which the human urge to appear can be aroused. The theoretical difficulty at this juncture, however, is that Arendt's account of modern world alienation and the rise of the social, culminating in a society of jobholders that demands no more than "a sheer automatic functioning of its members," is so totalizing that it is hard to form any materially grounded realistic hope for the revitalization of public life (*HC*, 322).[28] Although our system of "global housekeeping," prevents us from returning to a condition in which more individualized family units tend to the needs of life,[29] we may, however, be able to secure spaces for the episodic appearance of human freedom. We may be able to imagine forms of collective life in which a difficult tension between the social and the political could be sustained so that the devouring-process quality of social forces is somewhat constrained in the service of more multidimensionality to human capabilities and experience in general, and to those of public-political life in particular.

It is with a sense of the importance of such possibilities that, in closing, I develop an argument for privileging a public sensibility attentive to the suffering involved in the insult of oblivion. In Arendt's reflections on compassion, the social question, and public freedom, I find the hint (that I extend) of a fascinating and nuanced mediation between concerns for social justice and for public appearance and freedom. Maintaining my ethical focus on the challenge of how to intensify our awareness of reality, I aim to sketch a model of political thinking about the social question that resists the categorical exclusion that Arendt's rigid distinctions imply but, in recognition of the seriousness of their underlying ontological concerns, simultaneously addresses the problem of the devouring nature of the social.

Compassion, the Social Question, and Public Freedom

The story I tell is about the struggle to sustain tragic pleasure, for our ability to understand and bring into view the full reality and meaning of our actions rests on maintaining a lively and difficult tension between the social question and politically relevant freedom. It rests on our ability to conceptualize and sustain in practice the plurality of our often conflicting irresolvable concerns. The point is, indeed, to affirm a way of life that allows us to be troubled and provoked. In what follows I look briefly at the different relationships Arendt draws between compassion, the social question, and public freedom in her comparative study of the French and American revolutions.

In *On Revolution,* Arendt argues that only the American Revolution was successful at constituting spaces for public freedom, although it failed to do so fully. The single most significant difference accounting for the respective courses of revolution in France and America was the extreme misery suffered in the Old World. America, she argues, enjoyed freedom from real want. The French effort to create a republican form of government based on consent foundered on the dramatic distance between the rich and the very poor classes. The reason this made such a difference was that once the French people were liberated from feudal tyranny, it became clear that public freedom would be enjoyed only by the few. Yet these few could hardly be legitimate representatives of the people, distinguished as they were from the suffering masses by social status. Unable to establish a constitutional form of government under these divisive circumstances, a great "effort of solidarization" was made by the rich toward the poor (*OR,* 74). And compassion for the poor's suffering was its instrument. As the ability to suffer *with* those who suffer, compassion appeared to be a natural, passionate bond between "men." The "natural goodness" of the miserable became the foundation of virtue, and the cohesiveness of the body politic was born of the single will to have compassion for the poor's suffering.

The problem, Arendt argues, is that this route to solidarity let the anguish felt by the heart toward suffering humanity overcome the effort at establishing spaces for public freedom. This passionate heart was indifferent to the suffering inflicted by the insult of oblivion; it could not, indeed, comprehend it. The reason for this is that when compassion leaves the realm of our private lives and becomes the foundation for political action and solidarity, it changes its character. Strictly speaking, we can have compassion only for particular people; compassion, in its nature, cannot be generalized. When we feel it we are "stricken in the flesh" by the sufferers in question (*OR,* 89). When compassion becomes the foundation of political life, however, it becomes the sentiment of pity.[30] And the problem is that, as a generalized feeling for the suffering of all, pity is boundless; it is unarrested by particular considerations. It has an inherent tendency to depersonalize all sufferers so that one can be "moved" by a whole class or people, moved by a single elemental force that gathers power from its reduction of the multitude to a single point of outrage.

As the foundation of political action, this boundless sentiment created what Arendt calls that "emotion-laden insensitivity to reality," both to reality in the general sense and to the reality of persons in particular (*OR*, 90). As such, however righteous, it is wholly unequipped to create enduring political institutions designed for freedom. All positive laws, in the face of the outrage at "the immensity of the people's misery," appear as callous and invidious examples of insensitivity and must fall before the just terror and the absolute morality of the good (*OR*, 92). Most significantly, in Arendt's view, this politics of outrage could not tolerate the difficult but important distinction between man-made politically induced suffering and the suffering we experience as a consequence of being "organic bodies" subject to "necessary and irresistible processes" (*OR*, 114). Without this distinction, the "abdication of freedom before the dictate of necessity" was assured in France (*OR*, 61).

Thus the politics of compassion overruled all other passions, and this immediate feeling for the suffering of the poor overwhelmed attentiveness to all other forms of suffering, for, as Arendt argues, pity cannot comprehend a multitude "whose majesty reside[s] in its very plurality" (*OR*, 93). That is, in the context of the revolution, pity could not comprehend the strong and the rich, but only the weak and the poor, and the latter only as a single will (*OR*, 89). Unable to "see" the strong and the rich *or* the weak and the poor in any terms other than through the sentimental lens of pity, the passion for public freedom that had driven and been experienced by some of both social classes during the revolution could not be illuminated. Suffering from the insult of oblivion was eclipsed from view, and with it, the passion for public freedom and the creation of spaces of appearance where alone the problems of social suffering might be intelligently addressed.[31]

Arendt sees the French as the first in the modern revolutionary tradition to fall victim to a pity-based, unconditional demand to be freed from necessity altogether. Her reading of the revolutionary experience of the French suggests that the emotions of the heart are entirely ill-equipped for establishing public freedom, and for this reason she argues (in an unmodulated manner that obscures somewhat the importance of her insight) that compassion is "politically speaking, irrelevant," that there are "disastrous results [when] emotions are displayed in public and become a factor in political affairs" (*OR*, 86). As we shall see in examining her analysis of the American revolutionaries' efforts, however, this does not mean that the heart and compassion are of no import in political affairs whatsoever.

The main argument Arendt offers concerning the relative success of the American Revolution is that, because the New World really did realize, although imperfectly, the dream of abundance, the American revolutionaries were never tempted by what Arendt calls, in a direct echo of Nietzsche, "the test of compassion" (*OR*, 95). Consequently, guided by common sense and a certain realism, the American revolutionaries remained committed to "the foundation of freedom" and to "the establishment of lasting institutions." The effort to "re-order society" did not distract and overwhelm them (*OR*, 69, 92).

This is the main theme. There is, however, an interesting and apparently contradictory counterpoint to this theme that comes in the form of a reminder. We must recall, Arendt notes, that abject misery did indeed exist in the form of slavery. In mid-eighteenth-century America there were approximately 400,000 African slaves as compared with 1,850,000 whites, and, she adds, "even in the absence of reliable statistical data we may be sure that the percentage of complete destitution and misery was considerably lower in the countries of the Old World" (*OR*, 71). Yet this destitution inspired neither compassion nor solidarity in the American colonists. Hence the realism that Arendt celebrates on the one hand she criticizes for being bought with indifference on the other. The price paid was tragically high.

The general outline of her argument is that the failure to be tried by this test of compassion, by "passion in its noblest form," meant that, their own experience and not infrequent expression of the passion for public life notwithstanding, the American revolutionaries remained confined within the liberal intellectual tradition they inherited (*OR*, 95). Following in this Enlightenment tradition, they understood government as the rule of reason over passion. Reason they equated with rationality, and passion they understood in terms of mere desire. The trouble was that this reduction of passion to desire belied the depth of their own experience of public freedom. Yet because they had no profound experience with compassion for the suffering poor, they were unable to forge new conceptual ground. And without doing so, their ability to understand and enshrine their passion in institutions failed: They could not succeed in giving constitutional recognition to those quintessential spaces for public freedom—the local town meetings.

We have arrived here at what at first glance appears to be a curious contradiction in Arendt's discussion of the relationship between compassion, public freedom, and the social question. On the one hand, the French revolutionaries were subjected to the test of compassion and failed miserably; their effort to found a stable political order was overwhelmed when compassion went public and pity for the impoverished took up residence in the public sphere. The Americans, by contrast, lacked all experience with compassion and consequently failed to save the "treasure" of their experiences—the spaces in which citizens could find public happiness and engage their "passion for distinction." The force of Arendt's argument is the following: Had the Americans been forced to wrestle with the test of compassion, they could have come to understand at a deep level the injustice of not being seen, "the crippling consequences of obscurity" (OR, 69). Had the founders felt not indifference but compassion toward their enslaved fellows, they might have developed a feeling of solidarity with them—a solidarity that would have made the political predicament, the "curse," of the enslaved painfully, even passionately clear. Simultaneously, this feeling of solidarity might have illuminated the novelty of the founders' own political experiences during the revolution; their indifference denied them the contrast through which alone they might have felt the full force of the nature and meaning of their public happiness.

But let me render this scenario with more power: Had the "men of the revolution," many of whom themselves owned slaves, experienced compassion, had they "suffered with" and felt the specific pathos of being a slave, the world they saw in all its terrible facticity would have been rendered in greater depth. That is, in looking at their own experiences through the eyes of the slave, in the conjoining of their perspectives and experiences, the founders would have seen the novelty and preciousness of their political passions. Likewise, the peculiar suffering of those confined to darkness and excluded from the play of arousal associated with public freedom would have been given definition and weight. In such conjoining of perspective alone, born of compassion, what was truly new about political possibility in the New World could be grasped: the passion for public freedom.[32]

Conceptually speaking, the founders' compassion might have moved them to break with their Enlightenment view of the role of government as the rule of reason over passion. As Arendt writes,

> Since passion had never tempted them in its noblest form as compassion, they found it easy to think of passion in terms of desire and to banish from it any connotation of its original meaning, which is...to suffer *and* to endure. This lack of experience gives their theories, even if they are sound, an air of lightheartedness, a certain weightlessness, which may well put into jeopardy their durability. For, humanly speaking, it is endurance which enables man to create durability and continuity. (OR, 95)

The revolutionaries' lack of experience with compassion kept them from forging the new conceptual ground that would match their new experience of public freedom and help provide an institutional home for it. Both conceptual and institutional achievements would have brought their experiences more fully into being, given them standing, reality, depth, and hence endurance. And this would have been an invaluable contribution to democratic thinking, for although the American revolutionaries were never subject to the test of compassion, the social question did, Arendt argues, influence them in a way that has profoundly conspired against democratic freedoms and practices. This came not in the form of necessity but in the form of the "fatal passion for sudden riches" (*OR*, 139).

Never was there, nor has there yet been in America, Arendt argues, a clear-cut resolution in favor of freedom or prosperity (*OR*, 137). Had the founders succeeded in endowing this political way of life and its passion for distinction with reality, they would have offered a powerful alternative to the passion for riches that has flooded the American polity in successive waves as the world's poor have crossed its borders. The tragedy of the American Revolution, as Arendt reads it, was that the founders came close to saving the republic from elevating life to the highest good and from embracing the passion for "conspicuous consumption," which has largely come to replace the passion to excel in public life (*OR*, 70). Very nearly did the American revolutionaries overcome the specifically "modern sensibility" among whose distinguishing characteristics is, once again, that it is "not touched by obscurity."

In these reflections on the relationship between compassion, the social question, and freedom we find, on the one hand, an absolute rejection of the uncompromising "inner processes of the soul" when it comes to the task of giving form and shape to political life. On the other we find an argument that it was precisely the absence of such inner stirrings that had serious negative consequences for political foundation. The problem with which Arendt wrestles is that we need compassion in order to have solidarity with the "oppressed and exploited," and yet this compassion is politically pernicious if it becomes the foundation of politics—and takes the form of pity. Arendt says that compassion is politically irrelevant because it destroys the distance between persons. In the intensity of identification with another's suffering, the compassionate person loses the capacity for argumentative speech, for talk about shared interests, for precisely those activities that arouse our urge to appear and that humanize the world. The compassionate cannot stand the suffering of others, and hence if they are moved to act, to go public, they eschew persuasion and negotiation in favor of violence. From this Arendt concludes that the heart needs to be hidden in darkness. Yet this darkness must not be a void. The human heart must beat—which is another way of saying it must be torn and ravaged by the world. The accommodation Arendt makes is that the compassionate heart must move us to formulate principles on which to act. The heart should "arouse" our sensibilities, wildly agitate our minds, but not directly move us to action.[33]

The argument here, then, is for privileging a public sensibility that is attentive to the suffering inflicted by the insult of oblivion. To become acquainted with this insult, as I have argued, the heart must beat, we must in some way manage to feel, be responsive to those who suffer the poverty of being left out of public affairs. Their being-in-the-world must be illuminated; they must be seen, noticed, and taken account of. To address this need, our thought should perhaps run in two directions. First, in our personal and private lives we can actively take account of others by exercising compassion. We can tend to the sufferings of those near. This gives us, among other gifts, an intimate knowledge of the deprivations others less fortunate than ourselves may suffer. Our heart can burn in the face of concrete injuries. We can minister to these injuries, but, and this is my second point, our manner of taking public-political account should be different. Although deeply informed by our concrete and personal experiences, our actions are best propelled by the insult of oblivion that others (including ourselves) may suffer.

What does this mean? Moved on the inside by social inequalities and deprivations, we should publicly frame our concerns in terms, as Arendt puts it, of "the relationship of men to their world," in terms of "the relativity of the world" (*MDT*, 29). Are others' positions and opinions sufficiently a part of public discourse? Do they contribute to the all-important "play of arousal" that gives rise to a shared world? Do we sufficiently yearn for forms of relations in which we can mutually encounter one another and better comprehend our world through that provocation? We continue to confuse things in not privileging radical democratic practices: the constitution of and access to those spaces of appearance that are their essence. We continue to confuse things if we attend to the many forms of suffering that social injustice takes *at the expense of* attending to the deprivations that accompany the insult of oblivion. In obscurity, our own as others' urge to appear is unaroused. The world inured against us, we are ripe for any manner of human depravation. We should privilege a specifically political, not social way of thinking.

This seems difficult, even cold-hearted and dangerous in a world such as ours, which, if not at the neighborly level, then on the larger scale, seems so lacking in concern for others, so ready to fortress. Yet it is tragic pleasure in our recalcitrant and plural world that this public sensibility for which I write induces. And this is a pleasure that draws us into, not away from the presence of others.

This reconfiguration of the relationship between social injustice and the passion for freedom captures a public-political language and uses that language to grasp the world, to name public passions and pleasures that were so relatively foreign to the modern age, and are even more foreign to our experience in late modernity. In so doing, it offers a way of life, perspectives and concerns that might be a bulwark against the spiritual consequences of modern world alienation—against civilization organized around the principle that life is the highest good. The point is, of course, not that life concerns, including those of social justice, are unimportant, but that we look at them differently when we are informed by public passions and concerns as Arendt articulates them, that we might, in our public-political life, succeed in better mediating the uneasy tensions between freedom and necessity, public concerns and private ones, mere life and a life worth living.[34] And finally, this may indeed enable us to more adequately address our social problems. What hangs in the balance is our capacity to be attentive to reality, to have a sense of what we are doing, and to resist the degradation of the human person.

4 Beauty, Durability, and the Practice of Judging

Our modern world, as Arendt describes it, suffers ethically and politically from the erosion of public spaces within which human beginnings can be initiated and human particularity countenanced. So thoroughgoing is our world alienation that we experience ourselves as caught in processes beyond human understanding, a condition that suppresses our impulse to freedom. Thus we have neither experiences nor social and political institutions that meaningfully "relate and separate" us, so that the otherwise inexorability of our organic appearance and disappearance can be humanized.

Yet, if anything, Hannah Arendt is a theorist of possibility. And the aesthetic dimensions of her political theorizing are the wings of political possibility as she invites us to envision it. Still, certainly the aesthetic sensibility of tragic pleasure in mutual provocation among plural beings in an appearing world, and among plural voices in the invisible world of thinking—certainly this pleasure alone cannot renew our faith in possibility. A sensibility alive to plurality and difference in general, one in which provocation and responsiveness in general are the achievements, is not cause to celebrate the possible renewal of a common world and a humanized sense of reality. By itself, such a sensibility provides little by which human existence might be anchored and ethically oriented. Pleasure in plurality in and of itself is as meaningless as is "life for life's sake." How, we might put the question, does Arendt reconcile the plural with the common?

In this chapter I turn to the other aspect of aesthetic experience relevant to the problem of ethically orienting ourselves in an appearing world—namely, to the relationship between beauty, durability, and our public or shared world. In Arendt's reflections on this relationship we encounter a thought of the common world grounded not in universality but in durability. Beautiful things provide us with meanings that can be shared not because they are the same to all of us—timeless and true in that universalist way—but because they are durable and lasting. As I shall argue, they endure and can be shared because of their capacity to illuminate the always historically specific *and* universal shape of our human dilemmas. As such, this aesthetic thought of the common may help us move beyond the sterile opposition between otherness and commonness that is so often a theme in debates between modern and postmodern reflections on politics.

In what follows I vigorously pursue the relationships in Arendt's work between beauty, our public or shared world, and durability. I do so in the belief that these elements are essential to renewing our ethical capacities insofar as this concerns a reconfirmation of the fragile beauty of human particularity and an intensification of our awareness of reality. I begin with an examination of her reflections on the relationship between beauty and durability. I then briefly discuss the practice of authority in the West through which human affairs were given a powerful degree of durability, arguing that what anchored this historical form of authority was the beauty of acts in a far distant past, one that became sacralized, deified. I argue that a different beauty must, for historical reasons, be deified in our times, and I examine Arendt's account of efforts to authorize new political bodies during the course of modern revolutions. Finally, I turn to judging as a practice in which we encounter our shared vulnerability, our profound need for one another if, through initiative, we are to constitute a common and relatively durable world. It is this vulnerability we must strive to find beautiful, moving. Judging demands a high degree of responsiveness to human particularity, and in so doing it fosters the ethical stance that Arendt's ontology demands. It is the central practice in which we take in and remain provoked by the real.

Durability: The Specific Power of Beauty

"Beauty is the very manifestation of imperishability" (*BPF*, 218). With this claim, we begin. What does Arendt mean by it, and why does she consider it so pivotal to our possibilities for political and ethical renewal?

The specific power of what we find beautiful is related to the quality of transcendence. Aesthetic pleasure or displeasure in a thing arises not from the thing's usefulness nor from its consumptive value. Rather, to define it first negatively, it arises out of our capacity to experience the way a thing transcends both these necessary dimensions of human life—the one in which things are consumed and immediately disappear, the other in which they are used and more slowly wear out. This quality of transcendence, superseding the temporal destruction of both tangible and intangible things, is inherent in all appearances. Arendt writes, "Everything that is, must appear, and nothing can appear without a shape of its own" (HC, 173). Everything in its very appearingness invites our aesthetic pleasure or displeasure, awaits, as it were, transcendence. Hence aesthetic involvement with appearances transports us from the perishable domains of consumption and use. As such, it at least seems to open a way toward durability. If, however, it takes us *from* these kinds of involvements, *where*, more precisely, does it take us, and why is beauty or aesthetic pleasure in appearances the very manifestation of imperishability?

Arendt's answers to these questions depend on the relationship beauty bears to illumination. Her most concentrated reflections on transcendence, durability, and aesthetic pleasure in what is beautiful emerge in discussions of art objects and culture on the one hand and of speech and action on the other.[1] Largely unconcerned with aesthetic pleasure in nature, she is preoccupied with the illumination that shines forth as we behold the products of human *poiesis* and the events of human *praxis*.[2] With Plato, Arendt calls the beautiful that which shines forth most and illuminates the darkness of human affairs (BPF, 112-13). Aesthetic experience transports us to the realm of illuminating understanding. So, as we concern ourselves with how art objects, speech, and action "look," with their appearingness, Arendt finds more than an idle gratification in appearances, although this is indeed one mode of intercourse with them. When we concern ourselves aesthetically, the power of our pleasure derives from the meaning the appearance emanates, and this requires that we perceptually transcend the relentless finitude which otherwise pervades human life. The imperishability or relative durability of beauty has to do with its capacity to carry us out from the midst of such modes of involvement with appearances and into the realm of illumination and meaning.[3]

If we look briefly at Arendt's discussion of the genesis of the work of art, this transporting capacity of beauty may become clearer. The immediate source of the work of art, Arendt argues, is thought. In creating beautiful appearances, thought transforms the "mute and inarticulate despondency" of feeling until it is "fit to enter the world and to be transformed into things, to be reified" (HC, 168). In artistic creation, as we engage with how things should appear in the world, a "passionate intensity" is released into the world from within the self (HC, 168). As the source of this creation of beauty, thought is thus deeply entwined with our "soul-apparatus"—with our feelings, wants, passions, and convictions as they arise in response to and have bearing on the world. Although Arendt's discussion in this context is restricted to the origin of the creative arts (*poiesis*), it applies equally to the performing arts and thus to the "arts" of speech and action, even though the nature of the artistic appearance differs dramatically—the one possessing durability as a consequence of the process of reification, and the other vanishing as soon as the performance ends. These differences are of course central to Arendt's accomplishment for our contemporary theorization of politics—namely, the recovery of an understanding of freedom as action (*praxis*) in strict distinction from freedom as making (*poiesis*).[4] They are, however, not important to my immediate point, which is that because thought is the direct source of art, our pleasure in the aesthetic experience of things—be they objects, words, or deeds—arises from the illumination they impart, our displeasure from the lack thereof.

As we read the following lines from Pablo Neruda's epic *Canto General*, this relationship between our pleasure and illumination may become clear:

> The jaguar touches the leaves
> with its phosphorescent absence,
> the puma bolts through the foliage
> like a raging fire,
> while in him burn
> the jungle's alcoholic eyes.

Here jungle and beasts radically transcend human utility and consuming need. These lines anoint the wild mystery of the Americas in a primeval time, honoring, sacralizing. And although the poet has a magnificent command of metaphor, this alone cannot account for the depth of pleasure we feel in the beauty of these lines. Our pleasure comes rather from what is in this case a radical suspension of human need and utility. The beauty Neruda's words impart cannot be disentangled from this suspension. It comes from an entirely different comportment with the jungle. And through it, human feeling, observation, the human heartbeat, and the jungle's overwhelming rich and nonhuman vitality burst into illuminating connection.

But what of a poem whose subject matter is more directly the human world? Let us consider Maria Iannacome Coles's "Time and Birch Bark":

> The tannery took the bark of hemlocks
> and left the trunks,
> the earth on which they once had stood
> the only thing more bare.

The chair factory took miles of oak and pine
and for miles the sky fell deep into the earth.

The windows on guest houses
and summer palaces have become opaque,
railings hang from balconies
like torn lace on fringes of old gowns.
Merciless use
is followed by merciless death.

Sagging roofs, leaning walls,
wide doors of barns stay shut,
surrounded by broken chairs and broken
tools laid down on the earth
as if the hope of the hands that used them
were left in them.

Here the poet entwines her readers in the sadness of merciless human use—
reckless, destructive, inexorable, only, in the last two lines, to offer some
small, still painful respite. The poem's beauty arises from the illumination
of the ineliminable implication of human hope in destruction, an illumination that, as the title suggests, comes only, or at least most readily to those
who follow in time. Here, our pleasure arises not so much amid a radical
suspension of human need and utility, but these are infused and transfigured with the plentitude of hope, and we are moved as we feel the sweet-
ness and the terror of human aspiration.[5]

So beauty is the very manifestation of imperishability because, as the result of a mode of involvement with appearances that transcends our sheer
need to use or to consume them, beauty brings about the pleasure of meaningful illumination. And this, which certainly still begs the question of why
such pleasure in illumination should be equated with imperishability, is
about as far as we can go. The question it seems is not really answerable. The
relationship simply seems quite richly to *be*. The most we can do is to lay
claim to a drive (Arendt calls it a quest) we all exhibit in ordinary life as we
endlessly narrate our experiences—as if to pluck from the relentless flux of
our existence a moment of eternity. And this is a quest, as Arendt calls it, for
meaning (*LMT,* 78).

If, in the foregoing senses, beauty is the very manifestation of imperishability, we might expect Arendt to believe, along with Plato, that the quality
in things that shines forth and makes them beautiful is their approximation
to a perfect mental image, to the *eidos* or idea that is thought to reside in a

realm of perfection and being-forever. We might expect Arendt to argue that the quality of beauty is eternal, that it is not tied to the fickle contingency of the public world and the vicissitudes of "taste." And indeed, Arendt argues that beauty is coercive, that, as a quality of relation between beholder and what appears, beauty is "beyond dispute" (*BPF*, 224). Moreover, for Arendt as for Plato, the standard for our judgment is the mental image seen by our inner eyes. However, this image by which we measure "the adequacy or inadequacy of what [a thing] should *look* like," emerges, in Arendt's view, from "the objective standards of the world," not from a vision of eternity beyond it (*HC*, 173). By "objective standards of the world" Arendt refers to a certain impartiality we can have with respect to the world we share in common, an impartiality that transcends subjective perception but simultaneously makes no claim to "correspond" transparently to its object. My point is that the mental image the inner eyes see is bound to a particular public, cultural world and as such is subject to change. The very standards, then, by which the beautiful is judged are, *contra* Plato, contingent and contextual.

That beauty is beyond dispute and yet is bound to the particular contingencies of cultures—how are we to consider these apparently incompatible arguments together as Arendt seems to do? And if they are both in some way true, don't they deflate the very relationship between beauty and durability that I am arguing Arendt attempts to establish? Arendt is trying both to account for a certain universality in our experience of beauty—a universality that enables us to save from time's ravages certain cultural works across cultures—and to argue that judgments of beauty must be regarded as time-bound discriminations of a particular people. Even more to the point, Arendt argues that to make our presence explicitly, to establish our space in time, we must avoid an indiscriminate love of beauty that she calls aestheticism and barbaric and develop, rather, an *active* love of beauty, a contextually specific way of discriminating. Beauty, she says, must be humanized (*BPF*, 215, 219, 224).

If we look to Kafka's parable "He," which Arendt discusses at two different points in her life's work, we can elaborate the complex and important relationship between these two contradictory aspects of our experience of beauty.[6] In so doing, my aim is to more precisely illuminate the specific and peculiar durability that aesthetic experience promises, as well as to begin to point to its ethical and political relevance.

The parable, which is about the "inner time sensation of the thinking ego" (*LMT*, 202), is relevant to this task if we bear in mind Arendt's claim that thought is the immediate source of all art, that the beauty shining forth in art is indeed thought reified or displayed. Thus, if we are seeking to comprehend the relationship between beauty and durability, the relationship of thought to time that is the subject of Kafka's parable needs elaboration. Kafka writes,

He has two antagonists: the first presses him from behind, from the origin. The second blocks the road ahead. He gives battle to both. To be sure, the first supports him in his fight with the second, for he wants to push him forward, and in the same way the second supports him in his fight with the first, since he drives him back. But it is only theoretically so. For it is not only the two antagonists who are there, but he himself as well, and who really knows his intentions? His dream, though, is that some time in an unguarded moment—and this would require a night darker than any night has ever been yet—he will jump out of the fighting line and be promoted, on account of his experience in fighting, to the position of umpire over his antagonists in their fight with each other. (Quoted in *BPF*, 7)

If we accept Kafka's parable as a rendering of the thinking activity, the following is suggested. Insofar as we are thinkers questing after meaning, our very birth causes a rupture in the otherwise peaceful and indifferent flow of eternity. In this rupture, temporality itself emerges in full battle regalia. And it is aimed at "him": The past fights to move him beyond its own failures and toward a "better" future, and the future, in fear of the unknown, tries to throw him back into the safety of the has-been. If he is to make his own presence, to widen the rupture into a gap, he must resist the relentless pressure of these antagonists, resist being violently compelled and buffeted by their hopes and fears. This battleground in which the thinker struggles in both directions to create "his" own *nunc stans*, his own track of non-time in time, as Arendt expresses it, is a metaphor for our home on earth (BPF, 13).

In Kafka's parable, however, this present appears in the form of a dream of jumping out of the fighting line into a region above where, having attained the distance necessary for reflection, he can be umpire over past and future. Here, Arendt critically observes, Kafka repeats the dream of Western metaphysics in which the region of thought is a "timeless, spaceless, suprasensuous realm" (*BPF*, 11). Arendt rejects this dream and amends the parable to imagine a space for reflection in and on the world, suggesting that, with the *event* of the thinker, the rectilinear quality of time is broken and the direction of the two opposing forces is deflected, causing them to meet not head on but at an angle. From the force of their angled encounters, the gap would become a "parallelogram of forces" from which a third force would issue. Situated equidistant from past and future, this is the space of thought. Thus when we accept the battleground as our home, it itself offers a space to which we can retire in order to take stock of and survey the field of forces, or, as Arendt puts it, to "properly see and survey what [is] most [our] own" (*BPF*, 12).

Because it is the event of the thinker who "himself" breaks up eternity into its battling elements, thinking cannot be inherited, simply passed down. Each human being must beat his or her specific track of "non-time-space" (*BPF*, 13). Our need to do so is as universal as our need to tell the stories of our lives. However, many, if not most, lose the battle. More often than not, the thinker will be unable to find the space that leads out of the fighting line. More likely, she will "die of exhaustion." Indeed, as Kafka's battlefield metaphor might suggest, our home is strewn with many wasted bodies. It is in those who survive, who are able to find the diagonal line *and* whose thoughts become reified in potentially durable form, that Arendt is interested. Their work endures through the centuries, achieves such relative permanence, she suggests, precisely because they are able to find that diagonal line and establish a present for *themselves*, that "timeless time in which men are able to create timeless works with which to transcend their own finiteness" (*LMT*, 211).

Critical to the durability or, as Arendt puts it, the timelessness of their achievement is that, paradoxically, they accept the past and the future as aimed at them, as *their* past and *their* future, as the forces against which they must throw their weight and out of which they must fashion a life. The key to Arendt's effort to answer why some works, some people's present *endures* lies precisely in their courage and their excellence in fashioning a response to the dilemmas to which they themselves, as beginnings, give birth. Indeed, it is the very acceptance of the specificity, the particularity of our own birth in time that grants to what we create in that space the possibility of being beautiful, of moving us. As we either reify thought in works of art or philosophy or act out of this self-same acceptance, what we are doing is gathering from our own *nunc stans* the saved past and our anticipated future into a meaningful whole that illuminates the now, the uniqueness of the problems and challenges of the present. And this illumination arrests as it moves the spectator.

Thus the imperishability of such creations arises not from the ahistorical or transhistorical, not from a realm of perfection and being-forever, but from a deeply contextual, deeply specific worldly engagement. Thought in its quest for meaning must be tied to incident if it is to illuminate. Precisely in this specificity lies the potential immortality of the works of art to which thought gives rise.

Yet this is not to say the whole of it, for insofar as the creator of works or the doer of deeds is able to *retain* the specificity of her *own* predicaments, she not only movingly illuminates the "enormous ever-changing time-space which is most [her] own" (*BPF*, 12); she gives us something more. The creator or the doer gives us the thrill of experiencing the beat of life as he inserts himself into the forces of past and future and treads a "track of non-time," a present. This beat moves us, draws us to itself again and again, for in its generality it "indicates" to us what we ourselves must also do; it illuminates the nature of the battle we must engage in. The pathos of this beat moves us: the nobility of the warrior's exertion, the heroism required for humans to claim a present and assert our specific dignity. These we find beautiful, want to be near, and they shine forth in great works and deeds, allowing them to transcend time's indifference.

It is this latter element of beauty that is coercive. Although we might fall under its spell, there need be no coercion, strictly speaking, in the *content* of what shines forth. This is time- and space-bound. Not the content, but the existential achievement and the illumination it offers of transhistorical dilemmas of human life move us in ways that Arendt refers to as coercive. Arendt's own engagement with Plato's political philosophy exemplifies these twin and apparently contradictory points about durability and beauty. I characterize that relationship briefly to better elucidate the specific power of beauty as I think Arendt sees it. Attending to the disagreements Arendt has with Plato's political philosophy also moves us on our way to clarifying the challenges she faces in attempting to theorize the conditions for a shared world whose law is plurality.

The sheer quantity of references to Plato in Arendt's work suggests she has "chosen his company among men," that she remains gripped and moved and spoken to by him (*BPF*, 226). And yet, in Arendt's view, Plato was the first to separate two modes of acting that had until then been interrelated in Greek thinking. In his effort to avoid "the moral irresponsibility inherent in a plurality of agents" (*HC*, 220)—the fact that the one who begins cannot entirely control the consequences and effects of that beginning—Plato separated the capacity to begin (*archein*) from the capacity to carry something through (*prattein*). Identifying the art of politics with the art of ruling, the ruler became the one who knows how to begin and who remains master of his beginning by ruling over those who, because they do not know, become mere executors of his edicts (*HC*, 222; *BPF*, 165). The model for action, thus, is that of artistic fabrication in which isolation from others, mastership over one's materials, violence, and a kind of stable predictability are central experiences that ensure against the moral frailty of action. And the authority of the rulers' knowledge is established by a claim of access to true knowledge imparted to them through the rarefied experience of philosophical contemplation. It is this substitution of making for action, buttressed by Platonic epistemology and undertaken to avoid the uncertainty and unpredictability which initiating action in a world of plural others inherently entails, that, Arendt argues, became authoritative for the entire tradition of political thought. As such, Plato's political philosophy is not only an argument against democracy. It is an argument against Arendt's understanding of the essentials of politics itself, insofar as it seeks to destroy the public realm in which plurality is actualized among humans, a realm that, Arendt argues, is relative, contingent, and unpredictable by definition. Hence Plato's thought is pitted against the ethical center of Arendt's entire intellectual effort, and he would seem to be her most serious opponent, her greatest nemesis. And yet what we find is not mortal enmity but dialogue and intellectual friendship. Why, despite an obvious repugnance, does she find, as she says she does, his work *beautiful* (*HC*, 223-30)?

We find the answer amid Arendt's effort to explain the durability of this part of Plato's work. She suggests that it is Plato's unique combination of "depth and beauty" (*HC*, 225) and the "*authentic perplexities*" to which he attempts to summon a response that give his work its ability to endure. That is to say, although Arendt emphatically rejects Plato's specific solution to the "frailty of human affairs," the way he responds to it greatly illuminates this perplexity endemic to the human condition. Her repugnance to his substitution of making for acting notwithstanding, Plato's work is beautiful because it shines light on our so human condition. As such, our return to his work again and again will be rewarded, and it is this reward of illumination that makes his work of such enduring relevance. More specifically, driven by the pain of the death of Socrates (who had been condemned by the *demos* of Athens), Plato, his thought deeply bound to incident, turns the force of his conceptualization and philosophical clarification on political action and produces works of great illumination (*HC*, 225). Arendt is moved, then, by what she, with Machiavelli, calls the *virtù* displayed by Plato. *Virtù* is "the response, summoned up by man, to the world, or rather to the constellation of *fortuna* in which the world opens up, presents and offers itself to him" (*BPF*, 153). This kind of admiration of another's virtù is of a formal sort—it is a response to the courage and heroism that beats forth in the works of those who successfully establish their own present. Such works "indicate" to us the general dilemmas we face.

Historically, however, the effect of Plato's conceptual moves was to eclipse from political memory and experience the earlier Greek understanding of action. And it is precisely this understanding that Arendt believes we so greatly need. She affirms the beauty and therefore enduring quality of Plato's work insofar as it illuminates through the ages real perplexities and dangers inherent in human action precisely by binding itself to its own present. But neither Plato's specific situation nor his response to it can adequately illuminate our own historically particular dilemmas with respect to this "authentic perplexity." These include the waning power of metaphysical thinking throughout the modern age, an end to the plausibility of metaphysical standards in political life that became evident with the experiences of totalitarianism, the near total failure of modern revolutions to establish new political foundations, the spread of first mass, then totalitarian politics in the nineteenth and twentieth centuries, and the sources of world alienation discussed in the previous chapter. All of these experiences suggest a radical loss of political belonging, of meaning, and of a sense of reality. In such a world, Plato's political philosophy, in which philosophers who alone possess knowledge of the Good that is thought to stand outside the realm of human affairs, and who mold their human material on the basis of this knowledge, is both irrelevant and politically repugnant. Appeals by political actors to a philosophically imagined world outside the realm of political experience have become unconvincing and, as such, more dangerous. Ethical and political life can no longer rely on the authority of transcendental standards.

So while Plato's response to the "moral irresponsibility" that Arendt agrees inheres in a "plurality of agents" must be rejected as decidedly unfit for our historical situation, the beauty of his work remains a source of illumination as we face the daunting challenge of fashioning a different response. We will need both to reject Plato's solution *and* to be compelled by the (beautiful) illumination we receive through encounter with his thought. We will need to do both if we are to summon our own response, create our own *nunc stans*. In this sense beauty is both contingent and coercive, and in the paradox of these qualities lies the specific power of the beautiful: its capacity to endure.

But now, turning to the substance of what Arendt rejects, are we not left with bearingless nihilism? Arendt insists not, and she formulates her hope thusly: "[All thinking egos are] limited, enclosed, as it were, by the forces of past and future, and thus protected against the void; [they] remain bound to and [are] rooted in the present" (*LMT,* 209). Protected against the void, we have perhaps, she writes with a decidedly phenomenological accent, "enough origin in [ourselves] to understand without preconceived categories."[7] That is to say, we may be in a position to share a world whose law is plurality, and to do it well. This is the possibility our present invites us to embrace. And it is, to follow her thought, a response to this challenge that alone should move us, arrest our attention, and, in the illuminating beauty our response may impart, achieve for our shared existence a certain degree of durability.

Yet how and how much durability are perhaps the questions. As we stand in the gap between past and future, we seem to find, as Arendt beautifully puts it, "no willed continuity in time" (*BPF*, 5). We feel exceedingly burdened by existential insecurity, an insecurity fought off for nearly two thousand years by the way authority was configured in the West. This form of authority rested, as Arendt magnificently if overdramatically puts it, "on a foundation in the past as its unshaken cornerstone [and] gave the world the permanence and durability which human beings need precisely because they are mortals—the most unstable and futile beings we know of" (*BPF*, 95).

By contrast, we appear condemned to eternal shiftlessness. The loss of authority in our time, Arendt writes, "is tantamount to the loss of the groundwork of the world, which indeed since then has begun to shift, to change and transform itself with ever-increasing rapidity from one shape to another, as though we were living and struggling with a Protean universe where everything at any moment can become almost anything else" (*BPF*, 95). Yet while we have lost the form of life that for millennia gave permanence and stability to human affairs, this loss need not, Arendt argues, "entail the loss of our capacity to build, preserve and care for a world that can survive us and be fit for humans" (*BPF*, 95). While the kind of seemingly unshakable authority of the West is no longer possible, we are not doomed to a "Protean universe" of rapidly changing shapes. Such a thing as a common world, renewable, with a specific shape and a certain durability is indeed not an impossibility.

I want to look briefly at Arendt's account of this historical practice through which futility was kept at bay in order to help further articulate the precise nature of our own predicament as it concerns the loss of worldly permanence and stability. The contrast is important because although authority has historically made life existentially secure in many respects and had, therefore, great political advantages, the tradition to which it gave birth "paved over" the gap between past and future. That is, it made it unnecessary for all but professional thinkers to think. And this entailed, in Arendt's view, a definite loss. We must learn to live in the gap where our thought can be tied to the incidents of our lives and where, therefore, our capacity for illuminating under-standing may grow. And by "our" I believe Arendt meant all of us. For reasons I will argue, I think Arendt believed this to be *our* challenge, *our* need, *and* our hope. And in this I read in the deep center of her work a radically democratic Enlightenment element. The result of this living in the gap might be an in-tensified awareness of reality and, therewith, a renewal of our ethical re-sources and practices. And this of course depends on our achieving concep-tually, and in practice, an alternative to the singular example of authority in the West. We must find other ways to create "willed continuity in time," to create alternative foundations for our public-political world. With this sense of possibility I approach Arendt's reflections on authority in order to prepare to unfold the practices and conceptualizations toward which I believe her thinking on the matter points.

Authority: "An Obedience in Which We Retain Our Freedom"

Conceptually, Arendt distinguishes authority from both power and vio-lence. While authority demands obedience, the mode by which it does so has nothing to do with coercion of any kind. Yet it is also distinct from persua-sion by argumentation and the equality that it implies. In contrast to per-suasion, authority implies hierarchy, although, paradoxically, it is a hierarchy that allows those who obey to retain their freedom, which is to say that the capacity to start something new is not eclipsed in this obedience (*BPF,* 106).

Authority, or *auctoritas,* has its origins in Roman political experience. It comes from the verb *augere,* meaning "to augment" or "to add to." Politi-cally it meant that those who had authority had it by virtue of the fact that they augmented or breathed fresh life into the original accomplishment of those who founded the city of Rome. Above all other conceivable achieve-ments of Rome was the unrepeatable enormity of the original acts that lay the foundations for the city's body politic. These deeds gave authority to the living as long as these citizens safeguarded and renewed the spirit of that original foundation. The shining beauty of this beginning was passed down through tradition, and it was sacred or religious in the sense that it was with the city's founding that the gods were given a home. It was the sacred and stabilizing cornerstone of the body politic.

This political experience of a glorious foundation in a far distant past, thus, was in Arendt's view the origin of the Roman practice of authority. Se-cured by both religious ties and a tradition that "willed it" to the future, this Roman "trinity," designed to immortalize the beauty of the founder's achievement, gave Roman political life its durability.

This "miracle of permanence" was repeated in the creation of the Roman Catholic Church. The Roman awe at a miraculous mundane beginning—this time the birth of Christ—became the foundational event for the authority of the Church, and Roman political experience was given new garb. The apostles became the authoritative voices that told of the event, and their testimony was passed through the ages by way of tradition, tying those who came after back to the fearsome beauty of the foundational event. And yet the authority of *this* event had a compelling quality. Moved by the Greek philosophical experience of beauty in that extraworldly, unalloyed dream state, as Plato referred to it, the Church followed Plato in "converting" these experiences into measures in the service of ruling. Thus in the Christian event a transcendent God descends to earth not to be given a home by mortals or to make the earth a home for them but, through a resplendent birth, to redeem their otherwise depraved and meaningless sojourn. The voice with which Christian popes, bishops, prelates, priests, and so on spoke had, like the philosopher-kings Plato envisioned, the authority of transcendent measurements and rules.

In this amalgamation of Roman and Greek experiences in the Roman Church, authority was anchored in the beauty of sacrificial acts of a transcendent God. The impact of this form of authority, Arendt argued, was far deeper than any previous effort at establishing authority. She writes, "General and transcendent standards under which the particular and immanent could be subsumed were now required for any political order, moral rules for all inter-human behavior, and rational measurements for the guidance of all individual judgment" (*BPF*, 127–28).[8]

In their efforts to authorize new political orders, modern founders also appealed to otherworldly religious sanctions. So, for example, Robespierre appealed to a cult of "the Supreme Being," John Adams to the "great legislator of the Universe," and Thomas Jefferson, in the Declaration of Independence, to "the laws of nature and nature's God" (*OR*, 185). Such appeals, Arendt suggests, were wholly inadequate under modern conditions in which secularization had already separated religious and political life. To the extent that they succeeded in legitimizing their foundational acts, the authentic location of the authority they commanded is to be found elsewhere. Focusing exclusively on the American experience, Arendt suggests that it is the beauty of the act of foundation itself that invested the resulting republic with a new kind of authority.[9] Arendt tells this bold story through a series of conjectures always prefaced with the phrase "one is tempted to conclude." In this form she formulates what I take to be her very unique contribution to the possible source of authority in our times, telling a tale that brings before us the beauty of the founder's beginning.[10]

The elemental political problem to which authority is a response is what Arendt called "the abyss of freedom": the mark of arbitrariness that the appearance of new things always bears because they do not fit causally into the temporal stream. They appear bizarre and without reason, and abyssal. They have, indeed, a frightening and sometimes miraculous quality. More specifically, the revolutionaries were faced with the problem of creating laws and institutions that would constitute a solid supporting structure for a new form of political life. How could the constitution-making of these mere mortal founders command the kind of reverence and respect needed to sustain some continuity in time against the initiatives of generations of citizens to come? How could durability be had?

Arendt begins her story by calling on a tradition of thinking about law that had been buried by the amalgamation of the Roman experience of foundation with Greek political philosophy in the Christian Church. Revitalized by Montesquieu and again in Arendt's own works, law establishes an "intimate connection" (the original meaning of the Latin *lex*) or *rapport* (Montesquieu) between two discrete entities that contingent circumstances bring together (*OR*, 187–88). If we conceive laws as *establishing relations* rather than as *commanding obedience*, it becomes far more plausible to understand the wellspring of laws as being collective, concerted human action. And from there Arendt seeks the source of authority for that concerted human action within the domain of human affairs itself—indeed, within the terrain of action. The Roman example is particularly fascinating to Arendt in this regard, for, as I have suggested, it was the acts of the founders of Rome, themselves mortals, that gave a home on earth to the *gods*. Those who came after venerated the *maiores,* the founders, for their (godlike) ability to forge relations and establish specific connections between formerly unrelated peoples, and hence to create something new in the way of human association. Here we might say, existentially speaking, that what received veneration, what inspired reverence was the superhuman ability of mortals to take into their own hands the haphazard and bewildering nature of their appearance in a strange and often estranging world by creating new possibilities for human relatedness. The magnificence of this initial act through which the city of Rome was brought into being became and remained the source of authority not only for the Roman Republic but also for the "augmentations" to the city through the expansions of the empire.

In an analogous manner, Arendt approaches Americans' curious reverence for their Constitution. Arendt suggests that it is both the substantive and verbal meaning of the term *constitution* that so connected the document with the spirit of the American people. The Constitution immediately became and has remained authoritative because it is a living embodiment of the achievement of the founding acts themselves. Despite the founders' own sense that they were "merely revolving back to an earlier period" (*OR*, 198), the "blind worship" of the Constitution, which seems to have begun almost immediately after its creation, points to the fact that what really held the American public in thrall was the experience—politically—of a new beginning brought about by acts, not of gods or demigods but of mere mortals. Americans had, as Arendt put it, "the extraordinary capacity to look upon yesterday with the eyes of centuries to come" (*OR*, 198). And this is suggestive of a kind of authority entirely different from that resting on appeals to a transcendent source, but also from that resting on a single set of grand acts whose magnitude can never again be approximated.

Inasmuch as the American revolutionaries consciously and successfully imitated the Roman example, their practice reflected the recognition that in the arbitrariness that accompanies all new beginnings itself lies the only absolute that might legitimate them. It is this absolute that the Romans, and the Americans after them, divinized, found godlike, if you will, for all new beginnings, by definition, possess an arresting transcendence. Arendt writes, "For a moment, the moment of beginning, it is as though the beginner had abolished the sequence of temporality itself" (*OR*, 206). To experience a new beginning is, for a "moment," to defy the relentless movement of temporality's natural inexorability. It was this arresting transcendence that appeared in the founding acts of the Roman *maiores*, giving their efforts authority and relative durability. Arendt writes, "Authority in this context is nothing more or less than a kind of necessary 'augmentation' by virtue of which all innovations and changes remain tied back to the foundation which, at the same time, they augment and increase" (*OR*, 202). In the amendment process in the U.S. Constitution we see the same kind of necessary augmentation of the founding acts of the American polity.

This conservative tenor of Roman authority goes only so far, however, in capturing the nature of the authority invested in the U.S. Constitution. What distinguishes the Romans is that they so divinized the founding of their city that no future acts could ever attain the greatness of those initial efforts. Moreover, they also enshrouded these "absolute" beginnings in legends that located the Roman political beginning itself in an earlier history: Rome was not a new beginning but the restoration of ancient Troy. Thus the impact of the arbitrariness, the abyssal quality inherent in all beginnings, was mitigated. Roman veneration for the ancestors and their heroic foundational deeds was a veneration advantaged and augmented by a fugitive beginning. Thus Roman authority rested on every new act being understood as but a reaffirmation of and addition to the original and never repeatable heroism of the founders—whose own acts lay enshrouded in an elusive past. Because the present could only augment, never equal or surpass the founding glory, the public-political world constituted by Roman authority was fundamentally conservative. And this, too, we ought to add, though Arendt does not, provided not only tremendous stability but also an ingenious justification for imperial expansionism. That is, if greatness was a one-time deal, the best we can do is to *expand* on it, "to found Rome anew" (*OR*, 212). In this sense, the Romans did not so much divinize birth as they did rebirth.

By contrast, the nature of the authority that Arendt suggested emerges from the American experience with political foundation does not rely on tying the present back through a venerating remembrance to legendary founding acts in an ancient, unreachable past. Nor does it depend on the veneration that grows as things persist and endure.[11] The American experience was not about founding Rome anew. It was about founding a "new Rome" (*OR*, 212). To use the imagery of Kafka's parable, the American revolutionaries were able to feel and respond to the particular way the past and future were aimed at them, to successfully battle *their* forces in order to create and claim their *own* present. And what dawned in that present, what drew the breath of reverence from those who participated in and bore witness to the American founding was the "absolute novelty" of the fact that a new beginning was born when simple mortals mutually promised to bind themselves together in the face of an uncertain future and shared the commitment to deliberate together. It was this mutuality that, in its vulnerable and illuminating beauty, arrested and moved the American revolutionaries and their contemporaries, canceling the arbitrariness in all beginnings.

This absolute contained in all beginnings, Arendt argues, is the principle, or the *way* the beginner begins, which appears in the world simultaneously with the new beginning. She writes, "What saves the act of beginning from its own arbitrariness is that it carries its own principle within itself, or, to be more precise, that beginning and principle, *principium* and principle, are not only related to each other, but are coeval" (*OR*, 212). Insofar as this principle or way of beginning inspires those who come after, there is authority, a perseverance in time that occurs not through coercion and violence but through an obedience in which we retain our freedom. And it is Plato, Arendt suggests, who most beautifully gathers the "innermost meaning" of this relationship between principle and beginning: "For the beginning, because it contains its own principle, is also a god who, as long as he dwells among men, as long as he inspires their deeds, saves everything" (*OR*, 213).

To peer into the misty enshrouded past or to stretch beyond the messy temporality to some putative eternal world—either of these moves to give legitimacy and weight to mere mortal doings looks, from this vantage point, like (humanly comprehensible) efforts to escape from responsibility for our own freedom, and from the dignity, even divinity, that our capacity to begin should bestow on human affairs. It is precisely this responsibility that was affirmed by the interconnected principles of mutual promise and common deliberation that inspired the American revolutionaries. The American foundation, Arendt argues, "told an unforgettable story" about a miraculous possibility: that "the most unstable and futile beings we know" can, through "deliberate acts of freedom," constitute political association, that in willing faith we can bind ourselves to one another against an uncertain future and, at least for some time, defeat human futility (*OR*, 213).

If the "way" the founders began, inspired by the principles of mutual promise and common deliberation, became authoritative for a new United States, it was, in Arendt's view, this event more than any other in modern history that affirms the possibility of politically relevant freedom and the ontological condition of natality to which it corresponds.[12] Moreover, the founding does so by revering the vulnerable mutuality of our being in time together. This, indeed, is the illumination by which its beauty moves us. To put this another way, what secured the American foundation, paradoxically, was that the inspiring principles enshrined in its founding documents and institutional arrangements were designed to augment *initium* itself, to add to and increase our human capacity for beginning anew. And this both spoke to and arose out of the deep dilemmas that the historically unique processes of the modern age I chronicle in Chapter 3 presented to its contemporaries. Thus it is these principles that Arendt hopes might yet prove authoritative in the general sense of the term in *a novus ordo saeclorum:* command our unquestioning respect and obedience without compromising our freedom, neither coerce nor persuade through argumentation, but rather inspire and speak to us *so that* freedom is augmented.

We might pause here to consider that Arendt's arguments are hardly novel, that it is almost axiomatic, even platitudinous, to assert that these two principles are the legitimizing sources of authority in modern polities, and that one or the other can be found in most contemporary theorizing, liberal and communitarian. But there are distinctions to bear in mind between mutual promise and mutual consent on the one hand and common deliberation and common good on the other. Both the liberal notion of consent and the communitarian notion of common good obscure the dynamic reality-constituting nature of our political life: consent insofar as it contributes to a forgetfulness that our world is never a preexisting whole to which we do or do not consent,[13] common good insofar as it seduces us to imagine the (timeless) preexistence of an entity rather than a sensibility constantly shaping and being shaped by human activity. These differences are all-important, for neither mutual consent nor common good speaks to a world such as ours, a world whose reality, without traditional authority, without religion or tradition, is in perpetual need of reaffirmation and reconstitution. Neither principle adequately addresses the fact that our world's durability is vulnerably dependent on political practices of mutuality—promising and deliberation—and rapport-establishing communication. Nor does either speak to the way in which this condition of vulnerability uniquely moves us, to the way in which we find it beautiful. Ours is indeed a too protean world without our intervention. It requires our initiative if it is to stay in being through time.

I have been discussing what it was about the American founding that Arendt suggests moved its contemporaries and continues to move us today—namely, the way America's founding illuminated how dependent we are on one another in facing the task of building a human world that can endure for those who come after us. And I have suggested that the *way* the founders began, guided by the principles of mutual promising and common deliberation, moves us aesthetically, that we find it beautiful because it illuminates something of the human predicament while it also responds to and illuminates our own postmetaphysical space in time. And for these reasons the American founding has had a certain durability. In the face of an uncertain future, mortals bound themselves to one another and kept that uncertainty from driving them back into the known but unfree past. They became, in this sense, the origin of their own future. But what of the dimension of the past? How do we keep the past from propelling us, in reckless hope, into a relatively bearingless future? How, to ask the question in a Nietzchean voice, can the past become useful to us?

This concern with the past was one Arendt felt deeply, arguing that, with the loss of tradition that had always secured memory and guided us through a "preestablished" past, we are in danger of losing the whole dimension of depth, and this because, as she writes, "memory and depth are the same, or rather, depth cannot be reached by man except through remembrance" (*BPF*, 94). But what is this depth, and why is its loss so threatening? Human perception gains depth when our efforts to comprehend something become flushed with and enlarged by the resonances of others' efforts. This certainly occurs, and importantly so, in the same time-space, although knowing the way in which those who have come before storied their experiences is probably what most expands our sense of depth. We experience awe when we feel ourselves in some way part of a far larger human story on earth. The experience of depth is important because the histories that render human experience meaningful provide us newcomers with touchstones as we make our way in a new and strange time, in an as yet unstoried wilderness. They help us think about what it is we are doing. "The mind," Arendt writes to drive home her point, "is helpless outside a pre-established frame of references" (*BPF*, 6). Indeed, Arendt argued that the loss of tradition that could anchor the present in a resonating depth made almost everybody far more vulnerable to the radical renarration of reality in the form of "organized lying," which occurred most systematically in totalitarian regimes (*BPF*, 227–64).

Arendt, however, complicates her thought concerning the mind's helplessness without a preestablished frame, arguing that the thread that secured memory and gave depth to the present was also a chain (*BPF*, 94). As long as tradition was intact, the present became flushed with the resonances of a predetermined past through echo and repetition. With the chain broken and pieces of the past strewn in wild disarray, we must learn how to retain a relationship to the past and on what basis. What should guide us as our "frame of reference?" The very way depth may be experienced by us, we might expect to be different.

Keenly aware of our need for depth and equally aware that we can no longer achieve the relatively orderly manner in which the past was secured by being passed through the "succession of time," Arendt insists that the past, as much as the future, must find its origin in us. It is we who must story our own *nunc stans*. We with *our* problems and questions must initiate conversations with persons, works, and events of the past, transforming the older "succession in time" into a "spatial juxtaposition" through the conversations whose origin we are (*MDT*, 79).[14] And this is no mean responsibility.

Indeed, the significance of the public realm arises not only because it houses the mutual promising and common deliberation of the future-oriented actor but also because it is the site for these conversations with the past—conversations that, transformed by the spectator into stories, illuminate what otherwise is a welter of bewildering occurrences. These stories are thus of necessity retrospective; they teach us to accept, which is to say to comprehend, a world already grown old. They engender an often difficult feeling of "gratitude for everything that is as it is."[15] Only by being responsive to the web of human understandings and the factuality of the world into which our own acts will reverberate can we as newcomers attain the reflective distance necessary first to question and then to act differently, to engage the world prospectively. Without such stories and the mental complexity they convey, the newcomer will know neither how to story anew nor how to act.[16]

The deepest essence of the public realm, then, is that it is the communicative site in which we give birth, through our own retrospective and prospective responsiveness, to the phenomenal richness of our shared world. The central practice through which we do so is judging. Arendt burdens judging with the ability, in our postmetaphysical condition, to bring into and keep in being a world sufficiently common *that* human particularity can appear and be cherished. As such, judging fosters the ethical orientation Arendt's ontology demands; it is the central means by which we intensify our awareness of reality. In what follows I unfold these arguments. To anticipate, judging demands a high degree of responsiveness toward the density within which the phenomenon in question resides. This high degree of responsiveness enables reconciliatory understandings, accepting comprehension of what is, precisely *through* certain practices of mutuality. In her idiosyncratic readings of Kant's representative thinking, Arendt theorizes these practices in suggestive ways. Judgment is the only mental activity that *requires* the presence of others. But this responsiveness is important in another crucial, interrelated, and perhaps more primary sense, and that is as a solicitation to others to respond, to act. In both senses, judging cultivates our attentiveness to, and perhaps our passion for, human particularity.

Our world can have a certain durability because the practice of judging confirms the spirit of the modern age that Arendt argues is so movingly beautiful in its illumination of our space in time: that we, in our own mutuality and particularity, are the origins. She writes,

> It was only in the course of the eighteenth-century revolutions that men began to be aware that a new beginning could be a political phenomenon, that it could be the result of what men had done and what they could consciously set out to do.... The *novus ordo saeclorum* was no longer a blessing given by the "grand scheme and design in Providence," and novelty was no longer the proud and, at the same time, frightening possession of the few. When newness had reached the market-place, it became the beginning of a new story, started—though unwittingly—by acting men, to be enacted further, to be augmented and spun out by their posterity. (*OR*, 46–47)

Judgment moves us insofar as it augments the human capacity to begin, augments natality. And in this it imparts to the world some of the imperishability that all things beautiful bear. Let me turn now to Arendt's thoughts on judging to argue my case.

Judging

Judgment received Arendt's sustained attention only in her final years. Her major writing on the subject, the proposed third book of *The Life of the Mind,* was scarcely begun at the time of her death. Indeed, it exists only as one quotation from Cato and another from Goethe, both found on the same page in Arendt's typewriter when she died. From Cato she quoted,

Victrix causa diis placuit sed victa Catoni.
(The victorious cause pleases the gods but the defeated one pleases Cato.)[17]

From Goethe's *Faust* she cited these lines:

Könnt'ich Magie von meinem Pfad entfernen,
Die Zaubersprüche ganz und gar verlernen,
Stünd'ich, Natur! vor dir, ein Mann allein,
Da wär's der Mühe wert, ein Mensch zu sein.
(Could I but clear my path at every turning
Of spell, all magic utterly unlearning;
Were I but Man, with Nature for my frame,
The name of human would be worth the claim.)[18]

We have on the authority of lecture notes kept by Michael Denneny what Cato's words meant to Arendt in this context.[19] Instead of the Hegelian tradition in which world history in the form of success is the final arbiter of all events, Arendt sides with Cato in suggesting that it is (or should be) the judgment of living spectators that renders events significant, giving them a "home" in human affairs. It is the quality of *their* attention that establishes an event as worthy of historical memory. And this quality of attention is of greater worth than the attention derived from success or power.

Yet this claim immediately raises questions about the origins and status of the spectator's attention. It is in the direction of these questions that the quotation from *Faust* tends, for with it Arendt suggests that if we were able to take fully in our disenchanted world, if we were able to stand nakedly before it, seeing and alone (ein Mann), then it would be clear how utterly important, how necessary it is that we turn to one another in the effort to humanize ourselves (ein Mensch zu sein) by making the world a place fit for humans (Menschen). This, to complete the circle and return to Cato, we can do only if we cease a fruitless and even dangerous search for guidance in an imagined otherworldly realm, or in nineteenth-century theories of progress, or in a deified and ever-receding past. If we are to take responsibility for our presence and accept the burden of freedom, it is to one another we must turn, and judging is the key form of this turning, as Arendt theorizes it. She writes,

> Without repeating life in imagination you can never be fully alive, "lack of imagination" prevents people from "existing." "Be loyal to the story... be eternally and unswervingly loyal to the story," means no less than, Be loyal to life, don't create fiction but accept what life is giving you, show yourself worthy of whatever it may be by recollecting and pondering over it, thus repeating it in imagination; this is the way to remain alive. (*MDT*, 97)

How do we story our experiences so as to achieve a kind of reconciliation from which action might spring? If our capacity to judge well depends on our ability, through our judgments, to augment the capacity to begin and thus potentially redeem a world decayed and fallen from neglect, and if this depends on our responsiveness, what is the nature of this responsive relationship? Arendt's gloss on the words of Isak Dineson quoted earlier clears a path. Here we are enjoined not to create fiction as we story our world but to remain loyal to "what life is giving [us]." This is an injunction to be attentive to the unique particulars of the world, to the phenomenal richness of our world as it has been gifted to *us*, and this depends on our capacity for imagination. Be imaginatively loyal, Arendt says through Dineson, and if you excel, if your imagination is active and vigorous, you will "remain alive." Indeed, your sense of existence will be intensified; your world, as I argue, will be renewed. The key is "imaginative loyalty," and it is Kant, in Arendt's view, who best understood the public-communicative preconditions for the kind of responsiveness on which this human vitality depends.[20]

Arendt turns to Kant because he is, in her view, more deeply aware of the political nature of judgment than any other philosopher.[21] His attention to the phenomenality of the world, to its spectacular appearingness spoke directly to Arendt's historically specific concern with world alienation. Arendt discerned in Kant's work a mode of public thinking suited to respond to *and* build, in the invisible space of the mind, the world's complex phenomenality or appearingness. Kant's "reflective judgment" emphatically concerns the world, and it is made possible only through a certain sociability.[22] In his work on aesthetic judgments of taste, Kant conceptualized, Arendt thought, a reflective communicative relationship to others in which one's idiosyncratic response to the world is neither wholly surrendered nor wholly subsumed. Rather, it is tested and potentially transfigured through the performance of the imaginative task of "representative thinking," whereby we think in the place of those with whom we share the world.[23]

The essence of this communicative performance is that, on the one hand, our taste becomes fit to appear in the world. Our pleasure loses its idiosyncratic quality and becomes "particularized," a possibility that depends on our ability to remain imaginatively loyal to the others with whom we share the world. On the other hand, we cannot judge anything in *its* particularity without ourselves reconstructing the complex, historical specificity that forms *its* realm of appearance. And this we do also through the communicative sociability in representative thinking. Thus Kant was powerfully attentive to the particularity of the phenomenal world in his conceptualization of judgment because the communicative sociability in representative thinking makes idiosyncratic feeling particular and worldly and gives birth to the public world, where alone any unique particular can appear and be perceived as such. In these two senses our attentiveness to particularity depends on the sociability inherent in judgment as Kant conceives it.

Judgment, then, is the means by which we join our "particularized" selves to and thereby help engender a specifically human world, which is to say a world we, in a strong and active sense, communicatively share. What we learn from Kant, Arendt thought, is that the sociability embodied in judgment is both the origin of the public sphere and its heartbeat, and the heartbeat, too, of our possible humanity. Let me briefly outline the features of Arendt's Kant-inflected account of judgment.[24]

Judgment requires two distinct mental operations: imagination and reflection. In imagination we close out the outside world and re-present to our inner world an object we have sensed in that outside world. Imagination shuts out the world's objectivity and makes sensing an inner and immediate experience. Furthermore, when we re-present the object, we also immediately feel pleasure or displeasure. In both respects judgment is similar to taste. Yet judgment also grows out of taste, for the immediacy of this pleasure or displeasure we feel is subject to reflection. Here we judge whether the pleasure or displeasure experienced in our immediate response *itself* pleases or displeases us.

These twofold operations of judgment establish a "proper distance" between ourselves and our object so that, for the first time, we can get a picture of the whole and the meaning of our object's place in it (*LK*, 67–68).

Arendt calls this the "condition of impartiality" because it makes possible a unique kind of interest: an interest in disinterestedness (*LK*, 73).[25] This interest concerns not our individual lives or our moral selves but the world itself (*BPF*, 222). In the distance won through judgment's two operations we can take pleasure in a thing's existence. *Volo ut sis:* "I want you to be."[26] I am interested in you not because you aid me morally or are useful to my individual life. I want you to be for the sake of the (meaningful) world.[27] It is this interest that may flourish in the impartiality judgment creates.

Yet, having identified the conditions in which impartiality is possible, the question now is how we attain this impartiality of judgment with respect to something as apparently idiosyncratic and private as our pleasures and displeasures. By what standards do we judge whether we are pleased or displeased by our pleasures and displeasures? What guides the operation of reflection? The criterion, Arendt argues, is publicness or communicability, and the standard to which we appeal is common sense (*LK*, 69). Drawing idiosyncratically on Kant,[28] she argues for the existence of a sense common to all without which our sensations would remain private and incommunicable. Common sense, Kant's *sensus communis,* is a transcendental requirement for human communication, and the fact that our feeling is "rooted in" it makes our subjective feeling *open* to communication. Indeed, in Arendt's view the *sensus communis* is the standard that allows us to assert the possibility of universal communicability.

The maxim of this *sensus communis* which enables communication is to think from the standpoint of everyone else. Through this mental practice we "enlarge" our mentality, shedding the private, idiosyncratic, and incommunicable aspects of our experience. Thus when we judge, the *criterion* by which we choose whether our initial feeling pleases or displeases us is the communicability we make possible through enlarging our mentality. And *this* occurs *in* community. In this context Arendt refers, in contrast to the *a priori sensus communis,* to a community sense: "When one judges, one judges as a member of a community" (*LK*, 72). The validity of our judgment is not universal but general, valid only for those "*judging* person(s)," those members of the public (*BPF*, 221; my italics).[29]

Thus in judging Arendt finds that "at least one of our *mental faculties*...pre-supposes the presence of others" (*LK*, 74). My ability to judge well whether I should be pleased or displeased with my feeling depends on being responsive to the uniqueness of others who, with me, live in and constitute *our* world. And through this responsiveness our feeling loses its private qualities and becomes "impartial." Arendt writes, "You see that *impartiality* is obtained by taking the viewpoints of others into account;

impartiality is not the result of some higher standpoint that would then actually settle the dispute by being altogether above the melee" (*LK*, 42).[30]

Let us look more closely at how Arendt conceives of this responsiveness while keeping the following questions in mind: If judgment requires the presence of others, what is it about their inexhaustible particularity that we must bring to presence? And how, in doing so, do we ourselves become transfigured? How do we lose the private character of our perceptions and pleasures so as to gain Arendt's impartiality?

The consistent point of departure for Arendt's answers to these questions is how to be concerned with the phenomenon in question "in *its own terms*, without relating it to any larger process; . . . with the individual event, the particular act" (*LK*, 56; my italics). How do we presence others so that the phenomenal richness of the event or act will be as fully flooded with light as possible? Because judgment is, as Arendt says, "one of the most important activities in which sharing-the-world-with-others comes to pass," the illumination of that particular world remains its touchstone (*BPF*, 221).

We presence others, Arendt argues, by traveling in imagination. We venture out to *them*, to their standpoint—meaning "the place where they stand, the conditions they are subject to, which always differs from one individual to the next, from one class or group as compared to another" (*LK*, 43). We "go visiting" the location that has inflected and engendered their specific outlook on the world, the place from which they view the spectacle. What we are doing, however, during such mental visitations is active. We are not engaging in empathy, in feeling or absorbing ourselves into somebody else. This would amount to passively exchanging our prejudices for theirs. Rather, Arendt describes this "activity" as "being and thinking in my own identity where actually I am not" (*BPF*, 241). Now, if we are not seeking to feel and be another, then what quality of that person's "presence" do we make present in the public space of appearances we have created in our mind? We presence, I suggest, their encroachment. Merleau-Ponty's description of how perception of what is sensible opens the world to us is relevant here. Like my perception of the sensible world, my mental presencing perception "initiates me to the world . . . by encroachment, *Ueberschreiten*. Perception is not first a perception of *things*, but a perception of *elements*, . . . of *rays of the* world, of things which are dimensions, which are worlds, I slip on these 'elements' and here I am in the *world*."[31] That is, in representative thinking, the other's view becomes a dimension, a world. It encroaches on mine, I am extended, I see what the world looks like from this particular spot, I slip on it, and, willy-nilly, the world threatens to be born anew. Representative thinking responds to and brings forth the essential dimensionality of the world. It propels me to ask whether my original view of the thing in question encompasses, speaks to, has seen, or can form some kind of communicative relationship with how the world appears in *this* dimension. Shouldn't this angle on the world, now that I am open to it and see it as part of my seeing, provoke me in my effort to determine whether I should be pleased by my pleasure or displeasure at the thing in question?

Through "sheer force of imagination," we re-create in representative thinking the rich phenomenality of the world, or, as Arendt puts it, "the space that is potentially public, open to all sides" (*LK*, 43). And this requires "our whole soul apparatus" (*LK*, 74). It requires that we *encounter* and *be responsive* to the way we might see, experience, and feel from the particularity of others' places in the world, that we embrace their encroachment.

The transfiguration Arendt describes as the achievement of this kind of mental presencing, impartiality and enlargement, is really an enhancement in our sense of reality. As we travel in imagination through the public, the light from our visits floods the thing in question, more deeply illuminating its distinctive and complex particularity, thus making our perception potentially far more potent and rich. It is toward such potency of perception that representative thinking leads us. Simultaneously, we receive a profound sense of perceptual intertwining, of belonging to and being an active participant in the world. Others become rays of a common world. And there is pleasure and great incitement of the human spirit in the impartiality this communicative responsiveness achieves.

Still, having won a greater sense of the world's density and richness through this mental practice, and having been transfigured through it in the process, we must still in fact make a judgment. The only possible counsel for how to do so, according to Arendt, is the maxim of enlightenment: Think for yourself. But, as we have seen, this is a self transfigured, a self who has an enhanced sense of the phenomenal reality of the world within which the thing in question is embedded, an enhanced sense of the world's density, and of the self's belonging to this density. And this enhancement and enlargement is a palpable *feeling*. Having taken the beat of our world, we feel we have achieved a community sense, a feeling for how our world should look, sound, and feel; what should be in it; and what it is to which we collectively belong. It is our pleasure in this feeling of enlargement that should guide our reflection.

Yet this feeling has a paradoxical quality. Having performed, in relation to an event or issue in need of our judgment, the difficult task of representative thinking, we emerge with the feeling that others ought to agree with us, see the issue just as we see it. Indeed, we emerge feeling *compelled* to make such a claim on others. And yet the mode in which we do so is persuasion, as if, though compelled by the rightness of our judgment, we are nonetheless oddly aware that it is uniquely and vulnerably *ours*. This paradox describes the following: Having traveled to many different others in the process of judging, and having emerged transfigured, the feeling with which we are left has, for us, the force of revelation. We literally see anew, and this seeing is compelling. And yet, compelled as we are, we emerge simultaneously moved by what this very experience has dramatically illuminated for us—namely, how profoundly difficult it is to comprehend any given phenomenon, and how dependent we are, in our effort to do so, on this communicative responsiveness to others. We emerge moved by this, perhaps feeling a certain gratitude or gladness toward the plurality of the human world, perhaps feeling Lessing's tragic pleasure, and finding, perhaps, a profound aesthetic pleasure in our experience of vulnerable dependence and interdependence.

Hence, although our feeling compels us, the claim implicit in our judgment is a claim to be heard, listened to, countenanced, and joined. We say, "Here *I* am in relation to *our* world. I offer you an invitation, a solicitation. Join me. I provoke you. I demand of you that you countenance me as I see our world. Respond." Embedded, then, in this arrogant (and inherently dangerous) feeling is a provocation to others to join in illuminating the appearingness of the thing in question. And this provocation in which we willingly expose ourselves to all others is not easy. Indeed, Arendt stresses the difficulty of judging: the courage needed, the frequency with which it is refused. She writes, "Of course, I can refuse to [judge] and form an opinion that takes only my own interests, or the interests of the group to which I belong, into account; nothing, indeed, is more common, even among highly sophisticated people, than the blind obstinacy that becomes manifest in lack of imagination and failure to judge" (*BPF,* 242).

Judging, as Arendt theorizes it, is a wide, forceful, and imaginative practice. The generosity, the gladness it implicitly displays toward the presence of others promises greater understanding as we perceptually forge relations we had not previously seen. And such understanding is a precondition for action. As Arendt wrote of the effort to understand totalitarianism, "Comprehension, in short, means the unpremeditative, attentive facing up to, *and resisting* of reality—whatever it may be" (*OT,* xxx; my italics). In short, comprehension is resisting. Propelled by a powerful imagination, judgments are capable of augmenting the human capacity to begin. Judgments such as these, paradoxically, impart to our world a certain durability, for we are moved by them, find them beautiful insofar as they illuminate the profound and difficult need we have for countenancing others if we are to make our world *comprehensible* and hence *resistible*. Thus we return to judgments that are forcefully imaginative. They in some sense compel us to return to wrestle with them. They possess, then, a kind of authority, for they command an "obedience in which we retain our freedom." We return to communicate with, to take up the specific *content* of their solicitation, and we also return because such judgments are moving examples of how to share the world with others. Both kinds of return, like the judgment itself, hold the space of a world together; they create and save the communicative space that is the essence of a shared world.

Judgments that reflect the "blind obstinacy" of parochialism, may, to be sure, invite response, but a response born of the threatened feeling of being excluded from the world. Such responses can almost only but be reactive: They reproduce enmity, mutual oblivion, and violent abysses; they are generative of neither human freedom nor a shared world.

In this account of judging we see the importance of the sheer force of our imagination as it holds our world in common by giving it a certain durability and spatiality. And this we must of course do over and over again. It is in this sense that I think Arendt goes a good way toward substantiating her claim that although authority, which for millennia gave permanence and stability to human affairs, is now lost, its loss need not "entail the loss of our capacity to build, preserve and care for a world that can survive us and be fit for human beings" (*BPF*, 95).

In closing I want to address the kind of validity that judgments can have, and this, in turn, raises the question of who we must visit, of what our responsibility in the matter is if we are to judge well. This question can only be addressed either in a formal, schematic manner or by way of example because of the acute specificity of all situations demanding our judgment. I do the former briefly and in Chapter 5 concentrate on the latter.

The validity of judgments, Arendt argues, is general, never universal, extending only to those in whose place the judging person has stood (*BPF*, 221).[32] Because it is always as a member of a community that we judge, the general validity of any given judgment is "closely connected with particulars, with the particular conditions of the standpoints one has to go through to arrive at one's own 'general standpoint' " (*LK*, 44).[33] Closely connected to this argument is the claim that judgments have "exemplary validity." That is, they claim to be examples in which others will recognize the public sense or taste that binds them together and arises out of their sharing the world together. Our responsibility, if we are to be examples in this sense, is to visit all "standpoints" from which concern about the phenomenon in question might arise. But because we cannot literally do so, can we schematize this point?

We are responsible for traveling to all standpoints that come to be part of the contested terrain of perspective and argumentation on the subject in question, including the standpoints of both individuals and organized groups. Additionally, because it is undoubtedly true that, especially under conditions of inequality, certain groups and possible concerns will never reach the public terrain, we are responsible, in the effort to address this absence, for visiting people whose judgments we have previously admired, not for *what* they think, but because they know *how to "take account of"* the world. From these exemplars we learn and are reminded of the difficult demands made of us as we attempt responsibly to venture into the public world.[34]

These seem to me to form a general schema of who we must mentally visit as a member of the community. These imaginative visitations give rise to the impartiality possible "inside the political realm," by which Arendt means the realm of engaged political actors (*BPF*, 260). Judgment's general (not universal) validity thus arises out of a complex responsibility "to visit" the contested and contestable worldly web of relationships that might sustain the reality of the phenomenon in question. To be unresponsive to the world's contestation and flux is the essence of irresponsibility and corrodes the validity of judgments. Thus judgments are always contestable and relative, if by "relative" we mean that because plurality is the law of the earth, we must be responsive to, must continually rethink our judgments on the basis of changing worldly events and opinions.

But this is far from a sufficient ground for a judgment's validity. How, for example, with these grounds in mind, could we argue against the validity of judgments in a polity whose public sphere had come to be largely based on lies and deceptions and various acute forms of collective oblivion?

Another kind of impartiality is also a crucial component of judgment, and that is the impartiality acquired, as Arendt says, "outside the political realm" (*BPF*, 259).[35] We attain it when we visit the world not as members of a community but in one of our many possible solitary modes—among which she includes reporter, philosopher, artist, scientist, witness, and historian. Such modes of being alone, she argues, are common to all men: They are modes of human existence as such (*BPF*, 260).[36] The impartiality they achieve is vital if we are to preserve the world's delicate factuality.[37] In these modes we engage in that retrospective, meaning-gathering moment of judgment that Arendt refers to as truth-telling. The truth-teller, committed to saying "what is" and unbounded by commitments to action in the present, must always at the same time be a storyteller, must transfigure in order to gather the contingent occurrences in human affairs into a story so that they might be saved. Arendt writes, "Reality is different from, and more than, the totality of facts and events, which, anyhow, is unascertainable. Who says what is—λέγει τὰ ἐόντα—always tells a story, and in this story the particular facts lose their contingency and acquire some humanly comprehensible meaning" (*BPF*, 261–62).

To take responsibility as citizens for the world and the public well-being, we must visit our world in the tension-filled, dual mode of community member and solitary being. The communicative involvements of each open us out upon different "worlds" that must be mediated *within each judging person* for judgment to foster the ethical orientation for which Arendt's ontological concerns call. She writes, "And this critic and spectator sits in every actor and fabricator; without this critical, judging faculty the doer or maker would be so isolated from the spectator that *he would not even be perceived*" (*LK*, 63; my italics).

Together these two modes sustain a larger plural base for the appearance of human particularity. Thus the complex impartiality we achieve through them serves the capacity to begin, and thereby the world's possible renewal. Renewal requires that the factual, plural web of the world be protected, remembered, and saved so that newcomers might establish their own relationship within the unique temporal forces that enclose their being in the world. For something new to appear, the old, the given must itself be secured, remembered, kept in being; it must be gathered before us—complex and provoking—that we may be adequately responsive.

And this recalls the fundamental existential challenge with which we began this chapter—that, without traditional guideposts to orient us in the contingent realm of human affairs, we must, nonetheless, as beginnings and beginners, accept the burden of the "divine gift" of action. Thrown into a world baby-faced, we must establish our own present, remain undetermined but not inured against the world we come, as strangers, to join. Neither must we, to recall Kafka's parable, be propelled out of fear into the past, nor driven in blind hope into the future. Our challenge is to claim our *own* present, to successfully battle the forces of past and future by accepting what the world is giving *us*, as Isak Dineson put it. And for this we need a powerful imagination, one that moves in the world both as a member of the community and as a solitary being.

5 Ethical Responsibility in Politics:
The Obligation to Renew

How does Arendt's work, lodged as it is in our postmetaphysical condition, help us to conceptualize our ethical responsibilities in politics? I now turn my attention to this question, taking my cue from Michael Denneny's account of the etymology of the word *responsibility*. He writes, "The word *responsibility* has three distinct but tightly connected elements of meaning: to declare the presence of that which is present; to declare oneself present; and to declare a bond between oneself and that which is present to one."[1] Inspiring, demanding, and paradoxical, the danger of such formulations as starting points is oversimplification—as if that which is present is always already there, unhaunted by absence, untroubled by concealments. To combat this possibility of oversimplification as we reflect on an Arendtian understanding of political responsibility, we must think carefully about the human condition of plurality. To help me do this I have used the term *density*, and I have suggested, perhaps somewhat cryptically, that to be in the place of ethics is to be in this density.

In what follows I make good and elaborate on this claim in the context of more concrete political judgments and events, beginning with an analysis of two of Arendt's judgments. The question I pose is, "To whom must we go visiting if we are to make responsible political judgments?" And, I might add, for what degree of impartiality, or better, what complex degrees of impartiality, must we strive as we visit others? In what "mode of existence" must we visit—member or solitary?

The question is how to stay alive *to* the density of the world. What kinds of worldly relations, public encounters, and mental traveling are required of us as citizens? What are the specific difficulties we face as we seek to dwell in this place of ethics? I have been arguing that what is an essentially aesthetic pleasure is a precondition of our capacity to do so. We must feel tragic pleasure in the encroachments, hostilities, tensions, and provocations of our plural world, for this pleasure invites our responsive provocation to the world in turn; it is our motor toward the world's density. And this movement, as I shall argue, is crucial to our successful pursuit of the more prosaic, pragmatic tasks of political life.

Arendt's theorizing gives us a language, a set of political understandings, principles, passions, and even utopian impulses through which to articulate and give conceptual shape to this pleasure as a possible active experience of political life. Still, of course, pleasures of any kind are not to be simply commanded at will. Tragic pleasure must be not only articulated but also cultivated, celebrated, and experienced in both mental and worldly *practices*. It must be made possible.

But we are beings located in a profound finitude. The densities of our unique place in the world profoundly challenge our capacity to feel tragic pleasure, to be provoked by the presence of different others, different histories. It is to the world's dense particularities that we must be drawn, but these same densities that open each of us out upon a world also claim us, causing ethically troubling forms of oblivion and inattentiveness. This is even more the case because our finitude is always already overlaid with and produced through human domination—through forms of power that create, institutionalize, and enforce various kinds of human oblivion and acculturate us to pleasures adverse to that of tragic pleasure.

In what follows I first analyze two examples of Arendt's own political judgments in order to discern further the challenges of remaining attentive to the world's plurality. When we "go visiting" others in the mental practice of judging, we create *in imaginatio* that public which is concerned with the thing in question. We seek to solicit in imagination the fullest presence of others' being in the world. Yet, as I argue, the challenges of doing this well are formidable. Practical engagement in a wider public world helps us meet these challenges. I will take up this argument in the context of a striking story of political friendship. This story shows that certain kinds of political togetherness can replenish and nourish our judging imagination because they hold open the space of the world in a renewing invitation to others to act, which is to say, to make their appearance explicitly. And without this erupting, eliciting self-display of others, our sense of the world rigidifies, too automatically reproduces itself, and our feeling for its reality as for the reality of others is diminished. Each move in this direction is a move away from the illumination and understanding that must accompany and support citizens as they engage in "the arts of public problem solving."[2] And while practical political engagement often, perhaps usually, is not possible in relation to most judgments we are called upon to make, we learn much from those selective engagements we do make. Ethical responsibility in politics involves, most centrally, the obligation to renew the space of the world so that others may begin.

Trials of a Difficult Seeing

In Chapter 4 I argued that mediation between the kind of impartiality achievable as a member of a political community and that won in solitude is a difficult but necessary one for good judgments. Taking responsibility entails complex demands on us as we mentally visit others in order to gain orientation for judgment. Looking at two different sets of judgments Arendt made—the one more, the other less valid—I aim to illuminate the nature and difficulties of our ethical responsibility.

The examples of Arendt's judgments I want to explore concern the quality and nature of Jewish political thinking and political acting. The first set of judgments arises in the context of her reflections on socialist Zionism and the kibbutzim. These judgments were made in the 1940s, when, as an activist-intellectual, Arendt was concerned with the fate of the Jewish people and the formation of a state in Palestine. She is explicitly and self-consciously speaking as an insider to members of a particular political community in the effort to persuade them to follow a specific course of action—namely, to create a federated state, not a Jewish one. Arendt made the second set of judgments in her report on Adolf Eichmann's trial in Jerusalem, and in response to those careful concerns that Gershom Scholem raised about the report.[3] These latter judgments were made in the early 1960s, when Arendt was a self-conscious reporter, an outsider. Uninvolved, in this case, with any urgent question of political action, Arendt wrote the report to illuminate.

I examine these very different kinds of involvements and degrees of impartiality to pursue the ethical nature of political judgments that sustain tension between our insider and outsider positions. In this difficult density alone, made palpable by who we visit, and in what capacity we do so, is or responsibility born.

In the early 1930s Hannah Arendt became a Zionist, not for cultural or religious reasons but for pragmatic political ones. Since the mid-1920s she had actively engaged the Jewish Question through her friendship with Kurt Blumenfeld, chief spokesman for the Zionist Organization of Germany, and it was at Blumenfeld's request that Arendt went to the Prussian State Library and illegally gathered a large collection of anti-Semitic remarks made in professional societies, business associations, private circles, and nongovernmental organizations. This "horror propaganda" was to be used at the Eighteenth Zionist Congress to help make the case that the path of civil emancipation and assimilation for Jews in Germany was closed.[4] It was for these illegal acts that Arendt was detained by the Gestapo in 1933, and this is what undoubtedly impressed upon her the impossibility of remaining in Germany. Fleeing to Paris in the fall of 1933, Arendt became director of the city's office of Youth Aliya, a Zionist organization that helped prepare young children for immigration to Palestine. Throughout the 1930s and 1940s, both in the exile communities of Paris and New York (to which she came in May 1941), Arendt remained active in Zionist politics.[5] She was deeply concerned with what she considered antipolitical tendencies embedded in Jewish self-understandings—namely, that Jews suffered and were blessed with a unique and uniquely Jewish fate and, relatedly, that anti-Semitism is best understood in quasi-metaphysical terms. Arendt vociferously opposed both because, in her view, they close off the world of concrete historical practice to human understanding—understanding that might open the present to action rather than lock humans into an incomprehensible historical inertia. They abdicate responsibility.

Arendt's assessment of socialist Zionism and the kibbutzim is both highly critical and laudatory. As an outgrowth of the nonnationalist trends in Jewish tradition in general, and more specifically of those of Eastern European socialism, the collective settlements were successful, in Arendt's view, in creating on a small scale a "new type of man and a new social elite" who held new values and established new practices based on a passion for justice (*JP*, 214). In the kibbutz way of living Arendt saw a viable alternative to "competitive and acquisitive" world-estranged modern society. Interestingly, she applauds the successful and unique combination of manual labor, a new form of ownership, and high culture. And it is the loss of this social experiment that, in 1948, Arendt wrote would be "the severest of blows to the hopes of all those, Jewish and non-Jewish, who have never made their peace with present-day society and its standards" (*JP*, 186).

Despite this enormous praise, however, Arendt is highly critical of these Zionists' lack of political judgment (*JP*, 207). By this she refers to their virtually exclusive focus on their own social experiment, and their abstention from politics, more broadly understood. Even their own understanding of the nature of their work was devoid of political sensibility, she argues, because it was governed by the notion that necessity (and not at least some measure of freedom) drives all action. More to the point, however, is the fact that these social experimenters were content to fully absorb themselves in the immediacy of their work, leaving the question of the native Arab population and the issue of state formation to others. The world held in common, as they understood it, simply did not include the native population; nor, for that matter, did it require that they entertain larger questions of political community—questions begged by their very presence in Palestine.[6]

This neglect, Arendt argues, has created a situation in which this moral "vanguard of the Jewish people" has, through its "innocent obliviousness," itself ended up supporting the very ugly nationalist and chauvinist policies that their ideal should disown (*JP*, 137, 140). And this soiled the glory of their experiments, as any successes have been won quite violently at the expense of others. Furthermore, their obliviousness has fundamentally threatened the survival of the "new social man" and the new values themselves because the support they give to neo-fascist policies makes a mockery of their work and destroys the very humanity they have tried to make possible.[7]

At the root of Arendt's characterization of their failure to think politically and to exercise good political judgment lies the insult of oblivion. The kibbutzim came to Palestine to realize their new social ideals as if to a barren land, as if, Arendt says, "to the moon; to a region beyond the wickedness of the world" (*JP*, 137). They came, in addition, armed with a revolutionary tradition that shared the modern sense of world estrangement insofar as it self-consciously eschewed explicit political thinking. At the same time, this Jewish nonnationalist vanguard was part of a larger Zionist movement whose leadership was preoccupied with the ideological thought of the Jews as "the people without a country [who] needed a country without a people" (*JP*, 203). Hence those to whom the kibbutzim ceded political responsibility themselves proceeded as if the native Arab population simply had no reality. Importantly, for both Zionist groups, this was all the more possible, Arendt argues, because the Jewish economic miracle in Palestine was built wholly from international charity and thus independent of the economic lives of the native population. This absence of concrete worldly interdependence made it even simpler to ignore the realities of life vis-à-vis the native Arabs in Palestine. In this practical ignorance, and in the illusion born of ideology, Arendt sees something frighteningly familiar—a refusal to face up to events, facts, the given; a way of thinking and acting that tries to restructure factuality itself.

I should add that Arendt is also, though in a less historically detailed manner, critical of a parallel difficulty on the part of many Arabs to engage in nonideological, practical thinking about the relations between Jews and Arabs. Each side, she argues, makes nationalistic arguments whose sense cannot extend outside the "closed framework" of their respective peoples, and legalistic arguments that discount the "concrete factors" of the situation at hand. Neither kind of argument, Arendt contends, is answerable; they do not constitute authentic *political* speech, premised as they are on a denial of central facets of reality.[8] Here the particular power of oblivion as an explanatory framework emerges clearly. Approaches that focus alone on specific aspects of the conflict—competing claims to territory or differences over religious beliefs, for example—do not address the various forms that the elementary inability *or* refusal to attend to others takes. For this reason, they cannot disturb either group's "closed frameworks," the hermetic worlds that are the deepest sustaining ground of their conflict.

As an active Zionist at the time, Arendt's judgments embody, I think, what she herself called "the hallmark of true patriotism and true devotion to one's people"—"intense discontent" (*JP*, 125). Such discontent arises in part from an insistence on seeing "what is," on encompassing as best we are able the discomfort, discontent, and pain that the world's shifting unruliness and multidimensionality provoke in us. Unable to sustain *this* kind of devotion to one's people, the "injury done to reality" is injury done to the possibility of upholding a world one is trying to remake: in this case, a world with a solid and even new vision of justice (the kibbutzim), and a world capable of renewing its own principles and institutions through the initiatives of others. Such renewal is not possible if one of the primary preconditions of practical-political life is to radically restructure factuality itself by denying the concrete and excluding the reality of those with whom we, in one way or another share a world in common—apart from whether we desire to do so or not. Oblivion invites reaction, not action.

The true patriot's "seeing" is essentially both ethical and political in the very broadest terms, and such seeing is crucial if we are to give shape to a world with some measure of permanence. With respect to morality and politics, Arendt writes,

> In a world like ours, however, in which politics in some countries has long since outgrown sporadic sinfulness and entered a new stage of criminality, uncompromising morality has suddenly changed its old function of merely keeping the world together and has become the only medium through which true reality, as opposed to the distorted and *essentially ephemeral* factual situations created by crimes, can be perceived and planned. (*JP*, 217; my italics)

It is the gift of the "true patriot" to attain an impartiality that is the consequence of successful mediation between membership in and loyalty to a particular community and concerns as an outsider, a truth-teller/storyteller whose loyalty is to the complexity and density of relationships and facts within which the issues in question reside. Such loyalty is to the reality of the real: to know it, to endure that knowledge, and to see what comes of that knowing.[9]

To sustain this kind of complex impartiality (which I think Arendt successfully did in this context) is to be responsive to declaring the presence of those who in fact *are* present, are involved in the issue at hand, and to declaring oneself present *in* creating a bond with those who are present. In taking this kind of political responsibility Arendt joined a minority of Jewish patriots who, throughout the first half of the twentieth century, tirelessly pursued a politics that was neither "innocent[ly] oblivious" nor nationalistically so. They argued for the great need of Arabs and Jews in Palestine for institutions of self-rule, for public-political spaces in which they could face one another in practical, political, nonideological talk, spaces in which they could appear to one another in their concrete specificity. They opposed the formation of a Jewish state created by the imperialist powers, feared the reactive anti-Semitism they believed would result, and they argued, as late as 1948, for the creation of a federated state in Palestine. Judah L. Magnes, president of Hebrew University, was early on integral to these efforts, and in the 1940s he became the most important political proponent of this position, founding in 1942 the Ikhud ("Unity") party, whose purposes were to facilitate Arab-Jewish understanding and to agitate for a binational state. In 1948, just after the state of Israel had been proclaimed, Arendt became directly involved with Magnes's efforts to work toward a confederated Jewish and Arab state with Jerusalem as the capital. Arendt and Magnes shared the kind of practical political realism whose achievement rests on mediation between insider-outsider positions and the impartial seeing this makes possible.[10]

In Arendt's judgments and in the stories of this small minority of Zionists, there is something moving, something beautiful—a certain generosity and simple realism whose infrequent historical appearance and fragility make them, paradoxically, utopian. To mediate, in response to the question "What is to be done?" between, on the one hand, the power to change "what is," which is intrinsic to political action, and the factual, given texture of the world within which the question is posed, on the other, is a utopian aspiration. Our responsibility lies in a double and irreconcilable loyalty—to the elemental plurality of the human world, to its recalcitrant and plural quality, and to the specific political community that forms our cultural home and about which we are most fervently concerned.

In this case, then, Arendt's political judgments are made self-consciously as a Zionist and a patriot, and their ethical power rests on her ability to accept and extend the boundaries of the political world within which she must think—beyond the actual political-cultural community whose fate is her central concern. Admirably "impartial," she is actively taking responsibility for accepting the factual conditions within which her own people's fate is tied. The "representative thinking" she engages in embraces the reality of the common world of the two peoples in Palestine rather than the respective fictitious and hoped for common world that, she argues, both Jews and Arabs in Palestine constructed. She "visits" those concerned, and she does so with her concerns as a member of her particular political community in provoking tension with her concerns as a storyteller/truth-teller. In so doing, Arendt is responsible to and expresses gratitude for, the extended plurality of her life as it has been given her and as, therefore, she must accept it, answer it, and be answerable to it. Such complex gratitude expresses and teaches acceptance and reconciliation in the interest of renewing freedom—that there may be a new beginning and not the repetitious and reactive cycles of aggression and violence that are the grave if understandable responses to being consigned to oblivion.

We take such responsibility so that, as Dagmar Barnouw put it so beautifully in the context of the conflict in Palestine, "we can be a future's past that will not have imposed the silence of the inevitable, the fated, the inexplicable: a past that cannot be used, as has been the Jews' and the Arabs' past, as the final, inarticulate, unremovable obstacle to communication."[11] Responsibility in this sense renews the human capacity to begin, and it is this that shines forth, movingly, in these judgments of the Zionist-patriot Arendt. There is, of course, irony in this claim, for obviously in the immediate term, this minority lost; it did not, within this temporal horizon, invite renewal in the context of Palestine. Still, its efforts stand before us as a moving example, one to which we return again and again in wonder, provoked by a kind of political judgment that refuses to inflict the insult of oblivion and, in so doing, helps to keep alive our sense of the possibility of constituting a world in and for freedom. In this we are Cato's descendants and find in our shared pleasure in the "defeated" causes a means of sustaining a more fully human world.

By contrast, if we consider Arendt's judgments of Jewish actions under Nazi occupation, we will, perhaps, not be moved in the same way despite the fact that the general content of Arendt's criticism concerning the lack of political thinking on the part of the Jews is the same, and despite the fact that, at least formally, Arendt seems to have achieved the impartiality won through a complex responsiveness to one's own political community.

The judgments in question concern primarily the actions taken by the Judenräte, the Jewish Councils, whose members cooperated with the Nazi selection process and who, therefore, Arendt argues, accepted the morally outrageous logic that some human beings be sacrificed so that other, more privileged human beings might live. The lens through which Arendt looks as she judges such cooperation is her determination to face, not be oblivious to, what humans were capable of under the novel conditions of total domination. She saw that the effect of living in a world organized by an unprecedented assault on human plurality, diversity, and mutuality was a disturbing blurring (though not disappearance) of the distinction between victim and victimizer. It was the totality of the moral collapse under totalitarian rule that Arendt believed was the most pressing issue, and for this reason she wrote critically and disturbingly of Jewish cooperation.[12] For example,

> Wherever Jews lived, there were recognized Jewish leaders, and this leadership, almost without exception, cooperated in one way or another, with the Nazis. The whole truth was that if the Jewish people had really been unorganized and leaderless, there would have been chaos and plenty of misery but the total number of victims would hardly have been between four and a half and six million people. (*EJ*, 125)

And again, in another example, she characterized the chief rabbi of Berlin as someone who was "in the eyes of both Jews and Gentiles the 'Jewish Führer' " (*EJ*, 105).

Let me explore these judgments by reflecting on the issue as it is framed in the letters exchanged between Gershom Scholem and Hannah Arendt following the 1963 publication of *Eichmann in Jerusalem*, for this correspondence will help illuminate the terrible difficulty of taking responsibility in the way Arendt strove to do herself and about which she theorized.

Scholem's criticisms center on the matter of "how to approach the scene of that tragedy" in which one-third of "our people" were destroyed. He finds Arendt's approach painfully inappropriate. It is, he thinks, flippant, heartless, and frequently laced with overtones of malice toward those Jews involved. Because he regards Arendt as a "daughter of our people," this tone is especially troubling to Scholem. In Arendt he finds none of the traditional "love of the Jewish people" that, in his view, ought to be a natural disposition of all Jews. Beyond Arendt's tone, Scholem finds her specific judgments against the Jews unbalanced, and challenges her presumption to pass such definitive judgments on, for example, the Judenräte, when she "was not there." He also does not believe that their generation can possibly attain the necessary objectivity with which to judge these events (*JP*, 242–43).

Arendt's response is direct and uncompromising. In her view it is imperative to judge the *arguments* with which the Jewish functionaries justified to themselves and to others their cooperation with the Nazis in the Final Solution. Without such an investigation of what was done and how it was justified, followed by our own judgment of their reasoning, the past will remain out of our reach, haunting and mysterious, and we will learn nothing. Judgment is the route to reconciliation based not on resignation to a fate that can neither be changed nor understood but on understanding that helps us orient ourselves toward the future and establish our present.

This response exemplifies much of the ethical power of Arendt's thought. In her refusal to abdicate the effort to take responsibility for "what is" by declaring a bond through judgment between herself and this past, she calls those to whom she speaks to face the tragedy of what occurred in such a way as to make renewal and renewed action possible. The difference in their respective views in this context is best seen by Scholem's recognition that he *must* answer the Israeli youth's inevitable and persistent questioning about why so many Jews "allow[ed] themselves to be slaughtered" and his simultaneous abdication when it comes to judging those very events:

> The discussion of these matters is, I believe, both legitimate and unavoidable—although I do not believe that our generation is in a position to pass any kind of historical judgment.... Nevertheless, we cannot put these questions aside. There is the question thrown at us by the new youth of Israel: why did they allow themselves to be slaughtered? As a question, it seems to me to have a profound justification; and I see no readily formulated answer to it. (*JP*, 241)

And specifically, concerning decisions by those on the Judenräte, he writes, "I do not know whether they were right or wrong. Nor do I presume to judge. I was not there" (*JP*, 243).

Scholem's abdication comes in the form of a dual plea—that it is both too early to judge fairly and objectively and that only those who were there have the knowledge needed to pass judgment. Although these are real issues, I suspect that Arendt is right that the effort to judge has to begin, and that Scholem's abdication is not unrelated to his feeling of love for the Jewish people. The strength of Arendt's effort lies in her courage to judge what occurred, to create a *bond* between herself and that which is present through whatever understanding might be wrought, in order to free the young from the weight of that past for their own political life and, to the extent possible, to free those who themselves experienced and had to make decisions under totalitarian conditions.

Yet both the magnitude and quality of the controversy that erupted over Arendt's report on Eichmann's trial raises questions concerning how well Arendt mediated the relationship between insider and outsider, between membership in the community of Jews and truth-teller/storyteller. And in so doing, it illuminates for us something of the difficulty involved in the kind of ethical responsibility in politics for which I am arguing.

Heedless of Scholem's deep concern about the tone of her judgments of the Jewish functionaries, Arendt chalks up the controversy entirely to the "campaign of misrepresentation" carried out by the Jewish "establishment" in Israel (*JP,* 274). Clearly this was in part true, as Arendt herself documents.[13] Yet did the manner with which she chose to report on the Jewish functionaries—that is, her tone—not perhaps itself contribute to both the intensity of the controversy that immediately followed the book's publication and the attenuation of her ability to command the ear of her readers and thus stimulate renewal through understanding?

Arendt defends her tone, rejecting Scholem's notion that Jews should love their own people. She suggests that the proper attitude ought to be "*Selbstdenken,*" independent thinking. Love, she says, should not be felt for something that is "part and parcel of myself" (*JP,* 247). For such things we can and ought to feel gratitude; only for that which we are not, Arendt argues, can and ought we feel love. Love is an outer-directed passion that links us through intimate ties to others. While we may grant this to Arendt (and I think we should), she seems, in the role of reporter she adopted for Eichmann's trial, to have tried so to locate herself outside her "given" community that she fails to inhabit the Jewish community's points of view with the same kind of understanding and clear-sightedness she shows toward the Nazis. And one wonders whether this is not an overreaction to her own givenness as a Jew and her sense of the tremendous discipline in thinking required for her to be, in this event, impartial. Arendt admits to Scholem that she feels with more grief the wrongs done to her own people than those done to others. But such emotional partisanship has no business seeing the light of day, in Arendt's view, although it may indeed be what drives us most deeply.

My point here is not to gesture towards a psychological reading of some purported difficulty Arendt had in relation to being Jewish. It is, rather, to argue that in mediating between insider and outsider positions, it is surely harder to rub, as rub we must, against some grains than against others, and that Arendt was, perhaps, overzealous with the rubbing she certainly had to do against the grain of what she felt as her natural sympathies as a Jew.

If I am right, these two examples of judgment show us the extreme difficulty of taking political responsibility as we judge, insofar as this demands of us movement out to visit others both as a member of an engaged community and as a differently engaged truth-teller/storyteller concerned with illuminating understanding. The density of the world whose law is plurality, and in whose place we must be if we are to be in the place of ethics, is a density that, as my analysis of this second set of Arendt's judgments suggests, claims us each in nontransparent ways. The particular densities of our own being generate their own species of oblivion. They make taking responsibility, understood as being responsive to the worldly density within which any phenomenon in question resides, a utopian aspiration. It is to beat our wings against features of our own irreducible finitude. Taking these examples as communicative events, we experience how difficult it is as engaged political actors "to receive" the relative impartiality of the outsider, how hard it is for the outsider to "give" or communicate that impartiality in ways "receivable," and how difficult but necessary is this demand to move between insider and outsider positions as we judge. To take responsibility for this aspiration toward impartiality, for making present that which is present, is to embrace the trials of a difficult seeing.

In this context, then, the relative failure of Arendt's judgments concerning the Jewish Councils is due not to the content of her judgment but, as Scholem intimates, to her tone, a tone that comes about because her thinking is too removed from one crucial part of the public world with which she is concerned. Even Gershom Scholem, her friend, cannot really deal (and I do not mean "agree") with what Arendt had to say. Having lost the necessary tension that the responsible judge must sustain between the outsider/truth-teller and the insider/political actor, Arendt fails not in loving the Jews, as Scholem suggests, but in speaking and thinking *with* them, and thus she fails to carefully inhabit their standpoints.

If we are to judge responsibly, to answer to the density of our worldly phenomenon, we must be attentive to the unavoidable particular densities our own location creates. In the cooperation of the Jewish leadership with the Nazi authorities, Arendt reads one more horrific instance of the absence of political thinking on the part of the Jewish people—an argument that, by 1963, she had been making for more than thirty years.[14] Did this make her less attentive, less sympathetically comprehending as she put herself, as judge, in the place of those who faced such decisions? Had her lengthy occupation of the outsider position made her impatient and thus less adept at communicating her thoughts in ways others could receive? As Arendt theorizes, the tension between "truth" and politics, outsidership and insidership *must* be sustained because at stake is the renewal of a world in which "we are free to act and to change."[15] In Arendt's ethically important effort to stand outside her own "natural" sympathies, did she stand too far outside? Does her example reveal to us something of the vital utopian (or alternatively tragic) nature of this injunction to assume responsibility through impartial seeing? I think that it does, and I suggest nonetheless that it is a crucial ethical effort. Had Arendt retained the substance of her judgments but adopted a tone less ironic, less harsh, one that instead reflected, through thinking "with" others, the enormity of the circumstances faced by the Jewish elders, her ability to facilitate renewing interrogation of Jewish action in the interest of understanding the proportions of the moral collapse under totalitarian rule would have been far greater. In the words of one of "the daughters," her people might well have found exemplified the awesome effort to take responsibility for "our" world; they might have been provoked by the "tragic pleasure" Arendt exhibited, by her deeply woeful pleasure in seeing "what is," in illuminating that the way may be held open for change, for the new. And this, as spectators, we should find moving—the way such responsiveness to others can renew, invite others' attentiveness in turn. In the final instance, it is the renewal of this fragile, mutual communicative need we have for one another that, in its courage and generosity, is beautiful and through which we both feel and constitute our world as a place specifically human and shared—open to action, renewed and renewable.

Political responsibility as I have been articulating it opens the world to those disparately located in it. It refuses to mentally inhabit a seamless world that we can win only on the terms of oblivion—oblivion to particular others and to the peculiar partial understandings and concealments that our own specific density unavoidably creates and in which it partakes.

If we are responsible for mentally moving toward the world's dense plurality in the activity of judging, what kinds of political engagements with others best stimulate and nourish the judging imagination? What mode of political togetherness best solicits others in ways that hold the world open to them so that we may be responsive to their particular presence and, by extension, to the world's density? What quality of political togetherness best intensifies our awareness of reality? How, in our direct political engagement with others, do we take responsibility in that threefold sense about which Michael Denneny writes, "to declare the presence of that which is present; to declare oneself present; and to declare a bond between oneself and that which is present to one"? I turn to these questions to complete my argument for an Arendtian-inspired understanding of ethical responsibility in politics. The story through which I pursue these questions is one of political friendship achieved by two people who had been made impervious to each other by the practices of power in which their lives were embedded. Their story shows the way in which institutionalized human domination creates powerful forms of oblivion to the reality and specificity of others—forms that are tremendously difficult to become aware of, much less to dislodge through mental activity alone. Such oblivion, as this story powerfully shows, impairs our capacity to understand our world, and thus also our capacity to engage in pragmatic political action with others. What did dislodge the mutual oblivion of these two people was the experience of a certain kind of political togetherness that, I argue, is essential to our capacity to renew the world as a place where the freedom "to call something into being that had never existed before" remains a lively possibility.

Trials of a Difficult Doing

Ann planted her large frame in the doorway and lit into the youths. "If you want to know where a person's coming from," she yelled, "you need to *read* this material, not tear it up! You got to *see* what makes him think what he *thinks!*" C. P. had seen Ann mad many times before, during protest marches and at City Hall. It occurred to him as he watched her in the doorway now that if someone had told him years before that someday she would be protecting his Klan material from a group of blacks, C. P. would have told them that they were crazy. Now he wasn't even sure what the word meant.[16]

Ann Atwater shouted these words at the young black youths who, incensed at the display of Ku Klux Klan material on their school grounds, were about to seize and destroy it. A tough, poor, and by this time, politically seasoned black woman and civil rights activist, Ann had recently agreed to co-chair a "charette" in Durham, North Carolina, with C. P. Ellis, the Grand Cyclops of the Ku Klux Klan of Durham. A series of extended face-to-face meetings among people with sharply opposing positions on an important issue, the charette was designed to open communication by first drawing into the public light people's raw fears and festering anger, their hopes and their longings, and then redirecting the unleashed energy in more constructive ways. The idea for this charette had originated with the state AFL-CIO, which had applied for and received an $80,000 grant from the U.S. Department of Education to help communities smooth the way for the court-ordered desegregation of North Carolina's public schools. The year was 1971, and this was the issue at hand in Durham. The man displaying the Klan materials was C. P. Ellis.[17]

Ann Atwater and C. P. Ellis had sustained a venomous political antipathy toward each other through the politically tumultuous 1960s and early 1970s, a period in which both of them rose to positions of community leadership: Atwater as a militant community activist among Durham's poor black population, and Ellis as the local head of the Ku Klux Klan, a man who not only skillfully cultivated working relationships with a large network of Durham's white middle-class city officials but also took the unusual step of going public with the Klan's views. Like Ann, C. P. was a frequent presence at city council meetings, and there they had confrontations that sometimes approached violence.

Their dozen or so years of deep animosity made Ann's deed, recounted above, all the more remarkable. What Ann Atwater did in that moment was to give C. P. Ellis the kind of recognition that he had always been denied. It was a kind of recognition that hauled him, allow me to say somewhat cryptically, immediately into the land of the real, that saved him from the fate of dirt-poor white laborers in the South, from a life that "slip[s] away, trivial and unnoticed." Ann saved him from the loneliness and irreality of worldly oblivion.[18]

To be sure, the Klan had already saved C. P. from the ignominy of total oblivion. It had given him a sense of importance, "a place to stand and feel he had a right to be there, a right to exist as he said."[19] But it was not to the land of the real that "citizenship" in the Ku Klux Klan gave C. P. entry. Rather, the Klan transported him through cheap feeling to an unreal world whose irreality is perhaps best captured in Ellis's own (transcribed) description of the moment when, as a young boy, he realized he was white:

In that moment he understood that blacks were not simply black. They were niggers. More than that, he realized (and thrilled to the recognition) that he, a white boy, poor as he was, was not a nigger—could never be a nigger.... The word had an electric crackle to it; saying it aloud produced the same feeling you got when you grabbed a snake in your bare hands.... C. P. felt a tingle coursing through his body.[20]

It is this feeling, and the sense of self-importance it imparts, that saves many poor whites of the South from the ignominy of total oblivion. But it does so only in the most self-deceiving sense, for it offers them an only slightly more remarkable fate than they otherwise would suffer—a life of hate and violence hardly distinguishable as a distinctive, individual life story worth telling. Indeed, membership in the Klan made of C. P., in the words of playwright Lorraine Hansberry, a "befuddled instrument" of powers he could not comprehend, helping to reproduce the mechanisms that had sustained the power structure of America's South for over a century. The genius of the South's "aggressive aristocracy" (V. O. Key's term) has always been to use the malignant solidarity wrought of the politics of white supremacy to subvert common cause among white and black working poor. This is, more specifically, a strategy that was designed to keep poor whites and blacks oblivious of one another and thus unequipped to grasp their shared oppression, the dawning recognition of which alone could begin a different story—one in which the lives of the poor might enter the register of history on their own wings, as it were. And the Klan has always formed the shock troops of this woeful strategy.[21]

So when Ann Atwater (assisted, of course, by all those who made the charette a reality) yelled at the black youths, she both called C. P. Ellis back from historical oblivion and made it difficult, in turn, for him to practice his own oblivion toward the lives of black Americans. And this was an awakening that indeed made Ellis uncertain of what it meant to be crazy, for Atwater launched him on a journey that would take him, the Exalted Cyclops of the Ku Klux Klan, to political friendship with a poor black woman, to resignation from the Klan, to work as a full-time organizer for the International Union of Operating Engineers, the union representing the maintenance staff at Duke University, where he worked and where 80 percent of the union members were black.[22] From violent enmity to a challenging common cause, C. P. (and Ann in her own way as well) awakened to the complex reality of the real. Less oblivion now, this is a story to be told.[23] It is indeed a story about redemption, about what Hannah Arendt would surely have called a new beginning. As such, it is a potent instance of what I believe she meant by political greatness.

Atwater and Ellis's story draws attention to a central paradox in Arendt's theorization of action, which is to say her understanding of freedom. The paradox to which I refer is that, according to Arendt, all great action is violent in the sense that it breaks through established routine and precedent, tears at the fabric of relationships. And yet freedom, only possible in the presence of others, is the hidden source of all great and beautiful things (*BPF*, 169). Thus, on the one hand, the defining characteristic of great action is its corrosive, tearing quality. It breaks open the known and the settled, destroys relationships, *appears* to have a heroic, almost sui generis quality. On the other hand, however, if freedom is its source, it requires the presence of others, some kind of political togetherness. Thus some particular sorts of relationships would seem to be its precondition.[24]

Meditation on these paradoxical observations will help us closely examine the way Arendt theorizes the presence of others. If what she means by it is fairly straightforward—that without politically organized others to bear witness to great deeds, they and thus freedom as well would have no reality, would pass into the evanescent—the paradox is less interesting. And this interpretation would certainly be supportable by Arendt's phenomenological understanding of reality. But if she is also identifying a more determining relationship between the quality of our presence to one another and the possibility of great action (and I think she is), a reconsideration of that quality of political togetherness should offer some fresh insight into Arendt's relatively hidden ethical concerns and contribute to my effort to articulate an Arendtian-inspired argument concerning ethical responsibility in politics.[25] I read her work here with these possibilities at the forefront.[26] In so doing, I think with Arendt and in some sense beyond her, for my reconsideration of this "presence of others" takes its cue first and foremost from the ontological reflections she made at the end of her life (see Chapter 2).

I proceed by considering Arendt's distinctive notion of political togetherness, elaborating on its political relevance, and finally arguing that ethical responsibility in politics centers on the obligation to renew the human capacity to begin. Throughout, the story of Ann Atwater and C. P. Ellis enriches, directs, and informs my thinking, for something of what Arendt attempted cautiously to articulate was manifest in the actions of Ann Atwater—a woman who had once in fact tried to stab C. P. Ellis while he spoke at a city council meeting—on that day she moved not merely to defend the right of the Exalted Cyclops to display Klan material but harangued her people about a certain obligation they had to the person and views of this "nigger-hating" Klansman. As their story tells, this was to be no small gift. As an instance of greatness and thus of redemption—of deliverance from the bondage of sin—their story dramatizes the abrupt, tearing end to routine and violent oblivion that is the precondition for holding a system of unjust power in place, an end made possible, indeed called forth by the particular (and audacious) public space of the charette.[27] Until the charette was created and summoned acts such as Ann's that renewed and sustained it, C. P. Ellis had been driven by a desperate hatred of black Americans that made both them and himself impenetrable phantasms. And as phantasms, no one can make political sense of their existence. To do so, in Ellis's case, would require illuminating the structure of power in the South and the complex oblivions upon which it relied. And this illumination was set in motion precisely by the peculiar kind of countenancing Ann Atwater enacted that day.

As will be clear, the principle inspiring this countenancing differs from "tolerance," the liberal moral principle that safeguards the sacred autonomy of the self in the interest of rich self-development. It also differs from the promise of truth that inspires a rationalist defense of free speech in a vigorous public sphere.[28] Arendt is concerned, rather, with our capacity to be responsive to the specificity of others in the interest of illuminations that renew the human capacity for freedom. And although the story of Ann Atwater and C. P. Ellis tells the tale of a miraculous new beginning, its positive outcome ought not to mislead. Ann's act is in and of itself, apart from outcomes, significant to politics and to an elaboration of our responsibility in politics. Behind it lies an understanding that power is best exercised not by persuasion or coercion but by, as Merleau-Ponty put it, "thwarting" others through appeals to freedom, by inviting them to *participate in* a "common situation."[29] This manner of thwarting neither mystifies nor ignores others. It invites them into the arena in agonistic recognition, thereby rejecting a politics of pure goodness because it is "a meek way of ignoring others and ultimately despising them."[30] Yet it contains a promise that through such countenancing the "walls of possibility" can be pushed back.[31] It is this promise, not its fulfillment, to which I suggest we must hold ourselves.

Political Togetherness: The Utopian Moment

For he describes the knot of collective life in which pure morality
can be cruel and pure politics requires something like a morality.
—MERLEAU-PONTY, "A Note on Machiavelli"[32]

Arendt theorizes a kind of togetherness she distinguishes as distinctively political. This is a kind of togetherness in which we are, as she says, "with others" by being "neither for nor against" them (*HC*, 180). This sounds ridiculously utopian to anyone whose political animus has been unleashed in response to some sense of violation that the political body could, if sufficiently mobilized, bring to an end. That politics is war by other means is confirmed day in and day out in the micro and macro political practices of any nation, and theorists offer few conceptual tools with which to grasp our own political experiences in any other manner.[33] To think political life can be otherwise is simply to be naive about its nature and content.[34]

From a different angle, Arendt's conception of political togetherness sounds equally naive, for, it might be argued, political togetherness is premised on a minimum of shared values, common principles, and mutual promises that must be vigilantly defended "against" those whose actions might undermine or otherwise subvert these foundations of political togetherness. If we think of today's dominant forms of political practices—party politics, interest-group pluralism, movement politics, even citizen initiatives— Arendt's conception of a specifically political space that rises up between people through a relationship in which they are "neither for nor against" one another seems to simple-mindedly miss the essence of politics (namely, conflict between at least minimally consensual, if shifting groups). It seems to dream up a state that appears closer to indifference than to the ever-muddy mixture of ethical outrage and pleasure in power that we more realistically know to be the essence of what drives people into political motion.

However true the many versions of these two arguments may *seem*, stories like that of the political friendship between Ann Atwater and C. P. Ellis controvert both and commend our attention to a form of ethical possibility in politics. Arendt's ethical concern, as I read it, lies with the conditions that make possible the strange, uncertain appearance of, as she calls it, not "what" one is but "who" one is, with the appearance before others of our distinct particularity. She claims that only when we are "neither for nor against" one another do we create the political conditions for the appearance of who the doer(s) is(are), without which the doing being done is really just another happening and not action in the fullest sense at all. Without this "revelatory quality," action has no meaning (*HC*, 180). Put another way, the agent's unique particularity that emerges as an enactment into the world must be disclosed if there is a story to be told, if something distinctive in the sense of great and radiant is to stand out and before human attention.

To be sure, it is not at all evident that Arendt's is an ethical preoccupation, and this performative disclosive aspect of her theorization of political action has been at the center of debate over the question of whether her aesthetic preoccupations result in immoral, at best amoral political theory. Formulations such as the following exemplify this troubling character of Arendt's work:

> Unlike human behavior...action can be judged only by the criterion of greatness because it is in its nature to break through the commonly accepted and reach into the extraordinary.... Pericles knew full well he had broken with the normal standards for everyday behavior when he found the glory of Athens in having left behind "everywhere lasting remembrance [*mnēmeia aidia*] of their good and evil deeds." The art of politics teaches men how to bring forth what is great and radiant. (*HC*, 205–206)

Arendt's use of Pericles's understanding of Athenian glory to illustrate political greatness is, on the face of it, disturbing, but the preceding passage is easily misread, and, as Lisa Disch so lucidly points out, this misreading appears plausible because scholars do what I have just done—they "[cut] off Arendt before she is finished"[35]—for Arendt concludes that "greatness, therefore, or *the specific meaning of each deed,* can lie only in the performance itself and neither in its motivation nor its achievement" (*HC,* 206; my italics).

What shall we conclude from this? Let me suggest that although great action violently breaks through everyday relationships and is, in contrast to them, novel, it is not found merely in a simple sense where there is something new, where change or innovation has occurred. Great action is radiant—it illuminates more than darkens, creates and perpetuates remembrance more than oblivion.[36] And for this illumination to occur, "who" the deed or deed doers are must stand out—their specific responses must shine out against the darkness of a world whose disabling forms of oblivion and domination are too often inclined against them. If we are to show ourselves as distinct to our world, we will need in some manner to interrupt, as we resonate, the web of human relationships of our world: traditions, standards of evaluation, seminal stories, cultural icons, lines of battle, places of sedimentation and ossification, and forms of oblivion, all of which constitute the fickle, uncertain, fragile field of receptivity. Arendt's "revelatory action" requires that we disturb some part of this web, not fit effortlessly into its awaiting form and movement. And for this, Arendt argues, the presence of others is necessary; a certain political togetherness must be achieved—one in which a kind of suspension of our goal-based hatreds and loyalties occurs. We must achieve a moment in which we are "neither for nor against" others, a moment that finds its difficult residence, in our story as in any political situation, in the tumultuous waves of hatred and pelting furies that also constitute and sustain political life.

If, then, we further explore this condition that Arendt theorizes for the possibility of great action, we can contribute to illuminating the ethical content of her theory of politics. Great action in Arendt's aestheticized sense—as a response to the world that promises more to illuminate than to darken—is born of a certain quality of responsive countenancing of political others. And this constitutes a kind of political togetherness in which the web of relationships of those concerned is resonated in ways that interrupt forms of oblivion and domination and thereby nourish a promise to renew the capacity of others to begin. I say "*forms* of oblivion" because, as I have argued, oblivion is an ineliminable expression of human finitude, although we may suffer from it in greater or lesser degrees and forms—such differences making all the difference, ethically speaking. Indeed, Ann's act must be seen as resisting features of human finitude that, unless resisted, drive us perpetually (back) into a closed world; it must be seen as resisting the forms of oblivion that accompany our own particular and group-based densities in the world. Thus it is important to pay attention to the various surprises experienced by both Ann and C. P. once they began to "see" each other. For example, having been locked in enmity, Ann was startled to learn that C. P. was scared to come to the charette because it was on "black" territory. Or, for example, both Ann and C. P. were astonished to find that their deepest concerns were the same: for the children of their respective communities. Or, perhaps most disturbingly because such an elemental oblivion, C. P. experienced an enormous shock when, after much stalling, he finally sat down for the first time with Ann and charette organizer John Riddick at a lunch booth and was overwhelmed by Ann's smell. Having so dehumanized her, he was shocked to realize she had, like other humans, a sensuous body.

If we are to articulate some notion of political responsibility that flows from Arendt's theory of politics, it will center on the obligation to renew the capacity to begin—that is, to diverge from patterns of existence that rely on the reproduction of certain vicious forms of oblivion. The seeds of this obligation can be found in Arendt's invocation of, as she puts it, "the original interdependence of action" in which the beginner "sets in motion" what others alone could "bear" to the finish, and in which these others depended on the beginner "*for an occasion to act themselves*" (*HC*, 189; my italics). To return to our story: What Ann Atwater offered, as she shouted to the youths, was a beginning that provided "an occasion" for C. P. himself to act.[37] To do so, he would have "to bear" to the finish what Ann's act had "set in motion." And what she interrupted was, first, her own oblivion toward poor whites like C. P. and, second, his oblivion toward people like herself.

I am focusing here on the miracle-like quality of Ann's gift as she countenanced C. P. In dramatizing this moment and insisting on the language of miracle, I risk mystifying the conditions of *its* possibility. Perhaps the first question is how Ann Atwater, a former domestic and impoverished single mother, received her own sense of self. Who bore witness to *her* being in the world? As for many African Americans, Atwater's church community was undoubtedly crucial.[38] In addition, she was visited in 1965 by Howard Fuller, the local organizer for the antipoverty program Operation Push. Operation Push offered her a space in which to be witnessed and one in which, with others, to act, to be not a "what" but a "who" in Arendt's terms. Such solicitations ought not to be underestimated. As Howard Fuller put it, "There are other kinds of poverty too, in addition to economic deprivation. There is the poverty of not knowing, of being 'left out' in community affairs, of lack of self-respect."[39]

These essentially ethical solicitations formed the basis of the strength Atwater would bring to the changed political conditions under which she and Ellis encountered each other again in 1971, during efforts to desegregate Durham's public schools. Unlike their earlier confrontations before the city council, their public encounter was backed by the coercive power of the state—in the form of court-ordered desegregation—and was mediated through the charette, an institution designed to open up a space of appearance between two deeply antagonistic and mutually oblivious social groups *so that* they might better engage in pragmatic political action. These two groups had to *see each other* better first before meaningful common action world be possible. Both state coercion and the constitution of the public space of appearance significantly shaped C. P.'s and Ann's willingness to work together.[40] Finally, considerable political support was being mobilized from the federal government down to the local city level for interracial dialogue (and in the cities this, of course, meant dialogue among poor and working-class citizens).

All of these things—both the profound ways in which others had solicited Ann Atwater's particular presence into the world as someone worthy of being witnessed and the political conditions just described—crystallized to form conditions of receptivity so that the miracle of which humans are capable—of beginning something new—might appear in the form of Ann's responsive engagement of C. P. during the charette. That day Ann created a kind of political togetherness in which she stood "neither for nor against" C. P. but "with [him]."

As a space of appearance in which we responsively countenance one another, however, the public sphere is vulnerable. We are subject to many sins and temptations—all forms of oblivion—that darken and foreclose this space: disregard, comfortability, indifference, stupidity, laziness, and active hatred, all of which make of others (and of ourselves) fictions and phantasms.

Such forms of oblivion have their deepest affinity with the figure of the tyrant. All are rooted in the pleasure of the tyrannical self who, Arendt argues, "hav[ing] no desire to excel and lack[ing] all passion for distinction" finds it "so pleasant to rise above the company of all men" (*OR*, 120). Hence, although the tyrant might emerge where politics had once been, and in this sense appear to initiate a new order of things, this emergence can never be action in Arendt's sense because tyranny has no capacity to illuminate human existence. In fact, all it inaugurates are further, more intransigent forms of oblivion. All of which is to say there is nothing, strictly speaking, new, certainly nothing miraculous, nothing redemptive about it. Indeed, the human world is ever threatened with drifting toward becoming tyrannically sutured, closed to the unique particularity of human strivings and overcomings. This "drift" is the background-normal against which the exceptional act appears. And such tyranny, and the oblivion upon which it depends, is one of the primary ways in which domination is sustained.

Arendt's conception of the political passion par excellence is precisely the antipode of this tyrannical pleasure: the passion for distinction or the desire to excel (OR, 119–20). This passion drives humans into the world with others, and it is this, she suggests, that makes us feel pleasure in the company of others and the world which we, together, constitute(OR, 120). But is this pleasure a pleasure in being countenanced? Is this desire a desire to make one's presence felt, a desire, as, for example, Bonnie Honig argues, to individuate? Honig writes, in her interpretation of Arendt's agonal passion for distinction, "This process of individuation is not *for* an audience, though any set of actions or performances may be witnessed by one. It is for the self who in concert with others like herself gains individuation, and for others who are 'enabled to do the same by way of these shared, if also conflicted, practices of support and struggle.' "[41] Here there exists too large an element of solipsism, and little of Arendt's generative notion of action. The passion to excel appears to be too easily exhausted by the desire to individuate, a desire that, for example, cannot capture Ann Atwater's driving passion in the moment I dramatized. The problem might be broached by asking the question, but at what, in contrast to apolitical or antipolitical tyrants, do political actors excel? They excel, following Arendt, at being together "with" others by being neither for nor against them; they excel at constituting a difficult "common" world. And for *this* kind of superiority we must see and engage with others. Seeing, or being a certain kind of active witness, is the indispensable excellence. Thus, in a move that transcends Arendt's work by thinking through it, we might formulate this nonsolipsistic political desire par excellence as the desire to be seen *because you see*. To excel is to excel at seeing one's world, at seeing the specificity of others' presence in the world.

To formulate political excellence in this way points us toward the ethical importance of the public sphere: as the place in which we are passionately driven, in the effort to make our own presence felt, toward the presence of others. In a comprehensive, even utopian sense, to excel at seeing means to countenance all relevant perspectives on any given phenomenon, to be attentive to the worldly density, including the dimension of the past, within which the political issue in question resides. This formulation of political excellence puts critical pressure on the so very common phenomenon that groups exhibit—on the one hand a kind of internal passion to excel in which they deeply desire to excel at seeing but only really care about seeing others in their group (although this itself requires constant policing of their members, as exemplified by the death threats that C. P. received from fellow Klansmen after agreeing to co-chair the charette), and on the other a tyrannical pleasure (that is, oblivion), toward nonmembers. Such group-based forms of oblivion are particularly pernicious because they have an exceedingly negative effect on our ability to illuminate the world when, as we so often need to, our understanding must extend beyond our group borders. The more ensconced we become within our group, the more difficult it becomes, however developed our political passion to excel might be toward *our* group, to sustain the imaginative resources necessary to have a sense of anyone else's being in the world. The group "rises above" the world of others and repetitiously confirms its own presence and perspectives.

To be successfully driven toward the presence of others is to heighten, therefore, our sense of their reality and of the world we together inhabit, however skilled some might be in refusing to acknowledge others. It is thus not merely your example of individuation (as Honig suggests) that allows others in turn to individuate themselves. For that, your own group might suffice. It is the *way* you *see*, the way you countenance others: that you make your presence felt by refusing to reproduce the oblivion of others, whether this oblivion arises from indifference, willed ignorance, fear, normalization, group-based tyranny, or some other source. To excel politically is to make one's presence felt by resonating the web of human relationships surrounding the phenomenon in question.

Transformative Solicitations

But what *way* is this? How should we countenance others? We best help engender the presence of others to us just as Arendt argues—by being neither for nor against them—for this kind of phenomenological attentiveness constitutes a space, to be sure, as Arendt says, of appearance but also, and more dynamically, a space of solicitation. And what we solicit is that those we countenance loosen their grip on *what* they are so as to enable them to become a more distinctive *who*. This we do by suspending our expectation that *what* we know them to be will determine their actions, while at the same time retaining our knowledge of the world out of which they struggle to rise, struggle to make a specific response to our particular solicitation. Thus the elusive quality of who someone "is" only arises out of and in relationship to our background expectations. Arendt sometimes obfuscates, in my view, this crucial relationship between what and who we are. She often appears to write as if what we are should be entirely left behind in specifically political appearance.[42] But to attempt to deliver political appearance of this background of "what" would simultaneously deprive it of the context within which "who" one is appears distinct. As others have adeptly argued, who we are emerges out of how we live our "whats," how we live what life has thrown at us—our class, our race, the specific nature of our times, political dilemmas, and so on.[43] Who we are is always about how we respond to that which has been given. So, for example, in suspending her deep political animosity toward C. P., the Klansman, as she engaged him, while simultaneously remaining fully aware of what his life had been and what it had made him,[44] Ann Atwater retained the necessary context within which, in turn, to comprehend C. P.'s response in its fullest meaning. For retrospective political understanding, this attentiveness to what someone is is also crucial. To know, for example, in great detail *what* in this sense was given to Ann Atwater and C. P. Ellis, respectively, is to really *see* the courage they both exhibited as they moved to countenance one another; it is to be confronted mightily with the exceptional quality of their action qua phenomenon.

Still, despite this important emphasis on retaining, as we countenance, a sense of *what* a person is, the utopian yearning in Arendt's basic argument for a kind of suspension of this "whatness" as key to countenancing another is crucial. In my formulation, to countenance another is to solicit the potentially unique way that person might live, might negotiate what life has given him or her. And to solicit this, our comportment cannot be governed by a disposition of opposition or favoring because we need to create a space in which to lodge our *own* hopeful, transformative expectation. We must strive toward an ideal of being "neither for nor against."[45] So, to countenance well is both to suspend our reliance on *what* we know others to be while simultaneously retaining the worldly context within which their lives have been embedded. Only then might great action or, the "specific meaning of each deed," emerge. Only in soliciting others' presence in this manner might we see manifest, in turn, particular responses that could renew our sense of what it means to be a human person, free in an inhospitable world that has more often than not succumbed to the sins and temptations of oblivion, to forms of domination.

I say only that this way of countenancing *might* renew our sense of human freedom, for we might indeed witness someone largely stamped by oblivion, someone who so greases the wheels of worldly tyranny that whatever is distinct about how they live what they've been given is politically trivial. This is, of course, our risk, and it is one of which we must become fully apprised in order to fortify ourselves against disappointment at our always too intransigent world. Hope lies in the solicitation, in a demand embedded in this kind of engagement with others that has the potential to transform the quality of our own and of others' being in the world. To elucidate that demand, we will return to C. P. Ellis's bewilderment when Ann Atwater yelled at the black youths. At this moment he was, as he said, no longer sure of what the word crazy meant. To have a black woman call out to those young black boys to learn about why the Klan thinks what it thinks turned his world upside down. All the primary stabilizers were removed. A deed was done, and it was simultaneously the creation of the kind of public space that Arendt theorizes—one C. P. characterized as "crazy." His description is apt, for it is the feeling of freedom, although it would take C. P. a whole year after the charette to understand it. Ann's deed helped C. P. to "act," provided him with, to recall Arendt's words, "an occasion to act," lodged a demand. It was a transformative solicitation. Why?

The recognition Ann Atwater gave C. P. Ellis created a novel quality of space for him in relationship to others—specifically blacks. Not a space for comfort, but one for dignity and legitimacy, it said, "You have your reasons; who are you? Let me learn how you see the world, that I can know why you do what you do. I *want* to see you, and that, my fellow citizen, is my freedom. It is also my excellence; it is what makes you, crazily, admire me, be inspired, feel solicited and challenged." The *deinon* quality of human particularity appeared in Ann's act. And C. P. responded by *wanting* Ann to see him.[46] To achieve this, however, he had to countenance her. And to do so he had to look at himself. Here we have a mutual provocation that engenders for each the specific particularity of the other, yet does so in a transformative fashion, for C. P. found it impossible to remain the same while showing himself to Ann. To look at Ann was to see a poor person with goals much like his own—to ensure that her children and her people's children got the best possible education. Furthermore, it was to see a person with great generosity, one who had engaged in an extraordinary act of freedom that itself illuminated, like no other deed had done, the specific nature of their shared world and the perpetuation of powerful mutual oblivion upon which it rested.[47] C. P. saw a person who had none of the demonic powers he had attributed to blacks, a person who, in fact, was transgressing and confounding all of what he had thought he knew about African Americans. Ann's act was transformative, redemptive. To return to Merleau-Ponty's formulation, it thwarted power by an extraordinary appeal to freedom.

There is something in the provision of the sort of countenancing that Atwater offered and Arendt theorized that calls forth others' will to action, something in the quality of presence that gives others courage to believe that their hope of being received—with all their particular failings, their poor responses to what their fate in time has slotted for them—will be fulfilled. And in this faith lies the first step toward the reality of others, and a reckoning with one's own failings, one's own oblivions. But this kind of countenancing also lodges a demand that I, the one who countenances, be included in that circle of humanity that matters, and in this, too, it solicits a free response in turn.

The specifically political kind of togetherness that Arendt theorizes promises that we need not remain latent as the particular unique beings we potentially "are" in relation to the specific world of others. Politically this means that this kind of mutuality (mutual countenancing) may enable individuals to resist being made by worldly formations of power into phantasms in the interest of manipulation and domination. And it may make individuals more able to resist turning others likewise into such phantasms, into instruments of their own design—a process that ultimately consigns the phantom-maker and the phantom to oblivion. It is this resistance and the promise it bears—that the human capacity to begin shall be rewarded—that constitutes the greatness of political action. Not mysterious in any absolute sense, though miracle-like, the mutual countenancing of Arendtian political togetherness stimulates great action and illuminates human existence.

Without this illumination the pragmatic purposes of politics are more difficult to pursue. Indeed, the power of Arendt's aesthetic theory of politics lies partly in the way it shows us that this "deeper" significance of the public realm makes the pragmatic art of politics more possible. Without the illumination of Arendtian political togetherness, the political world will be less a space for common action and concerted movement, for the generation of the power that comes through the initiating acts of free citizens, more a place of world alienation. Whatever banding together is possible will remain too enclaved, too group-fortified against the kind of transformative political effects needed for change to be pragmatically and effectively pursued.[48]

To return, once again, to our story, the ultimate practical political effect of the charette on C. P. was that he went on to organize black *and* white workers across North Carolina. In so doing, he helped generate power between these two historically hostile groups by making them visible to each other. Such generation of power is the only means by which our "civilization of productivity" and the forms of domination on which it depends can be resisted. Before the charette, C. P.'s capacity to effectively engage in pragmatic political action aimed at economic and political change was deformed by the distorted nature of the public world in which he lived. The charette illuminated his world, as I have argued, in novel and vital ways, opening possibilities for action heretofore absolutely closed to him. And although the history of unionism in the United States and elsewhere shows that the great temptation is to use union power alone to bargain for a larger piece of the pie and not to contest the organization of our shared lives around life as the highest good,[49] if anything can counter the process character of our world, it is the generation of power between formerly hostile or indifferent groups of people. The great power of the story of C. P. Ellis and Ann Atwater, *as* of Arendt's aesthetic theory of politics, is the way they singularly identify the insult of oblivion as the greatest of political sins and thereby keep the practical and ethical focus on the relations of power that sustain our capacity for freedom.

Arendt relies heavily on the faculty of imagination as the capacity that will enable us to make present in the interior space of our mind the complex web of human relationships that give rise to the rich phenomenality of the issue in question as we seek to know how to act in relationship to it. The story of Ann Atwater and C. P. Ellis certainly suggests that the oblivion that sustains human domination cannot be fought with a mental faculty alone. Nor can it be fought with a mental faculty informed by just any kind of knowledge of others. Despite the fact that Ann and C. P. had encountered each other in public many times over a period of ten years, they were unable to hold the space of the world open to each other until they were brought abruptly face to face in the intense public space the charette created. This itself, it seems to me, points to the power of Arendt's conception of public togetherness in which we are neither for nor against one another. There, in the context of public conversation concerning the fate of Durham's public schools, Ann and C. P. could ask the preeminently political question: How are *we*, your people and mine, going to *be* together? This kind of political experience, together with imagination, makes redemptive action possible.

The question remaining is what excelling at both this mental and worldly kind of presencing requires of us in the way of specifically political responsibilities.

The Obligation to Renew

> Without knowing the other's "world," one does not know the other, and without knowing the other one is really alone in the other's presence because the other is only dimly present to one.
>
> —MARIA LUGONES, "Playfulness, 'World'-Travelling and Loving Perception"

Here Maria Lugones attempts to draw attention to a feature of contemporary life that Hannah Arendt believed was indeed a mass phenomenon—

loneliness. Sharing a belief in the importance of political responses to this widespread problem in the form of creating public-political space and forms of togetherness, both Arendt and Lugones theorize such isolation and loneliness in order to draw attention to it *as* an experience. They share the belief that we live in a world ill-equipped to recognize it as such, a world little able to feel its deprivation as a specific form of suffering. We might recognize this kind of pathos in the story of the man recently arrested in New York City in connection with the brutal attack and murder of several women. John J. Royster beat his victims' heads into the pavement. This was his signature. Yet when people who knew him were asked to describe this man, it appears he made "no particular impression on anyone."[50] This is an extraordinary fact in relation to a man who confessed to doing these things. As I say, we who read about this man may feel the pathos of *his* loneliness, but do we feel, are we attentive to a kind of chilly loneliness in how "dimly present" this man and others like him are to *us*? To ask *this* question is to move toward an understanding of a loss that, once identified, calls for intensive reflection on the nature of our political responsibility, on our responsibility to a kind of political togetherness that is an ethical response to such loneliness and that feels liable for it. We must better feel the liability for us of indifference. That there is such a liability Patricia Williams expresses in the context of white indifference to black existence: "I was left with the impression that no one existed for them [a group of whites] who could not be governed by their intentions. While acknowledging the apparent lack of malice in their behavior, I can't help thinking that it is a liability as much as a luxury to live without interaction. To live so completely impervious to one's impact on others is a fragile privilege."[51] Two questions interpose themselves here: What is the liability that we, in our "loneliness," suffer, and what responsibility do we have to countenance the existence of others? For what are we liable?

In the most essential sense, Arendt's thinking bends us toward loss of meaningfulness as the answer to the question of what liability we suffer in enacting oblivion toward others and thus proliferating loneliness. In suffering loneliness as an individual or as a group, we are without the experience of others that might help us understand them, ourselves, or events in our not-too-common world. Alone, unresponsive to the always complex and changing human plurality relevant to any political question or problem, we can only recapitulate the world as we see it, a world that, by definition, will be dimmer, not merely partial. Both why we think what we do and how others think, what makes sense to them, will be beyond us. So a dimly lit world, a world we fail to adequately comprehend and thus to which our particular presence remains largely impervious, will make *us* its instruments. We do not, as free beings might, establish, as Arendt puts it, "a reality of our own" (*OT,* xxi). Full of oblivion toward ourselves and others, we reproduce a world too opaque and unopened to us as potentially free particular beings.

If such are our liabilities, for what are we liable? What, politically speaking, are our essential responsibilities? What key ethical demands does being a political being place upon us?

Anything we might wish to say about an Arendtian understanding of political responsibility has to be qualified by the twofold character of human action in a world of plural others: action's irreversibility and its unpredictability. When we broach the question of responsibility we are not talking, therefore, about sovereign responsibility, responsibility on the model of mastery, but about responsibility as it arises out of the complex condition of human plurality. And in this sense the two moral precepts that, Arendt argues, arise out of "the will to live together with others" and that are not imported from outside the realm of action—promising, in which we bind ourselves to one another in the face of an uncertain future, and forgiveness, in which we release each other from the inevitable unforeseen effects or trespasses of our acts—are both primary practices of political responsibility that take as their central condition that of plurality (*HC,* 246).

Oblivion, then, is endemic to the condition of human plurality. Tangled in our complex finitude, we know not, in any exhaustive sense, what we do; we cannot master this density. Our political responsibility is, however, *to* that density in the sense that we hold ourselves liable for not perpetuating old or inaugurating new forms of oblivion *by* moving *toward* that density of plurality. It is right to feel rage at a world that radically relegates some to enclaves and actively nourishes oblivion on the part of others. We must publicly identify the liabilities in these conditions, feel their insult, and let that feeling move us toward others and toward public ends. We need to prioritize the effort to create political structures in which public communication—be it over schools, plant closings, pollution, traffic, or foreign sweatshops—can vigorously occur, in which all those party to the concern at hand can seriously and deeply pursue *the* political issue of how the "we" in question is going to *be* together. There, in such political structures and spaces, we can struggle to interrupt those forms of oblivion that repetitively keep others' specificity barely if at all present to us. And we can name and cultivate public pleasures and sensibilities.

Our political responsibility is, then, to hold the space of the world open to the possible communicative presence of others so that we become more vividly, more comprehensibly present to one another. As citizens we have an obligation to renew our ability to share the world with others by stimulating and soliciting the capacity of others to begin. And this is potentially, as the story of Ann Atwater and C. P. Ellis shows, redemptive in the sense of inviting illuminating comprehension of the forms of oblivion upon which human domination inevitably depends. Political responsibility is responsibility to the possibility of this kind of redemptive renewal.

The existential reward for taking responsibility in this manner is a sense of relatedness, a sense of belonging of a particular type: the kind we feel when our sense of reality is made fuller, deeper. Enacting this kind of responsibility and being active witness to its various forms as they appear on the human stage should draw us. As instances of the difficult freedom of which humans are capable, they speak to us of the fragile beauty of our need for a kind of politics in which we may, in soliciting display, make our appearance before others and bear witness, in turn, to theirs. In this vulnerable mutuality the reality of our elementary living-together can shine.

The story of political friendship between Ann and C. P. is a story to be told because it is a story about the difficult—indeed, miraculous—assumption of this kind of political responsibility on the part of free beings. And if we are to continue to actively shape a world we can hold in common, not only must we struggle to assume this kind of responsibility, but we must tell the stories of others whose acts exemplify it as well. We must "retrieve memories of public action"[52] that cultivate political pleasures and passions, memories that promise that our ability to belong to one another, care for our lives together, and act deliberately together has not abandoned us in our times.

Notes

Chapter 1. On Gates and Oblivion: Ethical and Political Challenges in Late Modernity

1. See "While You Were Sleeping," *Harper's*, December 1995, 44–52.
2. Ibid., 51. A handful of Juarez's journalists have been risking their lives to document and publicize the extremity of the city's violence. Their photographs have been recently published in *Juarez: The Laboratory of the Future*, ed. Charles Bowden, Eduardo Galeano, and Noam Chomsky (New York, 1998).
3. "While You Were Sleeping," 52.
4. Ibid., 51, 52.
5. I am drawing heavily on Charles Bowden's description.
6. The existing literature on gated communities is small but growing. See Edward Blakely and Mary Snyder, *Fortress America* (Washington, D.C., 1997); Evan McKenzie, *Privatopia* (New Haven, Conn., 1994); Michael Pollan, "Town Building Is No Mickey Mouse Operation," *New York Times Magazine*, 14 December 1997, 56–88; and Timothy Egan, "Many Seek Security in Private Communities," *New York Times*, 3 September 1995, 1, 10.
7. These groups were conducted by researchers Mary Gail Snyder of San Francisco and Professor Edward Blakely of the University of Southern California. See Egan, "Many Seek Security," 10.
8. Ibid.
9. Residents of gated communities have an exaggerated sense of vulnerability to crime, although they share this with their fellow citizens. In a 1995 Time/CNN poll, 90 percent of Americans reported believing that crime rates were rising. In fact, for all categories of crime surveyed except simple assault, household larceny above $50, and car theft, crime rates have declined since 1981. Notably this is true for all violent crimes: rape, robbery, and aggravated assault. See Jon D. Hull, "The State of The Union," *Time*. 30 January 1995, 63; and Bureau of Justice Statistics, "Highlights from Twenty Years of Surveying Crime Victims," *National Crime Victimization Survey* (Washington, D.C., 1993).

10. See Mike Davis, "Hell Factories in the Field," *Nation*, 20 February 1995, 229–34.

11. Ibid., 234.

12. Ibid.

13. In California as in many states, this number contains especially high percentages of black and Hispanic citizens.

14. Ibid.

15. See Robert Putnam, "Bowling Alone: America's Declining Social Capital," *Journal of Democracy* 6 (January 1995): 65–78.

16. For work on social capital that resists such commodification and is attentive to qualitative distinctions between kinds of social capital, see Theda Skocpol's historical analysis of civil associations in the United States from 1790 to the present. Skocpol argues that what has declined is not civil association per se but associations that facilitate cross-class interaction, that link face-to-face relations through a federated organizational structure to state, regional, and national ones, and organizations that facilitate two-way communication between leaders and those led. See "Civic America, Then and Now," paper presented at the Ninety-Fourth Annual Meeting of the American Political Science Association, Boston, 1998.

17. Berel Lang develops this point briefly but succinctly in his essay "Hannah Arendt and the Politics of Evil," in *Hannah Arendt: Critical Essays*, ed. Lewis P. Hinchman and Sandra K. Hinchman (Albany, 1994). For Arendt's most concentrated articulation of this point, see *The Origins of Totalitarianism* 456–57.

18. I use the term, as does Arendt, in a very elemental sense, referring to our ability to take in or countenance "everything that happens on earth" (*OT*, xxx). That is to say, it refers to our capacity to experience, to feel the impact of what comes to pass. The frame of reference remains for Arendt the emancipation from reality that she thought totalitarian ideology together with totalitarian practices of terror made possible. See especially her final chapter "Ideology and Terror" in *The Origins of Totalitarianism*.

19. The revised text of the speech, "On Humanity in Dark Times: Thoughts about Lessing," appears in *Men in Dark Times*.

20. See Lisa Disch's excellent essay "On Friendship in 'Dark Times,' " in *Feminist Interpretations of Hannah Arendt*, ed. Bonnie Honig (University Park, Pa., 1995). My discussion is deeply indebted to her analysis.

21. For a full discussion of this point see *The Origins of Totalitarianism*, 209–302.

22. Deceptive because Arendt is finessing entirely Lessing's deep embroilment in Enlightenment faiths and (ingeniously) rewriting the tradition to which she is heir. Lisa Disch calls this maneuver "a delicious irony." See "On Friendship," 288.

23. In the context of her speech it was, of course, Arendt's own "opinion" and the experiences of her group and generation that were embattled.

24. I am paraphrasing here the work of Jean-François Lyotard. See *The Postmodern Condition: A Report on Knowledge* (Minneapolis, 1984).

25. *Deinon* is difficult to translate into English. It is etymologically related to *deos*, "fear," but it has many sides. In different contexts it can refer to "the dazzling brilliance of the human intellect, [to] the monstrousness of evil, [to] the terrible

power of fate." I am following both the translation and the insightful discussion of *Antigone* and "things *deinon*" in Martha Nussbaum's *The Fragility of Goodness: Luck and Ethics in Greek Tragedy and Philosophy* (Cambridge, 1986), 51–82.

26. Ibid., 52.

27. Plato, *Symposium*, in *The Collected Dialogues*, ed. Edith Hamilton and Huntington Cairns (Princeton, N.J., 1961), 563.

28. *Signs*, trans. R. C. McLeary (Evanston, Ill., 1964), 180.

29. I might add that this was true not only for the citizens of Hamburg but for Arendt herself. Her willingness, even gladness to enter into relationship with this "stained" people was not unmixed with a feeling of foreboding.

30. George Kateb argues that the aesthetic feeling that forms the "substratum of Arendt's thought" is gratitude, a kind of holy appreciation for everything that has been given. He calls this a "non-aesthetic sense of beauty" in which things are "beautiful in the sense of being worthy of acceptance and fit for gratitude." In this focus on a nonaesthetic relationship to things as worthy of acceptance, Kateb captures something essential about both Arendt's feeling and about the aesthetic sensibility of tragic pleasure as I elaborate it in what follows. He reads Arendt, however, as a theorist of reconciliation and quietistic acceptance of the human condition, confusing her call to face up to "what is" with a politically and ethically problematic acquiescence. See *Hannah Arendt: Politics, Conscience, Evil* (Totowa, N.J., 1984), esp. 163–78.

31. This is the phrase Merleau-Ponty uses to describe the level of experience phenomenological work seeks to reach. See *Phenomenology of Perception*, trans. Colin Smith (London, 1962), vii.

32. For an insightful account of Arendt's method of thinking, see Ernst Vollrath, "Hannah Arendt and the Method of Political Thinking," *Social Research* 44 (1977): 160–82. See also the excellent discussion in Ronald Beiner's "Hannah Arendt on Judging," in Arendt's *Lectures on Kant's Political Philosophy* (Chicago, 1982).

33. All of what I say about reading tragedy is, of course, true for spectators of tragic drama.

34. The greatness of *Antigone* goes even beyond this, for if we read as authentic and not interpolated the much disputed passage in which Antigone reveals her absolutely idiosyncratic and thus impious understanding of her divine duties, we see how masterfully and fully Sophocles sensed the difficulties of political life. Not only is its field constituted through perspectives born of differences of power and worldly location, differences that are group-related and inflected. But its density and perspectival quality is born also of our vexing and miraculous idiosyncrasy. For a discussion of the passage in question, see Robert Fagles, "Introduction" to *Three Theban Plays by Sophocles* (New York, 1982).

35. Another way to put this is that what Mary McCarthy called "the medieval element" in Arendt's thinking, her vexing and stimulating propensity for categorical distinctions, is far less pronounced in this later work. See Arendt's "On Hannah Arendt," in *Hannah Arendt: The Recovery of The Public World*, ed. Melvyn A. Hill (New York, 1979).

36. Quoted frequently in chapter 1 of *Thinking* are Merleau-Ponty's *Signs* and *The Visible and the Invisible*, trans. Alphonso Lingis (Evanston, Ill., 1968), and Adolf Portmann's *Das Tier als soziales Wesen*, (Zurich, 1953).

37. *Political Theory and Postmodernism* (Cambridge, 1991), 20.

38. See Hanna Pitkin, "Justice: On Relating Private and Public," in *Hannah Arendt: Critical Essays*, ed. Lewis P. Hinchman and Sandra K. Hinchman (Albany, 1994).

39. Arendt herself sometimes seemed puzzled by this problem. See "On Hannah Arendt," 215–38.

40. In this respect, my argument goes a good way in addressing Mary Dietz's claim that despite the power of Arendt's theory of politics as a kind of theater in which freedom can appear, her public realm theory is "vulnerable to charges of aestheticism, sentimentalism, and self-defeat... *not* because it rescues theatrical performance in the face of reductive and routinizing life processes but because it celebrates the 'practical purposelessness' of speech and action and the transcendence of 'mere productive activity' in politics *as it does so*." See "The Slow Boring of Hard Boards: Methodical Thinking and The Work of Politics," *American Political Science Review* 88 (1994): 880.

41. In light of this fact it is remarkable that a good deal of Arendt scholarship barely mentions her aestheticization of political life. See Margaret Canovan's very early book, *The Political Thought of Hannah Arendt* (London, 1974), and Leah Bradshaw, *Acting and Thinking: The Political Thought of Hannah Arendt* (Toronto, 1989). Other scholars of her work set her aestheticization of political life at the center of their inquiry but either fail to develop their initially bold assertions about the relationship between politics and aesthetics or do so until what they hold to be its amorality is no longer tenable, at which point Arendt must be rescued, her notion of public citizenship "stripped" of its "theatrical dressing." See Bhikhu Parekh, *Hannah Arendt and the Search for a New Political Philosophy* (Atlantic Heights, N.J., 1981), and Shiraz Dossa, *The Public Realm and the Public Self: The Political Theory of Hannah Arendt* (Waterloo, Ontario, 1989).

42. Lionel Abel, "The Aesthetics of Evil: Hannah Arendt on Eichmann and the Jews," *Partisan Review* 30 (1963): 211–30.

43. Daniel Bell, "The Alphabet of Justice," *Partisan Review* 30 (1963): 417–29.

44. Martin Jay, "Hannah Arendt," *Partisan Review* 45 (1978): 348–68.

45. Kateb, *Hannah Arendt*, 28–44.

46. See Seyla Benhabib, "Models of Public Space: Hannah Arendt, the Liberal Tradition, and Jürgen Habermas," in *Habermas and the Public Sphere*, ed. Craig Calhoun (Cambridge, Mass., 1992), 178. See also Habermas, "Hannah Arendt's Communication Concept Power," *Social Research* 44 (1977): 3–24.

47. Dana Villa, "Beyond Good and Evil: Arendt, Nietzsche, and the Aestheticization of Political Action," *Political Theory* 20 (1992): 274–308.

48. Bonnie Honig, *Political Theory and the Displacement of Politics* (Ithaca, N.Y., 1993), 80.

49. "Beyond Good and Evil," 276.

50. *Arendt and Heidegger: The Fate of the Political* (Princeton, N.J., 1995), 106.

51. "Beyond Good and Evil," 288.

52. This Villa shares with Margaret Canovan and Ronald Beiner, among others. See Canovan, *The Political Thought of Hannah Arendt*, and Beiner, "Hannah Arendt on Judging."

53. This is the essence of George Kateb's argument. See *Hannah Arendt*, especially Chapter 1.

54. See Villa, "Beyond Good and Evil," and Parekh, *Hannah Arendt and the Search*.

55. See Habermas, "Hannah Arendt's Communications Concept," and Benhabib, "Models of Public Space."

56. See, for example, her speculative reflections at the end of *On Revolution* as to whether a political elite, self-selected from an open public sphere on the basis of their demonstrated concern for public over private life, might not be a more realistic way of saving public life from the corrosion of private individuals than universal representative democracy (277–81).

57. For the best argument about this theoretical and practical deficiency in Arendt's work, see Mary Dietz, "Slow Boring of Hard Boards."

58. For such critiques see Pitkin, "Justice"; Benhabib, "Models of Public Space"; and Mildred Bakan, "Hannah Arendt's Concepts of Work and Labor," in *Hannah Arendt: The Recovery of the Public World*, ed. Melvyn A. Hill (New York, 1979).

59. Her endorsement of radical democracy takes, of course, explicit form in her celebration of the public sphere created by council politics, the student antiwar movement, the civil rights movement, and even, though in accommodated form, in her advocacy for global federalism. For an extended defense of Arendt as a theorist of grass-roots democracy, see Jeffrey Isaac, "Oases in the Desert: Hannah Arendt on Democratic Politics," *American Political Science Review* 88 (1994): 156–68.

Chapter 2. Aesthetic Provocation, Plurality, and Our Sense of the Real

1. The most significant, though incomplete exception being *The Life of the Mind*.

2. "On Hannah Arendt," 313.

3. Compare this formulation from her final work with the following call from the preface to *The Origins of Totalitarianism*, her first published book: "Human dignity needs a new guarantee which can be found only in a new political principle, in a new *law on earth*, whose validity this time must comprehend the whole of humanity while its power must remain strictly limited, rooted in and controlled by newly defined territorial entities" (*OT*, xxxi; my italics).

4. For a critique of Arendt's conception of nature, see Fred Dolan, "Strange Power: Philosophy and the Image of a Break with the Past: Arendt, Valery, Benjamin, Kant," paper presented at the American Political Science Association's annual meeting, San Francisco, 1996. Dolan draws on recent developments in physics and biology and suggests that instead of eternal laws and automatic functioning, nature is more like "a world of sheer becoming, eventfulness and irreversability" (13). This does present an important challenge to Arendt's work and points to a simplification in her understanding of nature. Nonetheless, the qualities she identifies also seem phenomenologically correct.

5. Throughout *The Human Condition,* Arendt evinces very little awe for the novel creations of *homo faber.* Their novelty is of a very different quality from that of the new beginnings inaugurated by those who act.

6. In *The Human Condition,* Arendt does provocatively argue that subjects are both actors and sufferers, but the argument concerns the nature of political action and is not intended as a general ontological account.

7. Hans-Georg Gadamer's discussion of play was likewise influenced by Portmann's new science. See *Truth and Method,* trans. Joel Weisenheimer and Donald G. Marshall (New York, 1991).

8. See *Signs,* 166–67, and *Visible and the Invisible,* 9, 133, 141, 204, 249, 245–47.

9. *Visible and the Invisible,* 139; my italics.

10. Ibid., 155.

11. Ibid., 260. For excellent commentary on Merleau-Ponty's "new ontology," see James Schmidt, *Maurice Merleau-Ponty: Between Phenomenology and Structuralism* (New York, 1985), and Romand Coles, *Self/Power/Other: Political Theory and Dialogical Ethics* (Ithaca, N.Y., 1992).

12. Those works are *The Visible and the Invisible* and *Signs.*

13. *Visible and the Invisible,* 170.

14. *Signs,* 22.

15. *Visible and the Invisible,* 259; compare *The Life of the Mind: Thinking,* 33.

16. That Arendt's ontology is thought directly to counter the problems that in her view define the modern age is clear from the following quote. Speaking about Cartesian doubt, she writes,

> It now turned out that without confidence in the senses neither faith in God nor trust in reason could any longer be secure, because the revelation of both divine and rational truth had always been implicitly understood to follow the awe-inspiring simplicity of man's relationship with the world: I open my eyes and behold the vision, I listen and hear the sound, I move my body and touch the tangibility of the world. If we begin to doubt the fundamental truthfulness and reliability of this relationship, which of course does not exclude errors and illusions but, on the contrary, is the condition of their eventual correction, none of the traditional metaphors for supersensual truth—be it in the eyes of the mind which can see the sky of ideas or the voice of conscience listened to by the human heart—can any longer carry its meaning.
>
> The fundamental experience underlying Cartesian doubt was the discovery that the earth, contrary to all direct sense experience, revolves around the sun. The modern age began when a man, with the help of the telescope . . . learned that his senses were not fitted for the universe. (*BPF,* 54–55)

17. Arendt's claim in this context may need clarification. Namely, that the only reality there is in an appearing world is that which appears to the senses. The philosophical idea of Being is just that—a thought-thing (*LMT,* 51)—and it is one of the metaphysical fallacies, as Arendt refers to them, that philosophers have concluded from the sheer activity of the invisible thinking process that there exist "things in themselves" that in their own intelligible sphere *are* as we "are" in a world of appearances (*LMT,* 44). This is *not* to say that thinking is nothing but rather that reality is not one of its properties, although its *effect* may certainly be, as I argue later in this chapter, to intensify our awareness of reality.

18. This was a central argument of Portmann's new science. See *Das Tier als soziales Wesen*.

19. It is easy to misunderstand Arendt here as having an expressivist theory of action relying on the notion of some essential kernel of truth buried deep within the self that is *pressed out* through theatrical self-display in speech and deed. Arendt distinguishes between two meanings of the term *self-display*, and it is crucial to understand that she relies on the first meaning of the term. She writes, "The word 'self-display,' like the German *Selbstdarstellung*, is equivocal: it can mean that I actively make my presence felt, seen, and heard, or that I display my*self*, something inside me that otherwise would not appear at all" (*LMT*, 29). I say this is crucial because it depicts the self's urge to make its being *in the world* felt.

20. Merleau-Ponty's "philosophy of depth" possesses far richer meditation on concealment, hiddenness, the "back side" of things than can be found in Arendt's work. This is true for both *Phenomenology of Perception* and *The Visible and the Invisible*. For an extended interpretation of the concept of depth in Merleau-Ponty in which dimensionality and the "back side" figure centrally, see Coles, *Self/Power/Other*.

21. While for humans language is the crucial medium in which this sensuous provocation that engenders the real manifests itself, not all language is in this regard by any means of a piece. Indeed, Arendt's reflections on speech might be understood as directed toward a revitalization of speaking's sensuous richness in its capacity to make real what occurs. She relates the wonderful story in which Demosthenes is told by a man how terribly he has been beaten. Demosthenes replies, "but you suffered nothing of what you tell me." On hearing this the man raised his voice and cried out, "I suffered nothing?" "Now," said Demosthenes, "I hear the voice of somebody who was injured and who suffered" (from Plutarch's *Lives*, quoted in *HC*, 26). Demosthenes' forthright denial on hearing the man drolly recount his hair-raising story speaks of the extent to which language can become drained of its evocative, engendering potential. The same thing is of course true for the written word.

22. As I have already noted, this ontological work receives no sustained elaboration until her final work, *The Life of the Mind*. As is evident from Arendt's account of action, however, the aesthetic provocation that governs free beings under the earthly condition of plurality and through which that very plurality and diversity is engendered is already in her political theory the unsaid ground.

23. Lest this sound too much like Rousseau's active and restless "artificial men" who, tyrannized by their passion for the esteem of others, have become emptied of any feeling of their own substantially, we should note the way Arendt thematizes this deliberately chosen "playing." She suggests that many of our choices (of how to play) are determined by the culture in which we live—that is, we choose them to please others. We are also inspired by the effort to please ourselves, or, alternatively, by the effort to persuade others to be pleased by what pleases us. Virtue, in any case, and the substantiality of the self as well, is constituted through a "promise to the world, to those to whom I appear, to act in accordance with my pleasure" (*LMT*, 36). As is evident from these multiple ways in which we experience pleasure, such a promise entails complex considerations, but the salient point in this context is that

the specific community by which we wish to be countenanced also importantly includes the self; our provocation with and in the world is always a response to our own appearingness as well. The extent to which Arendt conceptualized a kind of autonomy for the self is best explored in her reflections on thinking (see *The Life of the Mind*). The issue of her conception of the self is, however, complex. For a reading that fruitfully exaggerates its multiplicitous character, see Bonnie Honig, "Toward an Agonistic Feminism: Hannah Arendt and the Politics of Identity," in *Feminist Interpretations of Hannah Arendt*, ed. Bonnie Honig (University Park, Pa., 1995).

24. In her explicitly political theory Arendt identifies this particularity that emerges in the interstice as "who" we are. This is neither an original invulnerable identity nor one that emerges as purely historical. It is nonreducible to either "origin."

25. The phrase is Adrienne Rich's. See *Of Woman Born: Motherhood as Experience and Institution* (New York, 1976), 250.

26. This is agonistic but certainly not essentially egoistic, as it is born amid an enormous yearning for and vulnerability to the sensuous provocation of others.

27. I do not wish, owing to my focus here, to underplay the fact that these cognitive-purposive interests are complex and crucial, and that their formation, content, and socioeconomic preconditions must be theorized. This is a task for which Arendt's theoretical resources are weakest. For a critique of Arendt on this point, see Dietz, "Slow Boring of Hard Boards," 873–86.

28. Certainly, although Arendt theorizes this at the level of urge, its quality, potency, and effect vulnerably vary with life's social and historical conditions. In Chapter 3 I address Arendt's account of this vulnerability as it takes form in the modern world.

29. Merleau-Ponty draws us more deeply into the mystery of this faith than does Arendt. He says it is this faith, this "unjustifiable certitude of a sensible world common to us that is the seat of truth within us.... Communication makes us the witnesses of one sole world, as the synergy of our eyes suspends them on one unique thing. But in both cases, the certitude, entirely irresistible as it may be, remains absolutely obscure" (*The Visible and the Invisible*, 11).

30. For a very similar formulation see *The Human Condition*, 57.

31. This objectivity is to be understood, of course, in strict contrast to the "eunuchic" objectivity governing the social sciences (*BPF*, 53). I hasten to add that Arendt's deepest concerns were not in any simple sense with ontological confirmation. It is not only the assurance of the realness of things but the fullness and intensity of our perceptual experience of them that is of ethical interest to Arendt, to us. As I discuss in the following chapters, this depends on achieving certain kinds of engagements with others. Merleau-Ponty's work on depth and reversibility, with its two moments of facticity and dimensionality, bears much affinity with Arendt's account of objectivity and also greatly develops and amplifies it. All sensibles are dimensional, are aspects of, openings out upon the world. Merleau-Ponty writes, "Perception is not first a perception of *things*, but a perception of *elements* . . . of *rays of the world*, of things which are dimensions.... I *slip* on these elements and here I am in the *world*" (*The Visible and the Invisible*, 218).

32. In the final section of this chapter I discuss the ways in which the invisible world also contributes to our capacity to share the world in common. This capacity depends similarly on a kind of aesthetic provocation within the thinking self.

33. This paradoxical insight is one that, usually implicitly but sometimes explicitly, informs much of the vital work by women of color in the debate over whether and in what sense we can speak about a common world of women. From this vantage point, the effort by many white women to substantiate the claim to women's common world by reference to some shared experience or condition qua identity corrodes the kind of dialogue through which the common world of women might possibly emerge. See Audre Lorde, *Sister Outsider* (Trumansburg, N.Y., 1984); bell hooks, *Talking Back* (Boston, 1989); and Bernice Johnson Reagon "Coalition Politics: Turning the Century," in *Home Girls: A Black Feminist Anthology*, ed. Barbara Smith (New York, 1983), 356–58. For fascinating dialogue between white women and women of color that bears directly on this issue, see Chandra Mohanty and Biddy Martin, "Feminist Politics: What's Home Got to Do with It," in *Feminist Studies/Critical Studies*, ed. Teresa de Lauretis (Bloomington, Ind., 1986); and Minnie Bruce Pratt, "Identity, Skin, Blood, Heart," in *Yours in Struggle*, ed. Elly Bulkin, Minnie Bruce Pratt, and Barbara Smith (Brookline, N.Y., 1984).

34. As I have already noted, I am not concerned here with the second moment of aestheticism in Arendt's work, with the relationship between beauty and permanence, political judgment and particularity. An elaboration of these issues is absolutely central to a full account of her understanding of the common world, and would anchor somewhat more firmly but in no way absolutely the parameters of the common. I take up these issues in Chapter 4.

35. The structure of figure-ground, taken from Gestalt psychology, formed the essence of Merleau-Ponty's early monumental study of perception, but he did not theorize it in this way. Arendt's "necessity" would have been, in his view, too relentlessly ahistorical and static, inadequate to render our thoroughgoing incarnation in history.

36. It might be argued that what has changed is not the extent to which privileged people can insulate themselves from necessity's compulsion but the proportion of people who can do so. Such insulation is undoubtedly no longer only an elite privilege. But the radical replacement of human labor by machines that has made this possible has also driven underground the older form of (cruel) testimony to necessity's existence—namely, human subjection.

37. To object here that it is wrong to speak in this context of factuality because science will, in the future, solve these problems seems to me to quite obscure both the basic and crucial distinction between the human artifice and the world not of our own making, as well as the pressing nature of these problems at the present time. Indeed, the first obfuscation propels the second.

38. I discuss the implications of such denial for certain key capacities and experiences important to our ability to be citizens in a democratic polity in "Hannah Arendt, Feminist Theorizing, and the Debate over New Reproductive Technologies," *Polity* 28 (1995): 159–88.

39. Michael Denneny, "The Privilege of Ourselves: Hannah Arendt on Judgment," in *Hannah Arendt: The Recovery of the Public World*, ed. Melvyn A. Hill (New York. 1979), 269.

40. This point often goes unnoticed by Arendt's most careful readers. So, for example, Margaret Canovan writes, "Human beings, as Arendt stressed, are plural beings, unique individuals capable of constant surprises. Nevertheless, this individuality does not manifest itself in all aspects of life." See *Hannah Arendt: A Reinterpretation of Her Political Thought* (New York, 1992), 77.

41. In all this focus on our sensation of reality we should not overlook the fact that there are many worthy and essential experiences that do not intensify our awareness of reality in the manner of fullness and that nonetheless are important to our being human, love being perhaps the most strange (*HC*, 50). To meditate on this is to realize the specificity of the reality-intensifying capacities of public-political togetherness as Arendt attempts to theorize them.

42. See Adrienne Rich, "Conditions for Work: The Common World of Women," in *On Lies, Secrets, and Silence* (New York, 1979); Jean Bethke Elshtain, *Public Man, Private Woman* (Princeton, N.J., 1981); Wendy Brown, *Manhood and Politics: A Feminist Reading in Political Theory* (Totowa, N.J., 1988); and Mary O'Brien, *The Politics of Reproduction* (Boston, 1981). For a different, more multivocal reading of the body in Arendt, see Linda Zerilli, "The Arendtian Body," in *Feminist Interpretations of Hannah Arendt*, and Bonnie Honig, "Toward an Agonistic Feminism." For an interesting interpretation and overview of developments in feminist readings of Arendt, see Mary Dietz, "Feminist Receptions of Hannah Arendt," in *Feminist Interpretations of Hannah Arendt*.

43. See Bakan, "Hannah Arendt's Concepts."

44. It is, let me briefly add, both plausible and promising in this context to "marry" Arendt's phenomenology to a historical understanding of labor indebted to Marx so as to conceive labor and necessity as both possessing an eternal unchanging relentless quality and as a profound historically productive activity. Marriage between existential phenomenology and Marxism was, of course, at the heart of Merleau-Ponty's early and middle period, but these were not the periods that influenced Arendt. He subtly theorizes both the necessary and historically incarnate moments of bodily being in *Phenomenology of Perception*, although he does so in ways that do not raise the provocative questions Arendt's work does.

45. I focus on this text alone both because it is her most sustained theoretical consideration and because her formulations remain relatively consistent in *On Revolution*, the other text in which necessity figures centrally.

46. See *Public Realm and the Public Self*, 59.

47. Bonnie Honig and Hanna Pitkin have made a similar point. See Honig, "Arendt, Identity, and Difference," *Political Theory* 16 (1988): 77–98, and Pitkin, "Justice."

48. If this is the case, as I think it is, Arendt's use of Greek and Roman thought is best read heuristically rather than as representative of Arendt's views. For those who see a far closer substantive accord, see Pitkin, "Justice"; Elshtain, *Public Man, Private Woman;* and Terry Winant "The Feminist Standpoint: A Matter of Language," *Hypatia* 2 (1987): 123–48. See also Margaret Canovan's interesting discussion, informed

by Arendt's unpublished lectures, of the complexities of her theory of action and her relationship to Greek thought in *Hannah Arendt: A Reinterpretation*.

49. I am suggesting that Arendt distinguished between specifically human capabilities—speech and action—and a conception of living a fully human life.

50. Largely uninterested in the former, Arendt's text offers little direct nuanced insights. Indeed, she entertains the perhaps honest but outrageous thought that because we are all subject to necessity we are "entitled" to violence toward others if it serves to free us from our subjection (*HC*, 31). For beings such as ourselves, whose capacities for oblivion to the reality of others is so highly developed, Arendt's is a supremely dangerous position to pursue. And, in that form, she did so no further. Nonetheless, her complacency on this issue is the most morally disturbing aspect of her work. It is possible that this can be partially understood as her reaction against the utopian impulses in Marx's understanding of the origins of violence in, alternatively, human exploitation and in necessity. See *On Revolution*, 61–66.

51. See her essay "What Is Freedom?" (*BPF*, 169), in which she writes that "we can find traces and signs [of freedom] in almost all [human] activities." See also *The Human Condition*, 9.

52. The fact that she does not do so is, as I have indicated, a real weakness of her work and is not coincidental. Rather, it grows out of the experiences that frame and give powerful focus to, but also limit, her ethical horizons. As I have argued, those experiences I refer to are ontological: the irreality and insubstantiality of things in a totalitarian world governed by ideology and terror.

53. Menstruation is a powerful example in this context, and feminist reinterpretations of "the curse" bear some affinities to this dimension of Arendt's thinking.

54. The idea that Arendt's deployment of these metaphors signifies a patriarchal notion of the private as negative and subordinate cannot be sustained by a nuanced reading of her text. It is true, however, that Arendt does not attribute equal value to the dimension of life represented by *animal laborans* and that represented by the actor. Yet her exploration of the "non-privative" traits of private life was of deep significance to her understanding of our capacity to live fully human lives. See *The Human Condition*, 62.

55. For the development of these arguments in relation to new reproductive technologies, see my article "Hannah Arendt, Feminist Theorizing."

56. Margaret Canovan refers to "necessity" and "artificial necessity" to make this distinction. See *Hannah Arendt: A Reinterpretation*, 122–27.

57. This formulation from her final work is the most measured form in which her thesis appears. In others, the qualifying phrase "among the conditions" is absent, and therefore a far more ambitious and, in my view, overburdened thesis about the moral relevance of thinking is advanced. See, for example, Arendt, "Thinking and Moral Considerations," *Social Research* 51 (1984): 418.

58. I would add to this question, although Arendt did not, whether thinking might also make us capable of experiencing the old or the familiar anew. This angle seems of great significance insofar as, with habituation and familiarity, the reality of things recedes. The question is whether the activity of thinking might allow us to see the familiar in new ways.

59. "Thinking and Moral Considerations," 425.

60. This lack of systematic account will be unsurprising to students of Arendt. It is characteristic of her style of thinking that she considers the performance of thinking alone and from the inside. The strength of doing so lies, as will be evident, in her ability to identify its sources of autonomy; the weakness is that she achieves neither a synthetic nor systematic account of the range of conditions that thinking must be "among" in order to have the ethical power she wishes to attribute to it.

61. This manner of theorizing the "fit" is, of course, quite similar to the way I have argued that Arendt theorizes the "fit" between the aesthetic-existential drive to display and the provoking-receiving world. In both cases the fit is complex, the promise uncertain.

62. This account of desensing should not be confused with that of Descartes. Arendt referred to his *res cogitans* as a "fictitious creature, bodiless and forsaken" (*LMT*, 49) and drew extensively on Merleau-Ponty's critique of Descartes's "reduction" of perception to the "thought of perception" in which what was seen or felt was considered "*inexistent.*" The principle point on which they both agreed was that Descartes's effort to clear the thinking field of all presumptions and thus attain certainty could, as Merleau-Ponty put it, "never restore to us the 'there is' of the world." See *Visible and the Invisible*, 36.

63. Arendt goes so far as to claim that thinking, like the other mental activities, is unconditioned, by which she means it neither *directly* corresponds to the conditions of life or the world nor is necessitated or conditioned by my individual life or by the world (*LMT*, 70).

64. Nor, of course, does the more plebeian *nil admirari* of Roman thought succeed in bringing itself to bear on worldly reality. To the contrary, Stoicism, Epicurianism, and Skepticism were responses to the disintegration of worldly reality in the form of escape.

65. As she says, the question does not seek to find causes, for ultimately there is no answer to the casual question beyond the answer "Life itself." If we strip the various answers of their "doctrinal content," all we get, she suggests, is the confession of a need (*LMT*, 166). Rather, she is trying to elaborate the mechanism and experience of thinking.

66. Richard Bernstein argues that Arendt actually proposed two examplars of thinking—the other being Heidegger. This is too extravagant a claim given that the written evidence for it comes alone from her tribute to Heidegger published in the *New York Review of Books* on the occasion of his eightieth birthday. Still, Bernstein provocatively challenges the sufficiency of Arendt's theorization of the moral relevance of thinking by raising the case of Heidegger. See Bernstein, "The Banality of Evil Reconsidered," in *Hannah Arendt and the Meaning of Politics* (Minneapolis, 1997), 297–322. See also Margaret Canovan's insightful account of Arendt's decades-long internal wrestling with the political implications of philosophy, which Canovan, too, argues became crystallized in the opposition between Heidegger and Socrates, in *Hannah Arendt: A Reinterpretation*, 253–74. I address the question of Heidegger at the conclusion of these reflections.

67. This movement and being at home in it constitutes the fundamental difference between Heidegger and Socrates. Although these things do not change the *structure* of thinking, they do indeed, as I argue in more detail, change the quality.

68. Indeed, Arendt's claim is even stronger—namely, that to mistake these propositions for moral insights is to try to draw our moral bearings from the insights of thinking alone, something that is wholly insufficient to guide action in the world. See *The Life of the Mind: Thinking*, 181.

69. See "Personal Responsibility under Dictatorship," *Listener*, 6 August 1964, 187.

70. Arendt believed that moral collapse in Nazi Germany was nearly total, a fact she thought would only be grasped by facing the extent to which the collapse occurred not only in the oppressor group but in the victims as well. Arendt's effort in her report on Eichmann's trial to bear testimony to this fact so that the full measure of what occurred could be countenanced was and continues to be one of the most controversial aspects of that work, particularly among Jewish communities. I discuss this controversy in Chapter 5.

71. This way of putting it certainly grossly simplifies the difficult practice of receptivity to God as it is variously conceptualized and struggled for in Christian practice, although it simultaneously illuminates its weakness.

72. For her concentrated discussions of conscience, see *Eichmann in Jerusalem* (esp. 83–150), "Personal Responsibility," Crises of the Republic (51–102), and *The Life of the Mind: Thinking*, (179–93).

73. "Thinking and Moral Considerations," 441.

74. I say more on the relationship between the friendship with oneself necessary to thinking and friendship with others in what follows.

75. Margaret Canovan summarizes the negative effects of the dialogical structure of thinking as it pertains to conscience as, "having to live with oneself, having to set limits to what one will knowingly do, and as questioning certainties, and thus making it impossible to 'drift with the crowd.' " See *Hannah Arendt: A Reinterpretation*, 269. I am making the broader point about thinking being the only remaining preserve in which plurality might be experienced. Here we can recreate something of the multiplicity of voices that living in a political world with some degree of freedom holds open to us, and carry on something similar to, though not the same as, an obligation to them.

76. I refer to Plato's relationship with the tyrant Dionysius of Syracuse as described by Plutarch. There is, of course, debate among scholars over the legitimacy of the surviving evidence concerning Plato's efforts to persuade the tyrant to redesign his state in accordance with the *Republic*. See Sir Ernest Barker, *The Political Thought of Plato and Aristotle* (New York, 1959).

77. I am therefore in agreement with Richard Bernstein's contention that Arendt never justifies her crucial claim that thinking has this liberating effect on judgment. As will be evident, however, I am discontent to let things rest here. See Bernstein, "Banality of Evil."

78. I address these issues in Chapter 5.

79. "Thinking and Moral Considerations," 425.

80. Children's discovery of this possibility for friendship with themselves may indeed actually first be a literal sounding out of this dialogue, as when my two-year-old daughter, responding to my mistaking her murmuring to herself as words directed toward me, said, with some exasperation, "Mom, I am *talking* to myself."

81. For a different discussion of this issue, see Bernstein, "Banality of Evil."

82. See "Martin Heidegger at Eighty," in *New York Review of Books* 17 (1976): 50–54, and "What Is Existenz Philosophy?" *Partisan Review* 13 (1946): 34–56. See also Elizabeth Young-Bruehl, *Hannah Arendt: For the Love of the World* (New Haven, Conn., 1982).

83. "Martin Heidegger," 52.

84. Ibid., 54.

85. See "What Is Existenz Philosophy?"

86. Arendt rightly and importantly insists that the plurality of the thinking ego is not the same as the plurality of we-in-the-world. See *The Life of the Mind: Willing*, 200. Nonetheless we see in her exemplar, Socrates, an important interrelationship, important ways in which these respective experiences have a bearing on one another.

87. See Dana Villa's study of the relationship between Arendt's theory of action and Heidegger's philosophy, *Arendt and Heidegger*.

Chapter 3. World Alienation and the Modern Age: The Depravations of Obscurity

1. *The Works of John Adams, Second President of the United States: With a Life of the Author, Notes and Illustrations*, vol. 4, ed. Charles Francis Adams (Boston, 1851), 234.

2. For example, she writes in her controversial chapter "The Social Question" in *On Revolution*, "All rulership has its original and its most legitimate source... in the old and terrible truth that only violence and rule over others could make some free" (114). The way her relative lack of distress in passages such as this borders on inattentive complacency has rightly disturbed many of her readers.

3. Nancy Fraser offers a useful typology of such injustices, including *exploitation* (having the fruits of one's labor appropriated for the benefit of others), *economic marginalization* (being confined to undesirable or poorly paid work or being denied access to income-generating labor altogether), and *deprivation* (being denied an adequate material standard of living). *Justice Interruptus: Critical Reflections on the "Postsocialist" Condition* (New York, 1997), 13.

4. See, for example, J. S. Mill, *On Liberty* (New York, 1956), 67–90.

5. The insult of oblivion is analytically distinct from what Nancy Fraser calls "cultural and symbolic injustices" that fuel the contemporary politics of recognition and its identity-based claims. Although the insult of oblivion probably always receives symbolic and cultural articulation, keeping it analytically distinct allows us to avoid too complete an immersion in debates over cultural value and cultural relativism that can divert our attention from theorizing our profound human need to be in the presence of others. See Fraser's *Justice Interruptus*, 14.

The insult of oblivion is also different from nonrecognition and the crippled self found in the works of Charles Taylor and Axel Honneth. Their vocabulary of integrity and respect is attentive to injuries to selfhood, whereas I am concerned, as was Arendt, with injuries to movement toward others. Again, these are not unrelated, but are importantly analytically distinct. See Charles Taylor, *Multiculturalism: Examining the Politics of Recognition,* ed. Amy Gutman (Princeton, N.J., 1994), and Axel Honneth, "Integrity and Disrespect: Principles of a Conception of Morality Based on a Theory of Recognition," *Political Theory* 20 (May 1992): 187–201.

6. These purges Arendt makes in order to isolate her phenomenon—politically relevant freedom—will strike and have struck the modern ear as perverse, and there exists a long and vigorous critique in this vein. See, for example, Pitkin, "Justice"; Elshtain, *Public Man/Private Woman;* Bakan, "Hannah Arendt's Concepts"; Dietz, "Slow Boring of Hard Boards"; and Habermas, "Hannah Arendt's Communications Concept."

7. In Arendt's early works it is not difficult to read freedom as a capacity that arises sui generis. With the help of her late ontology, however, we understand this "original interdependence" at a deeper level. I amplify it further as I discuss the concept of dimensionality in the context of Arendt's work on judging in Chapter 4.

8. Arendt argues that Greek philosophy had no concept of freedom at all, as it was founded in opposition to a politics that, for the Greeks and Romans, was the (rightful) home of freedom. See *Between Past and Future,* 157.

9. *What Is Found There: Notebooks on Poetry and Politics* (New York, 1993), 6.

10. It may appear that the very experience of Christianity suggests otherwise, for precisely this inner freedom burned, Arendt herself argues, through the long centuries of the Christian world, during which politically relevant freedom was nowhere in evidence (*BPF,* 165). What makes these questions serious for us, however, is a singular distinction Arendt rightly draws between the Christian world and our own. Both were profoundly worldless times, but the Christian principle of charity alone created a kind of community in which worldless people felt a bond to one another. This "political principle" established not, to be sure, a public sphere but a kind of relatedness that gave rise to a "worldless world" in which initiating action of a kind could occur. A corollary to this "Christian political principle" we do not have (*HC,* 53). In this sense we seem more completely lacking in bonds of relatedness and are thus more vulnerable to losing, in our anomie, the derivative forms and experiences of freedom.

11. I follow Arendt in distinguishing poverty from abject misery. The suffering of the emmiserated is qualitatively different.

12. Here I am in full agreement with Jeffrey Isaac's arguments concerning the humanistic foundations of Arendt's political theorizing. See "Arendt, Camus, and Postmodern Politics," *Praxis International* 9 (1989): 63–68.

13. As I write, for example, the world, having been presented with Dolly the sheep, attempts, rather feebly thus far, to render meaningful and therewith register the reality of the practice of cloning.

14. Here Arendt uses a version of the phenomenological reduction that, in the effort to grasp the "living relations of experience," requires that we "break with our familiar acceptance of things," that we "suspend" our relationship to the whatness of the world. Merleau-Ponty calls this a suspension of our common sense or, alternatively, our natural attitude toward the world. The need for suspension in order to see this living essence, together with Arendt's fierce faith in the spiritual dimension of public life, perhaps helps explain the sense it made to her to exclude those too governed by interest or need from public life. See Merleau-Ponty, *Phenomenology,* xiii–xiv.

15. This notion was developed by Husserl and stands in contrast to Kant's transcendentalism in which the world is imminent in the subject. See Merleau-Ponty, *Phenomenology*, xiii–xiv; my italics.

16. The worldly nature of Arendt's conception of spirit is obscured in certain passages. Compare, for example, *The Human Condition* (179–81) with *Men in Dark Times* (71–75).

17. I am drawing heavily on Arendt's "Karl Jaspers: A *Laudatio*" (*BPF*, 71–80).

18. Christian Bay, for example, charges that there is "a certain lack of seriousness about modern problems in much of her work." And Albrecht Wellmer argues that "these distinctions [labor, work, and action and the private, public, and social] have proved extremely fruitful with regards to criticizing ideological fixations: particularly those which represent the prevailing of 19th century traditions.... On the other hand... I always have the feeling that these distinctions are designating limiting cases to which nothing in reality really corresponds." See the discussion in "On Hannah Arendt," 307, 325. For the most sustained argument concerning Arendt's failure to appreciate modernity's strength, see Kateb, *Hannah Arendt*, especially 115–48.

19. Bonnie Honig contends that Arendt's rigid distinction between public and private conflicts with her theory of action and politics, and that her (Honig's) "radicalized" reading is truer to Arendt's central insights than was Arendt herself. See "Toward an Agonistic Feminism: Hannah Arendt and the Politics of Identity," in *Feminist Interpretations of Hannah Arendt*, ed. Bonnie Honig (University Park, Pa., 1995).

20. See the important and lively discussions in *Habermas and the Public Sphere*, ed. Craig Calhoun (Cambridge, Mass., 1992).

21. This is true of her interest in Aristotle and Cicero, but by no means is it limited to their work. See especially the chapter "Labor" (*HC*, 79–174).

22. By contrast, the central effort of Adolf Portmann's new science is to revive scientific interest in seeing by becoming "more susceptible to the special features of visible appearance." *Animal Forms and Patterns* (London, 1948), 28.

23. Her argument is that the life of *animal laborans* triumphs over *homo faber* because the modern reversal between the *vita contemplativa* and the *vita activa* occurs within a Christian society whose fundamental belief is the sacredness of life. See *The Human Condition*, 313–20.

24. This liberation has undergone three stages. The first stage of modern world alienation occurred as peasants were thrown off the land and back on their own labor power. Under the duress of living from hand to mouth, that surplus inherent in the biological process was freed. The second stage was reached when the life process became the concern of society, and property the concern of the nation-state with its antagonistic social classes. The final stage occurs in the twentieth century with the decline of the nation-state and the global penetration of capital. As the collective subject of the life process supersedes all territorial bounds, world alienation is reaching a new level, since the national territorial organization interferes less and less with the devouring processes of liberated labor.

25. Marx was Arendt's paradigmatic thinker because, as she said, he was most brilliantly true to phenomenal reality in making the relation between labor's productivity and natural abundance explicit. Labor is, he argued, man's *metabolism* with nature. For an extended discussion of Arendt's critique of Marx, see *The Human Condition*, 79–135, and Canovan, *Hannah Arendt: A Reinterpretation*, 63–154.

26. The phrase is William Connolly's. See *Politics and Ambiguity* (Madison, Wis., 1987). Michel Foucault's work remains among the most insightful in identifying these normalizing processes. They are a function of what he refers to as "modern bio power." See *Discipline and Punish: The Birth of the Prison*, trans. Alan Sheridan (New York, 1979); *The History of Sexuality, Volume One: An Introduction*, trans. Robert Hurley (New York, 1990).

27. The language of naturalism has become problematic as Arendt herself sometimes pointed out. See, for example, her discussions in *The Human Condition* (10) and *The Life of the Mind: Willing* (158). On this point, of course, there is an abyss between Aristotelian and Arendtian frameworks.

28. Margaret Canovan notes that Arendt appreciated neither the contribution civil society has made in the modern age in facilitating plurality nor the opportunities for personal freedom that market economies offer. See *Hannah Arendt: A Reinterpretation*, 121–22.

29. Arendt believed that we should encourage the older form of private property where at all possible, arguing, for example, that taxes are a "sweet" way to carry on the process of appropriation. See "On Hannah Arendt," 320.

30. There is, in my view, a clear debt to Nietzsche in her account, although it is developed from an explicit concern with the political world and hence fruitfully builds out from Nietzsche's own analysis. See especially part 4 of *Thus Spoke Zarathustra*, trans. Walter Kaufmann (New York, 1954).

31. Arendt argues that the social question is not an appropriate subject for the public realm, belonging in the private household or in public administration. Neither of these arguments is compelling, although her articulation of the concerns that lead her to these conclusions is highly compelling.

32. Such an experience of compassion undoubtedly also would have ended the personal involvement of some with the enslavement of their fellows. For others, it may have positively effected the substance of their participation in (especially) state constitution-making. I am thinking here of efforts to abolish slavery at the state level, among other things.

33. In this sense I think Leon Botstein is quite right when he suggests that "Arendt's implicit psychology (psychology is consistently absent from her considerations in a formal sense) is more akin to Rousseau's (despite her distrust of compassion as a political virtue) than to Locke's." See "Opposing Views," *Partisan Review* 45 (1978): 375.

34. Arendt identifies such tensions with considerable acumen, although her work contains astonishingly few instances in which mediation is achieved. Her categorical bifurcations are both, that is to say once again, stimulating and problematic.

Chapter 4. Beauty, Durability, and the Practice of Judging

1. See "The Permanence of the World and the Work of Art" (*HC*, 167–74); "Action" (*HC*, 175–247); "The Crisis in Culture" (*BPF*, 173–226); and *Lectures on Kant's Political Philosophy*.

2. I say she is "largely" unconcerned because in *Thinking,* where her primary effort is to reestablish the essential fit between earthly existence and human thought, to persuade that there is essential belonging between the two, Arendt discusses, as I have shown, the way in which metaphors carry us from the sensuous world of the seen to the world of the unseen, where although an invisible world, illumination breaks forth. Although Arendt does not explicitly say so, her examples and language suggest that it is sensuous experience of the nonhuman natural world in all its eternal yet cyclical change that is the deepest wellspring of this metaphorical power in language. The example she chooses from Homer's *Iliad*—in which Homer evokes our experience of the raging storms at sea to illuminate what fear and grief can do to the human heartbeat—beautifully illustrates this point. Arendt makes no effort, however, to relate this discussion of metaphor directly to the relationship between aesthetic pleasure and durability. See *The Life of the Mind: Thinking,* 98–110.

3. The difficulty with putting the point this way is that I seem to be suggesting that involvement with things as consumable goods or as more durable-use objects cannot be meaningful. My point is, rather, that when we involve ourselves with the meaning of things, as per the meaning of a thing's usefulness to us, we are drawn into a different quality of involvement, and it is this quality I am trying to single out. Arendt's own work battles this same difficulty perpetually.

4. The most concentrated texts in this regard are *The Human Condition* and *Between Past and Future* (143–71). See also Habermas, "Hannah Arendt's Communications Concept of Action."

5. Maria Iannacome Coles, *Intimate Weapons,* unpublished manuscript.

6. The parable occurs in the preface to *Between Past and Future* (7–14), and once again in *Thinking* (202–11). The span of time between these two works alone indicates its importance for Arendt's thinking.

7. See "Understanding and Politics," *Partisan Review* 20 (July–August 1953): 391. Compare this passage from Merleau-Ponty's *Phenomenology of Perception:* "To return to the things themselves is to return to that world which precedes knowledge, of which knowledge always *speaks,* and in relation to which every scientific schematization is an abstract and derivative sign-language" (ix).

8. There is a very Nietzschean feeling in Arendt's writing about this historical form of authority. Her unabashed awe and admiration for the sheer magnitude of the Roman, but even more, the Christian establishment of authority is reminiscent of passages in *The Genealogy of Morals,* in which Nietzsche extols the affirming will of Christianity and all it was able to build. Nietzsche and Arendt share a pathos for the enormous stability and permanence as well as beauty brought forth in a world made meaningful throughout the centuries of Christianity. This pathos wells out of their deep appreciation of the elemental problem to which it was one grand response—the problem of establishing some kind of durability and stability. Both also are, however, extremely critical of the specific costs of this achievement: Nietzsche expressing extravagant repugnance toward a (Christian) will that saves itself from existential despair by willing the void, and Arendt elegantly critical of the way in which the Christian world circumscribed the practices of political freedom. See Friedrich Nietzsche, *The Genealogy of Morals,* trans. Walter Kaufmann (New York, 1967), 97–163.

9. For a reading that contests this point in an interesting manner, see Bonnie Honig, "Declarations of Independence: Arendt and Derrida On the Problem of Founding a Republic," *American Political Science Review* 85 (1991): 97–113.

10. The allure of Arendt's story lies in part in the ambiguity she sustains about the experiences and self-understandings of the American revolutionaries and the American public. Despite the revolutionaries' conservative sense that they were merely "revolving back to an earlier period," Arendt implies that the story she tells more profoundly identifies the source of authority they were able to create. And yet, as I have noted, her story is always told as a conjecture. With this, Arendt spins a tale she hopes can *become* our truth, or better yet, having gathered the essential meaning of these events, she offers us a truth that she hopes can become useful to us.

11. Although the United States' capital-driven expansionism in the form of imperialism has often occurred under the banner of "making the world safe for democracy," a banner that has gained the legitimacy it has enjoyed, without doubt, from the founders' greatness and a kind of Roman-like veneration for their acts, Arendt's interpretation of the true spirit of the authority to which those events have given rise is different. Indeed, she finds policies legitimized or authorized by veneration of this kind misguided, a good example of this being, of course, her opposition to the imperialist war that the United States waged in Vietnam.

12. It is also, as I have said, a central argument of *On Revolution* that the American experiment failed insofar as it did not give real power to the town-meeting level of public life, did not institutionalize this space for the enactment of human freedom. See especially chapter 6.

13. For an excellent presentation of these arguments, see Samuel Bowles and Herbert Gintis, *Democracy and Capitalism: Property, Community and the Contradictions of Modern Social Thought* (New York, 1987).

14. This is also the essence of genealogical interpretation. See Nietzsche's brilliant and disturbing essay "On the Uses and Disadvantages of History for Life," in *Untimely Meditations*, trans. R. J. Hollingdale (Cambridge, 1983); and Michel Foucault's "Nietzsche, Genealogy, History," in *Language, Countermemory, Practice: Selected Essays and Interviews*, trans. Donald F. Bouchard and Sherry Simon (Ithaca, N.Y., 1977).

15. "On Hannah Arendt," 246.

16. Making a similar point about Arendt's work, George Kateb writes, "By willed definition, however, political action, more than any other human activity (except thinking), is traceable to gratitude, in spite of the fact that changing the course of things defines its greatness." Kateb's discussion of gratitude is incisive and subtle. Yet despite his careful recognition of the complex interrelationship between gratitude, acceptance of being, and action to change the world, in his effort to defend life in modernity, gratitude becomes a signifier for what Kateb quite wrongly sees as Arendt's effort to erase all alienation, to be at home in the world. See *Hannah Arendt*, 167.

17. Translation in Michael Denneny, "The Privilege of Ourselves," 246.

18. Translated by Walter Arndt in Johann Wolfgang von Goethe, *Faust.* (New York, 1976).

19. See "Privilege of Ourselves."

20. Arendt's two primary texts are "The Crisis in Culture" and *Lectures on Kant's Political Philosophy.* In the former Arendt draws on Greek, Roman, and Kantian sources. In the latter the primary text of Kant's on which she relies is, of course, *Critique of Judgment.* But as her task is to inquire into the political philosophy that Kant never wrote, she draws on works from both his precritical as well as his critical period.

21. For an astute account of Arendt's departures from the *Critique of Judgment,* see Lisa Disch, *Hannah Arendt and the Limits of Philosophy* (Ithaca, N.Y., 1994), 146–64.

22. The question of why Arendt did not turn to Aristotle, and whether Kant's work is sufficient for a theory of political judgment, has been the subject of much debate. See especially Ronald Beiner, "Hannah Arendt on Judging," in *Lectures on Kant's Political Philosophy,* ed. Beiner (Chicago, 1982), and *Political Judgment* (Chicago, 1983). See also Gadamer, *Truth and Method,* 3–81, for an extended critique of Kant's aestheticization and depoliticization of judgment.

23. Some commentators have argued that Arendt finds aesthetic judgments interesting only as a *model* for political judgment, but as others rightly note, Arendt makes no firm or consistent distinctions between aesthetic, political, or moral judgments per se. See Ronald Beiner's perceptive discussion in "Hannah Arendt on Judging," 131–44. Furthermore, because Arendt's concern is with our ability to disclose the phenomenality of things through the practice of judgment, our aesthetic experience of them is a central aspect of our performance. In this context Michael Denneny's suggestion that Arendt was interested in thinking jointly about two dimensions of experience that have, since the eighteenth century, been held apart—ethics and aesthetics—is just to the point. See "Privilege of Ourselves," 261.

24. For extended discussions, see Disch, *Hannah Arendt and the Limits of Philosophy,* and Beiner, "Hannah Arendt on Judging." Scholars have rightly noted that there are tensions in Arendt's reflections on judgment. Sometimes she seems to be concerned with it as a capacity of political actors, at other times as a capacity of the uninvolved reflective spectator. I read these as tensions between two "moments" of judgment—the prospective and retrospective—and argue that these moments must mutually inform each other, as they represent ethically fruitful conflict between ways of life and within selves. For contrasting views, see Beiner, "Hannah Arendt on Judging"; Richard Bernstein, *Philosophical Profiles: Essays in a Pragmatic Mode* (Philadelphia, 1986); Canovan, *Hannah Arendt: A Reinterpretation;* and Seyla Benhabib, "Judgment and the Moral Foundations of Politics in Hannah Arendt's Thought," *Political Theory* 16 (1988): 29–51.

25. Arendt might be understood here as accepting Nietzsche's critique of the disinterested, removed philosopher, but also as attempting to positively define a pleasure that was of extreme political relevance and about which Nietzsche seemed to know nothing. See *The Gay Science,* trans. Walter Kaufmann (New York, 1974).

26. Quoted in Beiner, "Hannah Arendt on Judging," 154. The phrase of Augustine's appears from time to time in Arendt's unpublished lectures.

27. This may appear to contradict Kant's own elaboration of disinterestedness when he writes, "Everyone has to admit that if a judgment about beauty is mingled

with the least interest then it is very partial and not a pure judgment of taste. In order to play the judge in matters of taste, we must not be in the least biased in favor of the thing's existence, but must be wholly indifferent about it." But to read it so would be to misunderstand that what Arendt trying to dramatize is that realness for us is never simply empirical but always contemplatively meaningful. See Immanuel Kant, *Critique of Judgment* (Indianapolis, 1987), 46.

28. Here I wholeheartedly agree with Lisa Disch that Arendt's is a self-conscious "creative interpretation" of Kant and not, as some argue, a retreat to philosophy at the end of her life. See *Hannah Arendt and the Limits of Philosophy*, 141–46. For the "retreat thesis," see Beiner, "Hannah Arendt on Judging."

29. Although Arendt accepts Kant's transcendentally derived *sensus communis*, I think Ronald Beiner is right when he says Arendt never seriously considers what force is to be given to this a priori in Kant. I disagree, however, with Beiner's assertion that Arendt does not "really confront the question of the nature of the judging community to which we appeal (*a priori*)." This is primarily because Arendt, in contrast to Kant, does not conceive this *as* an a priori appeal. See "Hannah Arendt on Judging," 170.

30. It is worth noting that this is one of Arendt's idiosyncratic departures from Kant, who actually conceives of representative thinking as "abstracting from one's own contingent situation to think in the place of *any* other man." Arendt, by contrast, is arguing for a more complex thinking that, as we shall see, is far more demanding of our imagination with respect to particular others than Kant's representative thinking. See Kant, *Critique of Judgment*, 136; my italics.

31. *Visible and the Invisible*, 218.

32. Arendt claims to be following Kant in claiming general but not universal validity for judgments of taste. As Ronald Beiner points out, however, Arendt persistently interprets Kant's *allgemein* to mean general, in a departure from all standard translations in which it is rendered "universal." This interpretive sleight-of-hand tells us something about the force she gives to the term *validity*, a point I am presently elaborating. On this point see also Dagmar Barnouw, *Visible Spaces: Hannah Arendt and the German-Jewish Experience* (Baltimore, 1990), 21–22.

33. Beiner argues that merely because Arendt claims that judgments are only generally valid, this still does not mean that, on her account, we relate judgment "to any specifiable human community, with all the particularity that would entail." My argument here is that Arendt's conception of judgment is acutely related to particulars and particularity, but in an unconventional sense. See "Hannah Arendt on Judging," 170.

34. In an echo of this on the level of activism, black feminist Bernice Reagon Johnson speaks, before a largely white all-women's music festival, of the importance of finding, supporting, and learning from people who have the gift of taking account of our world. She says,

Watch those mono-issue people. They ain't gonna do you no good. I don't care who they are.... Now, there [are] a few people who [keep] up with many...issues. *They are very rare.* Any time you find a person showing up at all of those struggles, and they have some sense of sanity by your definition, not theirs (cause almost everybody thinks they're sane), one, study with them, and two, protect them. They're gonna be in trouble shortly because they are the most visible ones. They hold the key to turning the century with our principles intact. (Quoted in "Coalition Politics," 363)

35. Arendt does not quite make this argument, which is to say she succeeds in distinguishing between these two types of impartiality, perceptively identifies the irreconcilable tensions between them, but fails to positively articulate the relationship between them. These "successes" and "failures" are characteristic strengths and weakness of Arendt's thinking more generally.

36. As spectators, while solitary, we are also essentially social. Arendt writes, "Spectators exist only in the plural. The spectator is not involved in the act, but he is always *involved* with fellow spectators" (*LK,* 63; my italics).

37. For Arendt's extended reflections on factuality and lying in politics, see "Truth and Politics" (*BPF,* 227–264) and "Lying in Politics" (*CR,* 1–48).

Chapter 5. Ethical Responsibility in Politics: The Obligation to Renew

1. "Privilege of Ourselves," 269.

2. The phrase is Harry Boyte's. "The Pragmatic Ends of Popular Politics," in *Habermas and the Public Sphere,* ed. Craig Calhoun (Cambridge, Mass., 1992).

3. Scholem sent his response to Arendt in a private letter to which she responded. Both letters were subsequently published at Scholem's request. The exchange has been printed in a collection of Arendt's writings on Jewish politics entitled *The Jew as Pariah: Jewish Identity and Politics in the Modern Age,* ed. Ron H. Feldman (New York, 1978).

4. For a discussion of Blumenfeld's "Postassimilatory Zionism," see Young-Bruehl, *Hannah Arendt: For Love of the World* (New Haven, Conn., 1982), 72–4, 105–10.

5. For an excellent account of the development of Zionism in its various forms, see Barnouw, *Visible Spaces,* 72–134. See also Young-Bruehl, *Hannah Arendt: For Love of the World,* 105–10.

6. These settlements began in the 1930s and continue to this day.

7. For a confirmation of these arguments from the perspective of contemporary Israeli politics, see Eric Alterman, "Israel and the Liberal Imagination," *Nation,* 4 May 1998, 24–26.

8. See "Peace or Armistice," in *Jew as Pariah.* See also Barnouw's excellent discussion of these issues in *Visible Spaces,* 126–34.

9. I paraphrase from Arendt's essay "On Humanity in Dark Times: Thoughts about Lessing" (*MDT,* 20).

10. For a full discussion of their relationship, see Barnouw, *Visible Spaces,* 94–126.

11. Ibid., 179.

12. It is quite important to point out, however, that Arendt deals only briefly with this issue. See chapter 7, "The Wannsee Conference, or Pontius Pilot," in *Eichmann in Jerusalem.*

13. See "The Formidable Dr. Robinson: A Reply to Hannah Arendt" (*JP*, 260–76).

14. Her argument with the Judenräte, as she clarifies it in her letter to Scholem, is not that they should have resisted. This, she argues, was not possible under such conditions. What was possible was noncooperation.

15. This is the all-important point of her essay "Truth and Politics" (*MDT*, 227–64, esp. 264).

16. Osha Gray Davidson, *Best of Enemies: Race and Redemption in the New South* (New York, 1996), 280–81.

17. The charette was held in an elementary school in Durham for ten days from 10 A.M. until 2 A.M. For an account of the organization and development of the charette in Durham, see Davidson, *Best of Enemies*, 245–59.

18. Ibid., 64.

19. Ibid., 283.

20. Ibid., 64–65.

21. Indeed, the Klan's original leadership had been from the Southern upper class, a class bent on wresting political power from the newly empowered Republican party of the Reconstruction South. To do so, they needed the support of the white lower classes. And to get it, they developed a divide-and-conquer strategy drawn on racial lines. See Joel Williamson, *The Crucible of Race* (Oxford, 1984).

22. Davidson, *Best of Enemies*, 291.

23. Although already familiar to many residents of Durham, North Carolina, this remarkable story is currently being told and retold, occasioned by the recent appearance of Osha Gray Davidson's excellent *Best of Enemies: Race and Redemption in the New South*, which richly contextualizes and embeds the story of friendship between C. P. and Ann in the complex political history of the city, the region, and the nation. C. P. Ellis and Ann Atwater also received national attention in 1973, appearing together on *Good Morning America* and *The David Frost Show*. There was also an article in *The Nation*. See Edward McConville, "The Prophetic Voice of C. P. Ellis," *Nation*, 15 October 1973, 361–66. See also Studs Terkel, *American Dreams: Lost and Found* (New York, 1980), 200–211.

24. So, although I begin with Ann's deed, with its drama and miracle-like unexpectedness, the questions it urges on us concern both the specific quality of Ann's presence to C. P. and the political conditions of its possibility.

25. Arendt's concern with responsiveness, with the kind of attention we give one another, has been creatively explored by Susan Bickford in the context of feminist debates over identity politics. She makes the important argument that while feminists have closely analyzed systematic distortions of attention, far less thought has been given to, as she puts it, "what emancipatory relations of expression and attention involve." See "In the Presence of Others: Arendt and Anzaldúa on the Paradox of Public Appearance," in *Feminist Interpretations of Hannah Arendt*, ed. Bonnie Honig (University Park, Pa., 1995), 315.

26. For a different and important reading of political responsibility that relies heavily on aspects of Arendt's political theorizing, see Melissa Orlie, "Forgiving Trespasses, Promising Futures," in *Feminist Interpretations of Hannah Arendt*.

27. The violent quality of this ending, the way it tore open previously solid relationships, is acutely evident for C. P.—first in the death threats from fellow Klan members he began to receive for agreeing to co-chair the charette, and then in the destitution he felt in severing himself and being severed from the Klan and, by extension, from the poor white community in which he had always felt at home. His experience of the violent nature of great action culminated one year after the charette when, in drunken and lonely suicidal despair, belonging now nowhere, he smashed a bottle over his head. For Ann, there was also violence accompanying this ending, but, although wrenchingly painful and for reasons that seem obvious, it was not as severe as that suffered by C. P. It took its greatest toll on her young daughter, who was taunted and beaten by her classmates and publicly condemned by her teacher because her mother was working with a Klansman. See Davidson, *Best of Enemies*, 275.

28. Both of these arguments are central to John Stuart Mill's liberal masterpiece, *On Liberty*.

29. I am drawing heavily here on Merleau-Ponty's incisive interpretation of Machiavelli's humanism. See "A Note on Machiavelli," *Signs* (Evanston, Ill., 1964), 215.

30. Ibid., 217.

31. This was the way John Riddick, the brilliant organizer of the charette, articulated the last of the three goals he hoped it would accomplish. See *Best of Enemies*, 263.

32. Merleau-Ponty, "A Note on Machiavelli," 211.

33. The influence on the Left of Karl Marx, Michel Foucault, and Friedrich Nietzsche, as well as Ernesto Laclao and Chantal Mouffe, among others, are important cases in point.

34. The critique, usually expressed as frustrated bewilderment, that Arendt is naive about the content of politics is a common one and owes much to her distinction between public and private life and her insistence on separating bread-and-butter concerns from real political concerns. Together, it is argued, these signature distinctions help constitute an understanding of politics that is hopelessly drained of conflict over specific material concerns. For versions of this argument see Dietz, "Slow Boring of Hard Boards," and Brown, *Manhood and Politics*, 23–31.

35. Disch also rightly argues that this argument about the immorality of Arendt's theory of action depends on interpreting this passage "out of the context of the new political lexicon of plurality, natality, and publicity." See Disch's nuanced argument in *Hannah Arendt and the Limits of Philosophy*, 76–77.

36. On this reading, then, what Arendt calls "the innermost meaning of the acted deed and the spoken word" is the same for both good and evil deeds—the way they break with everyday standards, and in this sense there are, indeed, as George Kateb points out, disturbing affinities between Arendt's ideal of action and totalitarian politics. What distinguishes them, however, is radiance, their capacity for world disclosure. See *Hannah Arendt*, 29–33.

37. She provided, to be sure, also such an occasion for the youths as well.

38. Thanks to Marion Orr for helping me think about the profound role that black churches have played in creating spaces in which African Americans can be witnessed. For one stirring recent account of this witnessing-confirming role in the

lives of poor and destitute black citizens, see Samuel G. Freedman, *Upon This Rock: Miracles of a Black Church* (New York, 1993).

39. See Davidson, *Best of Enemies*, 160.

40. State coercion was particularly important in C. P.'s case, as it convinced him that the writing was on the wall, that therefore if Durham's poor white children were going to be protected, participation was the only way to go.

41. See "Toward an Agonistic Feminism," 160.

42. This is most evident in *The Human Condition*, least so in her "On Humanity in Dark Times: Thoughts about Lessing," *The Origins of Totalitarianism*, and her 1963 letter to Gershom Scholem. For excellent readings of these texts on this point, see Disch, "On Friendship," and Morris Kaplan, "Refiguring the Jewish Question: Arendt, Proust, and the Politics of Sexuality," in *Feminist Interpretations of Hannah Arendt* (University Park, Pa., 1995).

43. See, for example, the very good discussion in Orlie, "Forgiving Trespasses," and in Bickford, "In the Presence of Others."

44. C. P. Ellis himself carries a profound and bitter sense of how growing up poor in East Durham "made" him, and how, as he says, it "equipped [him] for joining the Klan." From a talk delivered by C. P. Ellis and Ann Atwater, Duke University, October 1996.

45. Honig rewrites Arendt here to say we are always both "with *and* against" in an effort, apparently, to refuse the utopian moment. See "Toward an Agonistic Feminism," 159.

46. As he put this point recently, in this moment, "she [Ann] changed my ideas about human beings, I mean about blacks and whites" (lecture, Duke University, October 1996).

47. Retrospectively, the act illuminates the specific glory of being human and the capacity to act so as to engage the freedom of others.

48. Thus the abyss between what Mary Dietz has called Arendt's celebration of "practical purposelessness" of speech and deed, and of mere productive activity in politics, is not so great as some (including Dietz) have argued. See Dietz, "Slow Boring of Hard Boards," 880.

49. This is the upshot of the accommodation between labor and capital after the Great Depression in the United States. For an excellent analysis of the history of the relationship between labor and capital, see Bowles and Gintis, *Democracy and Capitalism*, esp. 27–63.

50. Richard Perez-Peña, "Man Said to Admit a Week of Savagery," *New York Times*, 16 June 1996, B16.

51. *The Alchemy of Race and Rights* (Cambridge, Mass., 1991), 72.

52. Boyte, "Pragmatic Ends," 350.

Selected Bibliography

Abel, Lionel. "The Aesthetics of Evil: Hannah Arendt on Eichmann and the Jews." *Partisan Review* 30, no. 2 (Summer 1963): 211–30.

Adams, John. *The Works of John Adams, Second President of the United States: With a Life of the Author, Notes, and Illustrations.* Vol. 6, edited by Charles Francis Adams. Boston: Little, Brown, 1851.

Alterman, Eric. "Israel and the Liberal Imagination." *Nation,* 4 May 1998, 24–26.

Arendt, Hannah. "What Is Existenz Philosophy?" *Partisan Review* 13 (1946): 34–56.

——. *The Origins of Totalitarianism.* New York: Harcourt Brace and World, 1951.

——. "Understanding and Politics." *Partisan Review* 20, no. 4 (July–August 1953): 377–92.

——. *Between Past and Future.* Middlesex, England: Penguin, 1954.

——. *Men in Dark Times.* New York: Harcourt Brace Jovanovich, 1955.

——. *Rahel Varnhagen: The Life of a Jewish Woman.* New York: Harcourt Brace Jovanovich, 1957.

——. *The Human Condition.* Chicago: University of Chicago Press, 1958.

——. *Eichmann in Jerusalem: A Report on the Banality of Evil.* New York: Viking Press, 1963.

——. *On Revolution.* Middlesex, England: Penguin, 1963.

——. "Personal Responsibility under Dictatorship." *Listener,* 6 August 1964, 185–87.

——. *On Violence.* New York: Harcourt Brace and World, 1969.

——. "Thinking and Moral Considerations: A Lecture." *Social Research* 38, no. 3 (Autumn 1971): 416–46.

——. "Martin Heidegger at Eighty." *The New York Review of Books* 17, no. 6 (1971): 50–54.

——. *Crises of the Republic.* New York: Harcourt Brace Jovanovich, 1972.

——. *The Jew as Pariah: Jewish Identity and Politics in the Modern Age.* Edited by Ron H. Feldman. New York: Grove Press, 1978.

——. *The Life of the Mind.* Single-volume edition. New York: Harcourt Brace Jovanovich, 1978.

——. "On Hannah Arendt." In *Hannah Arendt: The Recovery of the Public World*, edited by Melvyn A. Hill. New York: St. Martin's Press, 1979.

——. *Lectures on Kant's Political Philosophy*. Edited by Ronald Beiner. Chicago: University of Chicago Press, 1982.

——. "Philosophy and Politics." *Social Research* 57, no. 1 (Spring 1990): 73–103.

——. *Essays in Understanding*. Edited by Jerome Kohn. New York: Harcourt Brace Jovanovich, 1994.

Atwater, Ann, and C. P. Ellis. Talk given at Duke University in October of 1996.

Bakan, Mildred. "Hannah Arendt's Concepts of Labor and Work." In *Hannah Arendt: The Recovery of the Public World*, edited by Melvyn A. Hill. New York: St. Martin's Press, 1979.

Barker, Sir Ernest. *The Political Thought of Plato and Aristotle*. New York: Dover Publications, 1959.

Barnouw, Dagmar. *Visible Spaces: Hannah Arendt and the German-Jewish Experience*. Baltimore: Johns Hopkins University Press, 1990.

Beiner, Ronald. "Hannah Arendt on Judging." In Arendt's *Lectures on Kant's Political Philosophy*, edited by Ronald Beiner. Chicago: University of Chicago Press, 1982.

——. *Political Judgment*. Chicago: University of Chicago Press, 1983.

Bell, Daniel. "The Alphabet of Justice: Reflections on Eichmann in Jerusalem." *Partisan Review* 30, no. 3 (Fall 1963): 417–29.

Benhabib, Seyla. "Judgment and the Moral Foundations of Politics in Hannah Arendt's Thought." *Political Theory* 16, no. 1 (February 1988): 29–51.

——. "Models of Public Space: Hannah Arendt, the Liberal Tradition, and Jürgen Habermas." In *Habermas and the Public Sphere*, edited by Craig Calhoun. Cambridge, Mass.: MIT Press, 1992.

——. "Hannah Arendt and the Redemptive Power of Narrative." In *Hannah Arendt: Critical Essays*, edited by Lewis P. Hinchman and Sandra K. Hinchman. Albany: State University of New York Press, 1994.

——. *The Reluctant Modernism of Hannah Arendt*. Thousand Oaks, Calif.: Sage Publications, 1996.

Bernauer, James W., ed. *Amor Mundi: Explorations in the Faith and Thought of Hannah Arendt*. Boston: Martinus Nijhoff Publishers, 1987.

Bernstein, Richard. *Philosophical Profiles: Essays in a Pragmatic Mode*. Philadelphia: University of Pennsylvania Press, 1986.

——. "The Banality of Evil Reconsidered." In *Hannah Arendt and the Meaning of Politics*, edited by Craig Calhoun and John McGowan. Minneapolis: University of Minnesota Press, 1997.

Bickford, Susan. "In the Presence of Others: Arendt and Anzaldúa on the Paradox of Public Appearance." In *Feminist Interpretations of Hannah Arendt*, edited by Bonnie Honig. University Park: Pennsylvania State University Press, 1995.

Biskowski, Lawrence. "Practical Foundations for Political Judgment: Arendt on Action and World." *Journal of Politics* 55, no. 4 (November 1993): 868–88.

Blakely, Edward, and Mary Snyder. *Fortress America*. Washington, D.C.: The Brookings Institute, 1997.

Botstein, Leon. "Opposing Views." *Partisan Review* 45, no. 3 (1978): 368–415.

———. "Liberating the Pariah: Politics, the Jews, and Hannah Arendt." *Salmagundi*, no. 60 (Spring–Summer 1983): 73–106.

Bowden, Charles. "While You Were Sleeping." *Harper's*, December 1995, 44–52.

Bowden, Charles, Noam Chomsky, and Eduardo Galeano, eds. *Juarez: The Laboratory of the Future*. New York: Aperture, 1998.

Bowen-Moore, Patricia. *Hannah Arendt's Philosophy of Natality*. New York: St. Martin's Press, 1989.

Bowles, Samuel, and Herbert Gintis. *Democracy and Capitalism: Property, Community, and the Contradictions of Modern Social Thought*. New York: Basic Books, 1987.

Boyte, Harry C. "The Pragmatic Ends of Popular Politics." In *Habermas and the Public Sphere*, edited by Craig Calhoun. Cambridge, Mass.: MIT Press, 1992.

Bradshaw, Leah. *Acting and Thinking: The Political Thought of Hannah Arendt*. Toronto: University of Toronto Press, 1989.

Brown, Wendy. *Manhood and Politics: A Feminist Reading in Political Theory*. Totowa, N.J.: Rowman & Littlefield, 1988.

Bureau of Justice Statistics. *Highlights from 20 Years of Surveying Crime Victims: The National Crime Victimization Survey, 1973–1992*. Washington, D.C.: U.S. Department of Justice, Office of Justice Programs, Bureau of Justice Statistics, 1993.

Calhoun, Craig, ed. *Habermas and the Public Sphere*. Cambridge, Mass.: MIT Press, 1992.

Calhoun, Craig and John McGowan, eds. *Hannah Arendt and the Meaning of Politics*. Minneapolis: University of Minnesota Press, 1997.

Canovan, Margaret. *The Political Thought of Hannah Arendt*. London: J. M. Dent & Sons, 1974.

———. "Politics as Culture: Hannah Arendt and the Public Realm." *History of Political Thought* 6, no. 3 (1985): 617–42.

———. *Hannah Arendt: A Reinterpretation of Her Political Thought*. New York: Cambridge University Press, 1992.

Coles, Maria Iannacome. *Intimate Weapons*. Unpublished manuscript.

Coles, Romand. *Self/Power/Other: Political Theory and Dialogical Ethics*. Ithaca, N.Y.: Cornell University Press, 1992.

Connolly, William E. *Politics and Ambiguity*. Madison: University of Wisconsin Press, 1987.

Curtis, Kimberley. "Hannah Arendt, Feminist Theorizing and the Debate over New Reproductive Technologies." *Polity* 28, no. 2 (Winter 1995), 159–88.

———. "Aesthetic Foundations of Democratic Politics in the Work of Hannah Arendt." In *Hannah Arendt and the Meaning of Politics*, edited by Craig Calhoun and John McGowan. Minneapolis: University of Minnesota Press, 1997.

Davidson, Osha Gray. *Best of Enemies: Race and Redemption in the New South*. New York: Scribner, 1996.

Davis, Mike. "Hell Factories in the Field." *Nation*, 20 February 1995, 229–34.

Denneny, Michael. "The Privilege of Ourselves: Hannah Arendt on Judgment." In *Hannah Arendt: The Recovery of the Public World*, edited by Melvyn A. Hill. New York: St. Martin's Press, 1979.

Derrida, Jacques. *The Other Heading: Reflections on Today's Europe.* Translated by Pascale-Anne Brault and Michael B. Naas. Bloomington: Indiana University Press, 1992.

——. *Specters of Marx: The State of the Debt, the Work of Mourning, and the New International.* Translated by Peggy Kamuf. New York: Routledge, 1994.

Dietz, Mary. "The Slow Boring of Hard Boards: Methodical Thinking and the Work of Politics." *American Political Science Review* 88, no. 4 (December 1994): 873–86.

——. "Feminist Receptions of Hannah Arendt." In *Feminist Interpretations of Hannah Arendt,* edited by Bonnie Honig. University Park: Pennsylvania State University Press, 1995.

Disch, Lisa. *Hannah Arendt and the Limits of Philosophy.* Ithaca, N.Y.: Cornell University Press, 1994.

——. "On Friendship in 'Dark Times.' " In *Feminist Interpretations of Hannah Arendt,* edited by Bonnie Honig. University Park: Pennsylvania State University Press, 1995.

Dolan, Fred. "Strange Power: Philosophy and the Image of a Break with the Past: Arendt, Valery, Benjamin, Kant." Paper presented at the American Political Science Association Annual Meeting, San Francisco, 1996.

Dossa, Shiraz. *The Public Realm and the Public Self: The Political Theory of Hannah Arendt.* Waterloo, Ontario: Wilfred Laurier University Press, 1989.

Egan, Timothy. "Many Seek Security in Private Communities." *New York Times,* 3 September 1995, sec. R1, p. 10.

Elshtain, Jean Bethke. *Public Man, Private Woman.* Princeton, N.J.: Princeton University Press, 1981.

——. "Hannah Arendt's French Revolution." *Salmagundi,* no. 84 (Fall 1989): 203–13.

Fagles, Robert. Introduction to Sophocles' *The Three Theban Plays,* translated by Robert Fagles. New York: Penguin Books, 1982.

Foucault, Michel. *Language, Counter-Memory, Practice: Selected Essays and Interviews.* Edited by Donald F. Bouchard. Translated by Donald F. Bouchard and Sherry Simon. Ithaca, N.Y.: Cornell University Press, 1977.

——. *Discipline and Punish: The Birth of the Prison.* Translated by Alan Sheridan. New York: Vintage Books, 1979.

——. *Power/Knowledge: Selected Interviews and Other Writings, 1972–1977.* Edited by Colin Gordon. New York: Pantheon Books, 1980.

——. *The History of Sexuality, Volume One: An Introduction.* Translated by Robert Hurley. New York: Pantheon Books, 1990.

Fraser, Nancy. *Unruly Practices: Power, Discourse, and Gender in Contemporary Social Theory.* Minneapolis: University of Minnesota Press, 1989.

——. "Rethinking the Public Sphere: A Contribution to the Critique of Actually Existing Democracy." In *Habermas and the Public Sphere,* edited by Craig Calhoun. Cambridge, Mass.: MIT Press, 1992.

——. *Justice Interruptus: Critical Reflections on the "Postsocialist" Condition.* New York: Routledge, 1997.

Freedman, Samuel G. *Upon this Rock: The Miracles of a Black Church.* New York: Harper Collins, 1993.

Gadamer, Hans-Georg. *Truth and Method.* Translated by Joel Weisenheimer and Donald G. Marshall. New York: Crossroad Publishing, 1991.

Goethe, Johann Wolfgang von. *Faust.* Translated by Walter Arndt. New York: Norton, 1976.

Gray, Glenn. "The Winds of Thought." *Social Research* 44, no. 1 (Spring 1977): 44–61.

Habermas, Jürgen. "Hannah Arendt's Communications Concept of Power." *Social Research* 44, no. 1 (Spring 1977): 3–24.

——. *The Structural Transformation of the Public Sphere: An Inquiry into a Category of Bourgeois Society.* Translated by Thomas Burger and Frederick Lawrence. Cambridge, Mass.: MIT Press, 1989.

Haraway, Donna. "A Manifesto for Cyborgs: Science, Technology, and Socialist Feminism in the 1980's." In *Feminism/Postmodernism,* edited by Linda Nicholson. New York: Routledge, 1990.

Heather, Gerald P., and Matthew Stolz. "Hannah Arendt and the Problem of Critical Theory." *Journal of Politics* 41, no. 1 (February 1979): 2–22.

Heidegger, Martin. *The Question Concerning Technology.* New York: Harper & Colophon Books, 1977.

——. *The Will to Power as Art.* San Francisco: Harper & Row, 1982.

Hill, Melvyn A., ed. *Hannah Arendt: The Recovery of the Public World.* New York: St. Martin's Press, 1979.

Hinchman, Lewis P., and Sandra K. Hinchman. "In Heidegger's Shadow: Hannah Arendt's Phenomenological Humanism." *Review of Politics* 46, no. 2 (1984): 183–211.

——. "Existentialism Politicized: Arendt's Debt to Jaspers." In *Hannah Arendt: Critical Essays,* edited by Lewis P. Hinchman and Sandra K. Hinchman. Albany: State University of New York Press, 1994.

Honig, Bonnie. "Arendt, Identity, and Difference." *Political Theory* 16, no. 1 (February 1988): 77–98.

——. "Declarations of Independence: Arendt and Derrida on the Problem of Founding a Republic." *American Political Science Review* 85, no. 1 (March 1991): 97–113.

——. *Political Theory and the Displacement of Politics.* Ithaca, N.Y.: Cornell University Press, 1993.

——. "Toward an Agonistic Feminism: Hannah Arendt and the Politics of Identity." In *Feminist Interpretations of Hannah Arendt,* edited by Bonnie Honig. University Park: Pennsylvania State University Press, 1995.

Honneth, Axel. "Integrity and Disrespect: Principles of a Conception of Morality Based on a Theory of Recognition." *Political Theory* 20, no. 2 (May 1992): 187–201.

hooks, bell. *Talking Back.* Boston: South End Press, 1989.

Hull, Jon D. "The State of the Union." *Time,* 30 January 1995, 63.

Ingram, David. "The Postmodern Kantianism of Arendt and Lyotard." In *Judging Lyotard,* edited by Andrew Benjamin. New York: Routledge, 1992.

Isaac, Jeffrey. "Arendt, Camus, and Postmodern Politics." *Praxis International* 9 (1989): 48–71.

——. *Arendt, Camus, and Modern Rebellion.* New Haven, Conn.: Yale University Press, 1992.

———. "Oases in the Desert: Hannah Arendt on Democratic Politics." *American Political Science Review* 88, no. 1 (March 1994): 156–68.

Jacobitti, Suzanne. "Hannah Arendt and the Will." *Political Theory* 16, no. 1 (February 1988): 53–76.

Jacobson, Norman. "Parable and Paradox: In Response to Arendt's *On Revolution.*" *Salmagundi*, no. 60 (Spring–Summer 1983): 123–39.

Jay, Martin. "Hannah Arendt." *Partisan Review* 45, no. 3 (1978): 348–68.

———. *Permanent Exiles: Essays on the Intellectual Migration from Germany to America.* New York: Columbia University Press, 1986.

Jonas, Hans. "Acting, Knowing, Thinking: Gleanings from Hannah Arendt's Philosophical Work." *Social Research* 44, no. 1 (Spring 1977): 25–43.

Kant, Immanuel. *The Critique of Judgment.* Indianapolis: Hackett Publishing, 1987.

Kaplan, Gisela T., and Clive S. Kessler. *Hannah Arendt: Thinking, Judging, Freedom.* Sydney: Allen & Unwin, 1989.

Kaplan, Morris. "Refiguring the Jewish Question: Arendt, Proust, and the Politics of Sexuality." In *Feminist Interpretations of Hannah Arendt,* edited by Bonnie Honig. University Park: Pennsylvania State University Press, 1995.

Kateb, George. *Hannah Arendt: Politics, Conscience, Evil.* Totowa, N.J.: Rowman & Allanheld, 1984.

Knauer, James T. "Motive and Goal in Hannah Arendt's Concept of Political Action." *American Political Science Review* 74, no. 3 (September 1980): 721–33.

Kohn, Jerome. "Thinking/Acting." *Social Research* 57, no. 1 (Spring 1990): 105–34.

Lang, Berel. "Hannah Arendt and the Politics of Evil." In *Hannah Arendt: Critical Essays,* edited by Lewis P. Hinchman and Sandra K. Hinchman. Albany: State University of New York Press, 1994.

Laqueur, Walter. "Re-reading Hannah Arendt." *Encounter* 52, no. 3 (March 1979): 73–79.

Lasch, Christopher. Introduction to special issue on Arendt. *Salmagundi,* no. 60 (Spring–Summer 1983): iv–xvi.

Lorde, Audre. *Sister Outsider.* Trumansburg, N.Y.: The Crossing Press, 1984.

Lugones, Maria. "Playfulness, 'World'-Travelling and Loving Perception." In *Making Face, Making Soul/Haciendo Caras: Creative and Critical Perspectives by Feminists of Color,* edited by Gloria Anzaldúa. San Francisco: Aunt Lute Foundation Books, 1990.

Lyotard, Jean-François. *The Postmodern Condition: A Report on Knowledge.* Translated by Geoff Bennington and Brian Massumi. Minneapolis: University of Minnesota Press, 1984.

———. *Just Gaming.* Translated by Wlad Godzich. Minneapolis: University of Minnesota Press, 1985.

MacIntyre, Alisdair. *After Virtue: A Study in Moral Theory.* Notre Dame, Ind.: University of Notre Dame Press, 1981.

Major, Robert. "A Reading of Hannah Arendt's 'Unusual' Distinction between Labor and Work." In *Hannah Arendt: The Recovery of the Public World,* edited by Melvyn A. Hill. New York: St. Martin's Press, 1979.

McCarthy, Mary. "The Hue and Cry." *Partisan Review* 31, no. 1 (Winter 1964): 82–94.

———. "Hannah Arendt and Politics." *Partisan Review* 51, no. 4, and 52, no. 1 (1984–85): 729–38.

McConville, Edward. "The Prophetic Voice of C. P. Ellis." *Nation*, 15 October 1973, 361–66.

McKenzie, Evan. *Privatopia*. New Haven, Conn.: Yale University Press, 1994.

Merleau-Ponty, Maurice. *Phenomenology of Perception*. Translated by Colin Smith. London: Routledge, 1962.

———. "A Note on Machiavelli." In *Signs*, translated by R. C. McCleary. Evanston, Ill.: Northwestern University Press, 1964.

———. *The Primacy of Perception and Other Essays*. Edited by James Edie. Evanston, Ill.: Northwestern University Press, 1964.

———. *Signs*. Translated by R.C. McCleary. Evanston, Ill.: Northwestern University Press, 1964.

———. *The Visible and the Invisible*. Translated by Alphonso Lingis. Evanston, Ill.: Northwestern University Press, 1968.

———. *Humanism and Terror*. Translated by John O'Neill. Boston: Beacon Press, 1969.

Mill, John Stuart. *On Liberty*. New York: Bobbs-Merril, 1956.

Mohanty, Chandra, and Biddy Martin. "Feminist Politics: What's Home Got to Do with It?" In *Feminist Studies/Critical Studies*, edited by Teresa de Lauretis. Bloomington: Indiana University Press, 1986.

Morganthau, Hans. "Hannah Arendt on Totalitarianism and Democracy." *Social Research* 44, no. 1 (Spring 1977): 127–31.

Nietzsche, Friedrich. *Thus Spoke Zarathustra*. Translated by Walter Kaufmann. New York: Penguin Books, 1954.

———. *The Genealogy of Morals*. Translated by Walter Kaufmann. New York: Vintage, 1967.

———. *The Gay Science*. Translated by Walter Kaufmann. New York: Vintage, 1974.

———. "On the Uses and Disadvantages of History for Life." In *Untimely Meditations*, translated by R. J. Hollingdale. Cambridge: Cambridge University Press, 1983.

Nussbaum, Martha. *The Fragility of Goodness: Luck and Ethics in Greek Tragedy and Philosophy*. Cambridge: Cambridge University Press, 1986.

O'Brien, Mary. *The Politics of Reproduction*. Boston: Routledge & Kegan Paul, 1981.

Orlie, Melissa A. "Forgiving Trespasses, Promising Futures." In *Feminist Interpretations of Hannah Arendt*, edited by Bonnie Honig. University Park: Pennsylvania State University Press, 1995.

Parekh, Bhikhu C. *Hannah Arendt and the Search for a New Political Philosophy*. Atlantic Heights, N.J.: Humanities Press, 1981.

Passerin d'Entrèves, Maurizio. *The Political Philosophy of Hannah Arendt*. London: Routledge, 1994.

Perez-Peña, Richard. "Man Said to Admit a Week of Savagery." *New York Times*, 16 June 1996, sec. B, p. 16.

Pitkin, Hanna. *Fortune Is a Woman*. Berkeley: University of California Press, 1984.

———. "Are Freedom and Liberty Twins?" *Political Theory* 16, no. 4 (November 1988): 523–52.

———. "Justice: On Relating Private and Public." In *Hannah Arendt: Critical Essays*, edited by Lewis P. Hinchman and Sandra K. Hinchman. Albany: State University of New York Press, 1994.

Plato. *Symposium*. In *The Collected Dialogues of Plato*, edited by Edith Hamilton and Huntington Cairns. Princeton, N.J.: Princeton University Press, 1961.

Plinius. *Naturalis Historia*. London: Islip, 1935.

Podhoretz, Norman. "Hannah Arendt on Eichmann: A Study in the Perversity of Brilliance." *Commentary* 36, no. 3 (September 1963): 201–208.

Pollan, Michael. "Town Building Is No Mickey Mouse Operation." *New York Times Magazine*, 14 December 1997, 56–88.

Portmann, Adolf. *Animal Forms and Patterns*. London: Faber & Faber, 1948.

———. *Das Tier als soziales Wesen*. Zurich: Rhein-Verlag, 1953.

Pratt, Minnie Bruce. "Identity: Skin, Blood, Heart." In *Yours in Struggle*, edited by Elly Bulkin, Minnie Bruce Pratt, and Barbara Smith. Brookline, N.Y.: Long Haul Press, 1984.

Putnam, Robert D. "Bowling Alone: America's Declining Social Capital." *Journal of Democracy* 6, no. 1 (January 1995): 65–78.

Reagon, Bernice Johnson. "Coalition Politics: Turning the Century." In *Home Girls: A Black Feminist Anthology*, edited by Barbara Smith. New York: Kitchen Table/Women of Color Press, 1983.

Reif, Adelbert, ed. *Gespräche Mit Hannah Arendt*. Munich: R. Piper, 1976.

Rich, Adrienne. *Of Woman Born: Motherhood as Experience and Institution*. New York: Norton, 1976.

———. "Conditions for Work: The Common World of Women." In *On Lies, Secrets, and Silence: Selected Prose, 1966-1978*. New York: W.W. Norton, 1979.

———. *What Is Found There: Notebooks on Poetry and Politics*. New York: W.W. Norton, 1993.

Ricoeur, Paul. "Action, Story, History." *Salmagundi*, no. 60 (Spring–Summer 1983): 60–72.

Rorty, Richard. *Contingency, Irony, Solidarity*. Cambridge: Cambridge University Press, 1989.

Schmidt, James. *Maurice Merleau-Ponty: Between Phenomenology and Structuralism*. New York: St. Martin's Press, 1985.

Scholem, Gershom. "*Eichmann in Jerusalem:* An Exchange of Letters [with Hannah Arendt]." In *The Jew as Pariah: Jewish Identity and Politics in the Modern Age*, edited by Ron H. Feldman. New York: Grove Press, 1978.

Scott, Joanna Vecchiarelli. " 'A Detour through Pietism': Hannah Arendt on St. Augustine's Philosophy of Freedom." *Polity* 20, no. 3 (Spring 1988): 394–425.

Sennet, Richard. "The Search for a Place in the World." In *Architecture of Fear*, edited by Nan Ellin. New York: Princeton Architectural Press, 1997.

Shklar, Judith. "Rethinking the Past." *Social Research* 44, no. 1 (Spring 1977): 80–90.

———. "Hannah Arendt as Pariah." *Partisan Review* 50, no. 1 (1983): 64–77.

Skocpol, Theda. "Civic America, Then and Now." Paper presented at the Ninety-fourth Annual Meeting of the American Political Science Association, Boston, 1998.

Smith, Barbara, ed. *Home Girls: A Black Feminist Anthology*. New York: Kitchen Table/Women of Color Press, 1983.

Steinberger, Peter J. "Hannah Arendt on Judgment." *American Journal of Political Science* 34, no. 3 (August 1990): 803–21.

Tamineaux, Jacques. "Phenomenology and the Problem of Action." *Philosophy and Social Criticism* 11 (1986): 207–19.

Taylor, Charles. *Multiculturalism: Examining the Politics of Recognition*. Edited by Amy Gutmann. Princeton, N.J.: Princeton University Press, 1994.

Terkel, Studs. *American Dreams: Lost and Found*. New York: Pantheon Books, 1980.

Thucydides. *The Peloponnesian War*. Translated by Richard Crawley. New York: The Modern Library, 1982.

Udovicki, Jasminka. "The Uses of Freedom and the Human Condition." *Praxis International* 3 (1983): 54–61.

Villa, Dana R. "Beyond Good and Evil: Arendt, Nietzsche, and the Aestheticization of Political Action." *Political Theory* 20, no. 2 (May 1992): 274–308.

———. "Postmodernism and the Public Sphere." *American Political Science Review* 86, no. 3 (September 1992): 712–20.

———. *Arendt and Heidegger: The Fate of the Political*. Princeton, N.J.: Princeton University Press, 1996.

Voegelin, Eric. "The Origins of Totalitarianism." *Review of Politics* 15, no. 1 (January 1953): 68–85.

Vollrath, Ernst. "Hannah Arendt and the Method of Political Thinking." *Social Research* 44, no. 1 (Spring 1977): 160–82.

White, Stephen K. *Political Theory and Postmodernism*. Cambridge: Cambridge University Press, 1991.

Whitfield, Stephen. *Into the Dark: Hannah Arendt and Totalitarianism*. Philadelphia: Temple University Press, 1980.

Williams, Patricia J. *The Alchemy of Race and Rights*. Cambridge, Mass.: Harvard University Press, 1991.

Williamson, Joel. *The Crucible of Race*. Oxford: Oxford University Press, 1984.

Winant, Terry. "The Feminist Standpoint: A Matter of Language." *Hypatia* 2, no. 1 (Winter 1987): 123–48.

Wolin, Sheldon. "Hannah Arendt and the Ordinance of Time." *Social Research* 44, no. 1 (Spring 1977): 91–105.

———. "Hannah Arendt: Democracy and the Political." *Salmagundi*, no. 60 (Spring–Summer 1983): 3–19.

Yarbrough, Jean, and Peter Stern. "*Vita Activa* and *Vita Contemplativa*: Reflections on Hannah Arendt's Political Thought in *The Life of the Mind*." *Review of Politics* 43, no. 3 (July 1981): 323–54.

Young-Bruehl, Elisabeth. *Hannah Arendt: For Love of the World*. New Haven, Conn.: Yale University Press, 1982.

Zerilli, Linda. "The Arendtian Body." In *Feminist Interpretations of Hannah Arendt*, edited by Bonnie Honig. University Park: Pennsylvania State University Press, 1995.

Index